All the Birds of the Bible

All the Birds

THEIR STORIES,

KEATS PUBLISHING, INC. • NEW CANAAN, CONNECTICUT

ALICE PARMELEE

author of *A Guidebook to the Bible*

of the Bible

IDENTIFICATION AND MEANING

To the Memory of
MY MOTHER
Who Enjoyed Birds

Foreword

THIS book is significant. First of all, it is a product of knowledge combined with enthusiasm. Alice Parmelee has long been a student of the Bible and has published a book and several studies which hold a high position in their field. She is also an enthusiastic bird watcher. Sound scholarship, deep feeling for the subject, and fine clarity of expression have united to produce a work of outstanding quality and interest.

All the Birds of the Bible gives a new dimension to Bible interpretation and also to the significance of birds. The Bible is approached with an appreciation of its spiritual message. But the emphasis of the book is on the natural phenomena of the Holy Land. When the author quotes biblical texts in which the birds appear, the familiar scriptural words act as little doors opening out upon the rugged and often desert country of Palestine.

In my own wanderings in most of the States of the Union I early came to love our desert country. There is a unique fascination in these great dry areas when their hills and mesas take on literally hundreds of colors from sunrise to sunset. Birds seem to adapt themselves to the eternal dryness and to wear the colors of these areas. In the entire country I know of no more interesting group of birds than desert species like the verdin, the phainopepla, the pyrrhuloxia, the roadrunner, and various hummingbirds and woodpeckers which must be counterparts of many Palestinian birds.

I want to emphasize another aspect of *All the Birds of the Bible*— its thoroughness and its freedom from any touch of superficiality. The author says in her Preface: "This book is the record of a journey through the Bible watching for its birds. There are surprisingly many of these lively creatures flitting through the Scriptures and I have quoted or referred to all the verses about birds in the Bible and many in the Apocrypha."

It seems to me that whether one's primary interest is the Bible or the birds, one will find here a thorough and imaginative treatment. Pertinent biblical texts are set forth simply and without straining their significance and the material on bird identification is excellent.

A number of singularly apt quotations from travelers in the Holy Land further enhance the scope and variety of the book. These quotations seem to me to open another entirely new area of interest in the subject.

Of course, as a bird man I am much interested in the illustrations which are selected from a wide variety of sources. One of the photographs I was happy to suggest personally. In reading over the manuscript, I noticed the illustration of six geese portrayed in the Egyptian frieze from Meidum. The markings of these ancient birds came out clearly and I saw that two of them were identical with a goose which caused some excitement on Martha's Vineyard Island in October 1958. This was a red-breasted goose *(Branta ruficollis)*. It flew in with some Canada geese and was photographed by Ann and Freeman Wallin. As many of these lovely geese are kept in captivity on Long Island, in Connecticut, and in Massachusetts, our little goose on Martha's Vineyard was undoubtedly an escape. Its photograph is shown on another page.

This book held my attention to the end and taught me much. I think it has wide appeal, for who, after all, is not interested in the Bible or in birds living amid unusual natural surroundings? Solely from the standpoint of vivid, enlightening reading I recommend the book. Beyond that, however, I think it qualifies as a permanently useful reference book in a field never before so thoroughly covered.

GUY EMERSON

Preface
and Acknowledgments

THIS book is the record of a journey through the Bible watching for its birds. There are surprisingly many of these lively creatures flitting through the Scriptures and I have quoted or referred to all the verses about birds in the Bible and many in the Apocrypha. Every journey through the Bible is an adventure, for the Bible is alive on every page. One travels in a spirited company of patriarchs, kings, and prophets who lead the most significant and best-known cavalcade through history. Bird watching on this journey has a unique charm. It might, however, seem frivolous in the midst of so much of spiritual importance in the Scriptures, were it not that the birds themselves are sometimes an integral part of the events. Whenever they appear they bring a vivid touch of reality and they can lead one to the heart of the Bible message.

First one must find the birds themselves and then determine what creatures they actually were by studying their Hebrew names and comparing the birds with those flying in Palestine today. The transliteration of Hebrew names in this book is from Robert Young's *Analytical Concordance to the Bible,* 1955. I used the Authorized or King James Version as my chief text, but consulted other English translations which often differ somewhat in their interpretations of bird names. Whenever a translation other than the Authorized Version is quoted I have noted the fact. I am especially grateful to The Division of Christian Education of the National Council of Churches for their permission to quote verses from *The Holy Bible: Revised Standard Version,* and *The Apocrypha,* copyright 1946, 1952, and 1957; and also to Harper & Brothers for their permission to quote from James Moffatt's *The Bible: A New Translation,* copyright 1922, 1935, and 1950. Dr. G. R. Driver graciously made available to me his translations of Hebrew bird names from "Birds in the Law," *Palestine Exploration Quarterly,* April 1955.

For the help I received in the research for this book I wish to thank the librarians and libraries of the National Audubon Society, the American Museum of Natural History, the New York Public Library, Princeton University Library, and the Robert E. Speer Library of the Princeton Theological Seminary.

Grateful acknowledgment is made for permission from the following individuals and publishers to use copyrighted material:

Victor Howells and Andrew Melrose, London, for a passage from *A Naturalist in Palestine,* 1956.

Colonel Richard Meinertzhagen and Oliver and Boyd, Edinburgh, for two passages from *Birds of Arabia,* 1954.

Robert Cushman Murphy, Dean Amadon, and McGraw-Hill Book Co., Inc., for two excerpts from *Land Birds of America,* 1953.

Mrs. George Bambridge and Doubleday and Co., Inc., for the second stanza of *"The Butterfly That Stamped"* in *Just So Stories* by Rudyard Kipling.

Edward A. Armstrong and Wm. Collins Sons and Co., Ltd., for a rhyme from *The Wren* in the *New Naturalist Library,* 1955.

The Macmillan Company, for a passage from Albert Schweitzer's *Memoirs of Childhood and Youth,* 1931.

To Eleanor Jordan of Harper & Brothers I extend grateful thanks for all she has taught me about the making of books and for her expert help in styling this manuscript.

Especial help in finding the illustrations was given by my sister, Mary E. Parmelee, and by Helen D. Alexander. Elizabeth Roth and Wilson G. Duprey, both of the Print Room of the New York Public Library, made valuable suggestions. To all these I wish to express my sincere thanks.

Dr. H. Mendelssohn of the Tel-Aviv Institute for Natural Science gave me helpful advice and said that bird photography is just beginning in Israel. It was possible, however, to obtain some superb photographs of living birds such as those mentioned in the Bible, for the well-known British ornithologist and photographer, Eric Hosking, made his photographs available to me. I am particularly grateful to him. Thanks are also due to Ann Wallin for her husband's photograph of the red-breasted goose, a bird the Israelites surely knew in Egypt.

To the following individuals, libraries, museums, collections, and art agencies and to their directors and staffs I wish to express grateful thanks for their very great help in supplying information and photographs and, in many cases, granting the reprint permissions noted in the credit lines of the various pictures: the New York Public Library; the Donnell Library Center; the Frick Art Reference Library; the Pierpont Morgan Library; the American Museum of Natural History; the New York Zoological Society; the National Audubon Society; the Massachusetts Audubon Society; the Metropolitan Museum of Art, New York; the National Gallery of Art, Washington, D. C.; the Fogg Art Museum, Harvard University; the Isabella Stewart Gardner Museum, Boston; the Museum of Fine Arts, Boston; the John G. Johnson Collection, Philadelphia; the Samuel H. Kress Foundation, New York; the Arents and the Stuart Collections, New York Public Library; the Pacific School of Religion, Berkeley, California; the British Museum; the National Gallery, London; the New York Graphic Society, Greenwich, Connecticut; Wm. Collins and Sons, Ltd., London; Fratelli Alinari, Florence; D. Anderson, Rome; Fiorentini-Venezia, Venice; Caisse Nationale des Monuments Historiques, Paris; and the Duke of Northumberland.

A Field Guide to the Birds of Britain and Europe by Roger Tory Peterson, Guy Mountfort, and P.A.D. Hollom was invaluable for identifying birds depicted in European art.

I owe a debt of gratitude to Guy Emerson, not only for giving encouragement and making helpful suggestions, but for writing the Foreword. Though a banker by profession, his interest in birds is attested by his "life list" which contains all but a handful of the birds ever seen in the United States. For nearly twenty years he served as a director of the National Audubon Society and from 1940 to 1944 he was its president.

In gathering material about the birds of the Bible, I found new insight into the Scriptures, a fresh perspective on art, and many deeper friendships both with ancient Bible people and with bird watchers today. May this book bring its readers some of the pleasures, satisfactions, and enlightenment it brought to me.

ALICE PARMELEE

Contents

List of Illustrations

Birds and the Bible

THERE were many bird watchers among the ancient Hebrews, for the Bible contains three hundred or so references to birds. These references are scattered throughout the various books from Genesis to Revelation and searching for them takes us along the main highway over which the cavalcade of biblical history passes. Here is new territory for a modern bird watcher to explore and an adventure which takes us far into the deeps of the past, and frees us from provincialism in time. Birds impart fresh delight to our reading of the Bible and they add a new dimension to our understanding of its message. Birds are extraordinarily vital scraps of feathered energy, defiant of gravity, undaunted by arctic cold, tropical heat, or all the immensities of space. With infinite grace they fly serenely through the world with its thousand dangers. No wonder such creatures can infuse life into ancient stories and bring us close to the Hebrews who, centuries ago, watched the lively actions of the same species of birds that fly in Palestine today.

Palestine is unusually rich in bird life and some 360 to 400 species have been recorded there in recent years. This is a remarkable number for an area of about 10,000 square miles. For all of the United States east of the Rocky Mountains, Roger Tory Peterson lists in *A Field Guide to the Birds* the 440 species commonly encountered by bird watchers. According to James Fisher, Great Britain with her over 90,000 square miles and 3500 miles of coastline has an official list of 424 species.

Without binoculars, cameras, field guides, scientific names, or phono-graphic records of bird sounds, the Hebrews saw and heard many of their birds and described them with surprising accuracy. In the Bible fifty different Hebrew and Greek names are used for birds in general or for particular birds, and there are fifteen distinct names for birds of prey, which are abundant in this region. One bird list in the Bible contains nineteen names and refers to many more species.

The Hebrews' keen awareness of birds may be partly due to the fact that they lived close to nature and were often dependent upon birds for food. They must have felt that same acute envy we experience when we see creatures free of earth and superbly alive in the limitless sky through which they have been flying for at least fifty million years. But there is another aspect to the Hebrews' accurate perception of flying creatures. From other ancient peoples they heard stories about birds that acted in unbirdlike ways or possessed magic powers, and they learned that some people actually bowed down before bird deities. But the Hebrews did not follow their neighbors down the blind alley of animal worship, for they believed in one Lord who created all living things. With this firm ground of faith beneath their feet they looked around them and saw birds, not as gods with power to act in unpredictable ways, but as creatures fashioned by the same Lord who controls the ordered harmony of the universe and who made man. This insight enabled them to perceive birds as they actually are. Two American ornithologists, Dr. Robert Cushman Murphy and Dr. Dean Amadon, pay high tribute to the Hebrews when they state: "To judge from the Old Testament, the inheritors of the Land of Canaan were extraordinarily good naturalists."

Time, however, has placed a barrier between the ancient Hebrews and ourselves, and even a good naturalist who uses names which have been out of circulation for some two or three thousand years is somewhat hard to understand. Hebrew bird names are not easy to translate, as footnotes in the Revised Standard Version constantly remind us. But fortunately the identity of many Bible birds can be discovered from descriptive notes about them in the Scriptures, for the ways of many birds and the patterns of their plumage continue virtually unchanged through the millenniums. When Micah spoke of the baldness of the *nesher* (1:16), he was probably describing a vulture, most likely one of the abundant griffon vultures of Palestine whose soft white down on head and neck gives it a bald appearance. Jeremiah's *nesher* (49:16) makes its nest high "in the clefts of the rock," a favorite nesting place of griffon vultures and a further confirmation of the *nesher's* identity.

Hebrew bird names are usually onomatopoetic, as Dr. G. R. Driver notes in his "Birds of the Old Testament" published in the *Palestine Exploration Quarterly,* 1955. Even when no descriptive clues can be found, the very sound of the name usually suggests the bird's song or call. Thus in *tor* (turtledove) we can hear the soft, repeated *"toor-r-r"* of the turtledove, while *qore* (partridge) resembles the grating *"krrr-ic"* a partridge makes when flushed.

Our spirits are somehow refreshed by watching birds and other living creatures, and the weariness caused by man-made things and by all the ugliness and confusion around us vanishes when a bird sings. The Hebrews felt the charm of birds and left us immortal stories about them and many a vivid word picture. They saw hawks soaring in the heavens. They recognized migration for what it is and left us our oldest account of it. The harsh cry of the swift was familiar to them. When an eagle mounted skyward they marveled at its mastery of the air. Owls hooting in the night made them shiver and imagine desolation and ruined cities. They told stories of a dove with a freshly-plucked olive leaf in her bill, of a miraculous migration of quails, of ravens bringing food to a starving prophet, of strange imported creatures from the East that may well have been peacocks, of a hen that gathered her chickens under her wing, and of a cock whose crowing one morning in Jerusalem caused an apostle to weep. All these and many more are biblical birds, small embodiments of life, akin to those we watch today. They bring the ancient stories close to our own experience and some of these birds have become part of the vocabulary of our spiritual lives and symbols of Christian realities. The flight of a bird in the Bible may mean more to us today than the outcome of some long-forgotten battle.

Where have they gone, these creatures imbued with such great intensity of life? It has been said that Palestine with its buried scrolls, its rubble of vanished cities, and its piles of broken pottery heaped one upon another through the centuries, is like a layer cake of history. Today a shepherd boy stands on the ruins of three kingdoms and two empires while around him a modern nation struggles toward maturity. But what of the sky above him which has been crossed and recrossed by innumerable birds in flight for millions of years? Here, too, is an ancient story, an invisible web of nature's weaving, known only to the imagination, for, as an apocryphal book says:

When a bird hath flown through the air, there is no token of her way to be found, but the light air being beaten with the stroke of her wings, and parted with the violent noise and motion of them, is passed through, and therein afterwards no sign where she went is to be found.

Wisdom of Solomon 5:11

Some of the ancient birds left traces of their flight and their songs in the hearts of those who saw and heard them and thence found their way into the writings of the ancient Hebrews. As we search the Scriptures we discover many of these long-dead, but once vital, exuberant creatures whose very lives seem to glorify God. Some are as visible as pigeons fluttering from the ledges of city buildings today, others are as well-hidden as a hermit thrush in a northern forest, while still others are merely a trace of a wing or a song.

All the ancient bird life in the Bible would be of interest mainly to specialists were it not that each of these creatures flies with a portion of the Bible message and enriches and adorns God's revelation of Himself to men. The Bible story, beginning in Genesis and coming to its triumphant conclusion in Revelation, is the entity that gives meaning to these birds and provides the groundwork and chief aspect of this book. It is the warp on which the brightly colored woof of birds is woven. Among all the voices in the Scriptures one hears each bird adding its note of praise to the cosmic symphony.

> O all ye fowls of the air,
> Bless ye the Lord,
> Praise and exalt him above all for ever.

Song of the Three Holy Children 58

PART I

In the Beginning

CHAPTER 1 ❧
Every Winged Bird

"IN THE BEGINNING," according to the Genesis story of creation, "the earth was without form and void, and darkness was upon the face of the deep." Silence and darkness prevailed. No bird sang and no wings moved through the vast empty spaces. But in the unimaginable nothingness there was God by whom all things were made. When His first Word of creation, "Let there be light!" rang through the primal silence, light began to shine. Even before day and night commenced their eternal ebb and flow, however, the ancient story suggests the fleeting image of a bird. Out of the silent darkness of nothingness in which only God's Spirit dwelt the picture of a bird is flashed before us in a single word. So delicate and insubstantial is the image that it is blurred or lost in many translations, but the original Hebrew of the Old Testament says that the Spirit of God was *hovering* upon the face of the waters. Here one can see, as it were, a bird with outspread wings fluttering protectively over its nest. Thus from the very beginning the Bible makes clear what God is like and what He does. Evidently the ancient writer intended to convey the idea of a brooding bird, for he uses the verb *rachaph* which in Deuteronomy 32:11 describes a parent eagle fluttering over its young.

Behind this brief bird reference in the second verse of Genesis may lie the story of the Egyptian sun god Ra who, in the form of a bird, flew over the primal deep spreading light by fluttering its wings. The image of a hovering bird in Genesis may have Egyptian origins, but our Bible story clearly leaves the Ra myth far behind and discards any suggestion that God assumes the guise of a bird. Genesis transmutes the crudities of the Egyptian story into the basic truth of our faith that God the Creator of all things hovers over His world with the loving care of a parent bird for its young. This age-old faith became the cornerstone of Christianity when Jesus taught His disciples the prayer beginning, "Our Father. . . ."

The story of beginnings continues with the creation of heaven, earth, and the seas. God made green things to grow upon earth and He set the sun, moon, and stars in the sky. When the fifth day of creation dawned both land and sea were prepared for living creatures and God said: "Let the waters bring forth abundantly the moving creature that hath life."

When God made "every winged fowl after its kind," the rhythm of wingbeats seems to echo from His words creating "fowl that may fly above the earth in the open firmament of heaven" (Genesis 1:20, 21). The primal silence became filled with the whir of wings, and with songs and calls as through the once-empty spaces of sky flew dark lines, precise formations, and massed clouds of birds etching wild patterns across the heavens. The earth became lively with feathered creatures, little brown birds, others resplendent in scarlet or yellow or blue, birds that whistle or twitter or croak or honk or chirp, that hop or run or strut, that flap their wings or soar or dive. Birds of every kind found homes and began their lives on the ground, on the water, and in the air.

Before the fifth day of creation ended God blessed His birds and the sea creatures He had made. The story gives only a vague impression of the latter as uncounted numbers of fishes swimming in the ancient seas, but the birds are mentioned by name. Surely they passed in joyous flight on their newly-created wings and rested upon the ground or perched in trees to receive their Creator's blessing:

> Be fruitful and multiply and fill the waters in the seas,
> And let fowl multiply in the earth.
>
> Genesis 1:22

Thus the myriads of birds of the Bible fly into its story in the first chapter of Genesis, before history began, even before Adam was created. They have been on earth a very long time—since the fifth day of creation, according to the Bible, about 125 million years, according to the scientists.

In the Bible, birds are the first creatures to be grouped in a class and given a name. In Hebrew this is *oph,* translated "fowl" in the Authorized Version and "bird" in more recent translations. The basic meaning of *oph* is "fliers" or "covered with feathers," two aspects of birds that set them apart from other creatures—they are feathered and they possess that ultimate and superb endowment of living organisms, the ability to fly. It was doubtless their flying power that made birds so attractive and fascinating to the Hebrews and gave them distinction as the first clearly-defined class of beings in the Bible. Primitive men observed many living creatures clothed in a variety of "feathers, furs, and fins"—creatures that swam, hopped, walked, galloped, crawled, or slithered over the earth, in the waters, or through the air—and soon men began the long task, which still continues, of classifying all the different forms of life on earth. Birds, fishes, beasts, "creeping things" including reptiles and insects, and men are all mentioned in the Genesis story as the five important groups of creatures. The prophet Ezekiel also mentioned them.

So that the fishes of the sea, and the fowls of the heaven, and the beasts of the field, and all creeping things that creep upon the earth, and all the men that are upon the face of the earth . . . shall know that I am the Lord.

Ezekiel 38:20, 23

In the apocryphal Book of Judith 11:7, four of these groups appear and in New Testament times Paul mentions them in one of his epistles.

All flesh is not the same flesh, but there is one kind of flesh of men, another flesh of beasts, another of fishes, and another of birds.

I Corinthians 15:39

The first brief phrases about birds in Genesis contain nothing fanciful nor imaginary, but are based, as are most of the Bible statements about birds, on accurate, clearly-observed facts. A bird's feathers and wings and its flight above earth through the spaces of sky are all implied in its name *oph.* As men watched birds build their nests, brood their eggs, and feed and protect their young, they interpreted these actions as faithful obedience on the part of His feathered creatures to the Lord's command to "multiply in the earth." The enormous hosts of creatures flying in the sky or covering the ground was evidence to men that birds were indeed multiplying in the earth. People began to see an almost endless variety of sizes, shapes, colors, and habits among birds and to hear a multitude of songs. They soon perceived that the general class of beings they called birds was divided into innumerable subdivisions. They found names for many birds, but they used the phrase "after its kind" to denote orders, families, and species.

In placing the origin of sea creatures before that of birds or of men, the Genesis story anticipated by several thousand years an accepted theory of modern science. Today we have evidence that millions of years ago reptiles climbed out of the water where they had been living and began to feed upon plants growing on dry land. From these sluggish, cold-blooded, earth-bound reptiles all birds are believed to have evolved. At first this idea seems strange, for birds are the most active, warm-blooded, free-flying creatures in the world. A bird, however, hatches from an egg, as does a reptile, and within its egg and even after hatching, a bird in many ways resembles a reptile, while the anatomy of these two classes of creatures shows similarity. Moreover, from the Mesozoic Era when dinosaurs roamed the earth come two clearly defined fossils. These vestiges of creatures that lived when the earth was young provide certain and dramatic proof of the theory that long ago birds descended from ancient reptiles.

The fossil *Archaeopteryx,* or "ancient wing," is the oldest bird so far discovered. It is estimated that this birdlike creature lived about 125 million years ago. *Archaeopteryx* is only an impression of feathers and bones in a block of limestone, a mere shadow of a bird, first recognized for what it was in 1861 when Hamberlein saw it in a rock cut from a Bavarian quarry. A second *Archaeopteryx,* better preserved than the first, was found in the same quarry. It was named *Archaeornis.* Doubtless this ancient bird fell into a shallow lake and was so gently covered by layer after layer of fine silt that its fragile bones and feathers were not disturbed, but left their delicate impression in the mud. Ages passed. The dinosaurs disappeared, mammals emerged, and finally man. Meanwhile the mud in which the *Archaeopteryx* was entombed became stone.

These two fossil creatures, which were about the size of pigeons, were certainly birds, for they were both clothed in feathers, and had wings for flying, and feet for perching. They also had lizardlike tails of twenty vertebrae, reptilian teeth, and claws on their wings. Today's birds are toothless, their tails are of feathers not bone, and wing claws have generally disappeared. These extinct fossil birds form a "missing link" between reptiles and birds and show that, as Thomas Huxley said, birds are "glorified reptiles."

After telling about the first creatures of the sea, the air, and the land, Genesis records the events of the momentous sixth day of creation when the heavens resounded with the songs of birds and all nature awaited the climax of God's mighty acts, the creation of man.

And God said, "Let us make man in our image,
   after our likeness.
And let them have dominion over the fish of the sea,
   and over the fowl of the air,
   and over the cattle,
   and over all the earth,
   and over every creeping thing that creepeth upon the earth."
So God created man in his own image,
   in the image of God created he him,
   male and female created he them. . .
And God saw every thing that he had made,
   and behold, it was very good.

Genesis 1:26-27, 31

The Hebrews had an unshakable faith that God was their Creator: "It is he that hath made us, and not we ourselves. We are his people and the sheep of his pasture." They believed that man, created in the image of God, was the highest among all other forms of life. Man is the crown of God's creation and God "gave him dominion over beasts and fowls" (Ecclesiasticus 17:4).

Man has exercised his "dominion . . . over the fowl of the air" (Genesis 1:28) in various ways. Some, like the pigeon and chicken, he has domesticated for his own use. Others, like canaries, he has caged and brought into his home so that he might enjoy their lively ways and their sweet singing. Still others he has, with unthinking selfishness and brutality, exterminated so that no one will ever again see a living passenger pigeon, a heath hen, an Eskimo curlew, a Labrador duck, or any one of many extinct species. Today some people acknowledge that "dominion" involves responsibility and they try to save the species threatened by man's encroachment upon the wild areas of the world. But more and more of the species which God created and watched over through countless ages while they were developing in all their perfection, beauty, wildness, and unique competence are endangered and are vanishing forever.

Birds are essentially wild creatures, though some have been tamed. James was obviously exaggerating man's ability to tame birds when he wrote in his epistle: "For every kind of beasts, and of birds, and of serpents, and of things in the sea, is tamed, and hath been tamed of mankind. But the tongue can no man tame" (James 3:7-8). One can only hope that should all human tongues be "tamed," birds will never be tamed so that they lose the splendor of their wild intensity.

Before the sixth day of creation ended and God rested from His mighty acts, one thing remained for Him to do. Out of the abundance of the earth, with all its grains, fruits, and green plants, the Lord provided food for "every fowl of the air" (Genesis 1:30), for every beast of the earth, and for all men. Then God saw that all He had made was very good and life began to flourish on the good earth.

All living creatures are truly marvelous, and there is glory in the sight of every winged bird, but man himself is the greatest glory and marvel of all.

> What is man, that thou art mindful of him?
>   And the son of man, that thou visitest him?
> For thou hast made him a little lower than the angels,
>   and hast crowned him with glory and honour.
> Thou madest him to have dominion over the works of thy hands;
>   thou hast put all things under his feet:
> all sheep and oxen, yea and the beasts of the field;
>   the fowl of the air, and the fish of the sea,
>   and whatsoever passeth through the paths of the seas.
> O Lord, our Lord, how excellent is thy name in all the earth!
>
> **Psalm 8:4-9**

CHAPTER 2 ✍

Animal Parade

THE first Bible story featuring both men and birds can be read in the second chapter of Genesis. In the familiar setting of the Garden of Eden, the chief actor is Adam who, when the story opens, dwells there alone. But God is with him and comes "in the cool of the day" to walk in the Garden. We read:

> Out of the ground the Lord God formed every beast of the field and every fowl of the air and brought them unto Adam to see what he would call them. . . . And Adam gave names to all cattle, and to the fowl of the air, and to every beast of the field.
>
> Genesis 2:19-20

Adam's naming of the animals must have been a lively occasion and one that marks the beginning of man's ancient friendship with birds. They and all other creatures appeared in a fantastic animal parade, and while the four-footed creatures trotted or hopped or lumbered along the parade route through the Garden, in the air birds were executing a variety of flying maneuvers. Adam watched each creature very carefully, for the name he gave to it must describe its unique quality. Adam was the first bird watcher and what an opportunity was his! The birds came swooping out of the sky, waddling across the grass, fluttering down from the trees of Eden, and the legendary fly-past began. It was a veritable bewilderment of birds and among those present were surely a mustering of storks, a sedge of herons, a spring of teal, a congregation of plover, a gaggle of geese, a charm of gold-finches, a watch of nightingales, and an exaltation of larks. The four hundred or so species of birds of Palestine would have been there, together with the eight or nine thousand different kinds of birds in the world, to say nothing of all other creatures! But one's imagination falters as the mighty parade streams past Adam and he continues with his immense task of nature study and dictionary-making.

Names were important to Adam and his early descendants and they did very well with their task of naming birds. Ancient people believed that by pronouncing a creature's name one could acquire some of its nature and power. They listened to birds and observed their habits carefully and some of this very ancient bird watching is enshrined in the Hebrew names. They called the dove *yonah*, a word which imitates its moaning. Ravens were named *oreb* for their black feathers. The rushing sound of *nesher* suggests the eagle's lightninglike swoop upon its prey. The harsh call of the swift can be heard in *sis*, while the twittering of sparrows and other small birds sounds in *tsippor*.

After the naming of the birds, Genesis says nothing more about them in the story of the Garden of Eden. One can imagine them, however, perched among the branches and watching with keen and wary eyes while Adam and Eve ate fruit from the forbidden tree. This opening act in the great drama of redemption, which is the subject of the Bible, in no way involved the birds, for they did not share man's willfulness and apostasy. They did not rebel against God, for these creatures were not entrusted with the choice. Within the appointed order of their lives, birds live faithfully according to the ordinances of God.

> Yea, the stork in the heaven
>   knoweth her appointed times;
> and the turtle [dove] and the crane and the swallow
>   observe the time of their coming;
> but my people know not
>   the judgment of the Lord.
> How do ye say, "We are wise,
>   and the law of the Lord is with us"?
> . . . .
> Lo, they have rejected the word of the Lord,
>   and what wisdom is in them?
>   Jeremiah 8:7-9

Cherubim with flaming swords guarded the gates of Eden when Adam and Eve went forth from the Garden to begin their life of toil in the world.

Many of their descendants settled in Palestine, a narrow land tucked

Palestine Is Unusually Rich in Bird Life

People of Bible times watched such birds as these: eagles, swallows, cocks, partridges, doves, and waders of various kinds. Though realistically portrayed here, the birds are believed to symbolize the souls of the faithful while the encircling vine suggests Christ's words: "I am the vine, ye are the branches" (John 15:5). This mosaic pavement, unearthed by workmen digging near the Damascus Gate of Jerusalem in 1894, bears a fifth-century A.D. Armenian inscription. The photograph shows the pavement after restoration. [Page 19]

They Marveled at Its Mastery of the Air

Majestically soaring on huge outstretched wings, griffon vultures such as this one were a familiar sight to the earth-bound men and women of Bible times. They must have watched with admiration as these superb creatures mounted high in a rising current of air, their wings and broad tail extended and the tips of their primaries widely fingered out. Among all of Palestine's great birds of prey the griffon vulture is the one most often seen. [Page 21]

"God Created . . . Every Winged Bird"

With a mighty gesture of His hand God creates the birds. As they hurtle through the air on untried wings, a tree bends in the turbulence of their headlong flight. Sea creatures gaze above them with a hint of envy. The primal darkness rolls away as the sun shines on a desolate coast and an ocean empty of boats. In this detail from one of Tintoretto's Bible illustrations, painted about 1550 and now in the Accademia di Belle Arti, Venice, the great Venetian painter uses light and shadow to convey immense energy, powerful motion, and the sublime beauty of a scene brought close to the spectator. [Page 26]

"And God Blessed Them"

God's sublime gesture of blessing dominates a scene portrayed with reverence and deep feeling. Though the English artist attempted to portray animals he had never seen, he clearly knew the birds, for he drew and colored them accurately. Beginning at the left they include: a peacock, a long-eared owl, a parrot, a lark, two birds not easy to identify, a blackbird, a swallow with a long body, a singing goldfinch, a magpie, a hawk chasing a heron, a peregrine preying on a smaller bird. A wren, a bird with a striped breast, and a robin are among the leaves. In the stream are a heron, a lapwing, a swan, and a duck. This page is from the fourteenth-century manuscript called the *Holkham Bible Picture Book*. [Page 26]

"The Earth Is Full of Thy Creatures"

Birds give liveliness to a scene in which God blesses His creatures. Paul Bril, the outstanding Flemish landscape painter of his time (1554-1626), filled his canvas so full of creatures that it became a veritable animated encyclopedia of animal forms. Only in the presence of God can one imagine so many hunters and hunted remaining together in peace. The painting, of which this is a detail, is in the Doria Gallery, Rome. [Page 27]

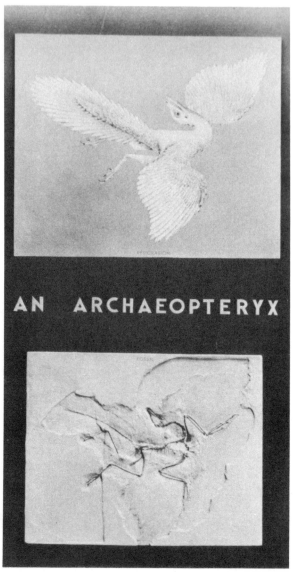

AN ARCHAEOPTERYX

A Bird That Lived About 125 Million Years Ago

The lower photograph shows a cast of the limestone block containing a fossil *Archaeopteryx*. The bones and even the feathers left such a clear imprint in the mud, later to become stone, that it was possible to reconstruct the creature shown in the upper picture. Its teeth, wing claws, and tail denote its reptilian ancestry, but its feathers, wings, and feet, which are adapted for perching are those of birds. [Page 28]

"Adam Gave Names to All Cattle and to the Fowl of the Air"

Adam, the first bird watcher, is using long scrolls for his animal "dictionary."
One of his two "secretaries" has evidently suggested a humorous name, for
Adam is unmistakably smiling. Of all the birds Adam named, only seventeen
are represented here, but half of these are identifiable. The vellum page is
from an English bestiary dated about 1250 and now in the library of Alnwick
Castle, England. [Page 31]

Birds of the Sea of Galilee

Near Capernaum at Tabgha, where Jesus is thought to have fed the five thousand, a Christian church was built about 400 A.D. Though it was destroyed two hundred years later, its damaged mosaic floor survives. This detail shows, amid lotus, papyrus, and other plants, three birds of the region. The curved neck of the larger bird indicates that it is a swan. Two smaller birds perch upright with their wings hanging half open in the characteristic **pose** of cormorants. [Page 50]

40

Above the Procession of Creatures into the Ark Fly the Birds

Hurrying to reach shelter before the storm breaks, Noah and his sons drive many kinds of animals into the Ark. Noah's daughters-in-law gather up their possessions while above them the birds, sensing the coming catastrophe, fly toward safety. Less wise than the birds, his neighbors jeer at Noah and his huge Ark, though already wind is tossing the trees. The engraver of this scene from *Historien des Ouden en Nieuwen Testaments,* published in Amsterdam in 1700, depicted an Ark curiously like the lower stories of the United Nations Building, New York. [Page 53]

"Two of Every Sort Shalt Thou Bring into the Ark"

Storks, pelicans, cranes, and ravens join the orderly march toward the Ark. With careful gait the storks step delicately through a winding, flower-bordered stream. Ungainly pelicans with huge yellow bills and pouches seem conscious of the gravity of the occasion. Little but the supercilious eyes of the dark cranes can be seen against a gold mosaic background. Following these birds of lakes and streams come two ravens pattering along on dry land. One of these was to be Noah's first scout. This thirteenth-century mosaic from the narthex of St. Mark's, Venice, is reproduced in *Mosaics of St. Mark's*, New York Graphic Society. [Page 53]

"He Sent Forth a Dove"

Swirling blue and white waves make patterns as they pound against the hull of the Ark. Noah opens the window and gently releases his fluttering dove, for the storm is over and the rain has ceased. Though water still engulfs the world, the raven has found food in the floating wreckage. The artist of this mosaic in St. Mark's, Venice, portrays Noah's anxiety for all those in his care and his eagerness to learn what God has in store for him. [Page 55]

43

"Go Forth from the Ark"

Noah and his family stand once more upon dry land as the rainbow of God's forgiveness arches above them. Preparing to fly away, the birds on the roof shake out their feathers. A handsome red-legged partridge looks back at the home it is about to leave. Noah helps a fierce-visaged lion scramble from the Ark to join its mate. The scene is one of the thirteenth-century mosaics in St. Mark's, Venice. [Page 56]

"Noah Built an Altar to the Lord"

Noah's wife is putting out a duck that is apparently reluctant to leave its strange home and follow the rooster, the stork, three other birds, and a great black bear across the gangplank. After the violence of the flood, the Ark rests safely on its splintered base upon Mt. Ararat. On a hillside bright with flowers Noah offers his sacrifice. From an upper window one of the daughters-in-law watches the birds fly away. The dove silhouetted against the roof still carries the leafy olive branch. This detail is from a Book of Hours made in France about 1423 for John, Duke of Bedford. [Page 57]

THE METROPOLITAN MUSEUM OF ART

The Shores of the Ancient Nile Teemed with Birds

Enormous flocks of waterfowl were netted in Egypt in the manner depicted here. Concealed behind a blind this Egyptian pulls his rope to raise the sides of the net trap and so imprison the birds floating within. The bushes in the foreground are drawn with conventional perspective, but one must look down as from above upon the zigzag lines of the water and into the trap itself. The artist, however, has presented a side view of the birds. This is a copy of a wall painting in the Tomb of Khnum-hotpe at Beni Hasan. At it dates from about 1900 B.C., Abraham may have been visiting Egypt when the artist drew these birds. [Page 62]

46

Pigeon Perched on a Stalk of Papyrus

The pigeon Abraham sacrificed was like this lively bird fluttering its wings in a papyrus swamp. The reproduction shows a fragment of a wall painting from the pharaoh Ikhnaton's palace at El Amarneh. The scene may illustrate the following lines from Ikhnaton's well-known hymn to his god Aton:

> The birds flutter in their marshes,
> Their wings uplifted in adoration to thee . . .
> All winged things fly,
> They live when thou hast shone upon them.

[Page 64]

47

"The Birds Did Eat Them Out of the Basket upon My Head"

While the butler serenely dreams of pressing the juice of a bunch of grapes into the pharaoh's gold cup, the sleeping baker is troubled. He dreams of three birds pecking at buns in the three baskets on his head—a dream containing a warning that Joseph will soon interpret. The scene is one of the Old Testament narratives depicted in the thirteenth-century mosaics of St. Mark's, Venice. [Page 67] away in the southeast corner of the Mediterranean, and here the chief scenes of the Bible drama took place. The actors were men and women like ourselves and the land in which they lived, with its stony hills and fertile valleys, still lies between the desert and the sea. Here flew the birds of the first animal parade, the birds to whom Adam and his sons and grandsons gave names and whose stories add a lively note of reality to the Scriptures. Many of these birds live in Palestine today obediently carrying out, in their own way, God's vast, inscrutable design.

From the heights to which an eagle soars one can see the Holy Land spread out below "from Dan to Beersheba" and from the sea to the Arabian Desert. It is a land of sudden contrasts of climate and terrain which create many different environments attractive to a wide variety of birds. During most of the year snow lies deep upon the nine thousand foot summit of Mount Hermon, standing like a sentinel above Dan on the northern border, while little more than one hundred and fifty miles to the south, beyond Beersheba, stretch the flat, arid wastes of the Negeb. On the west the salt waves of the Mediterranean break upon a seashore only fifty miles from the deep Jordan-Dead Sea chasm and some one hundred miles from the vast Arabian Desert farther east.

Aloft with an eagle and with eyes as keen as his, one can see that between the sea and the desert four parallel bands run north and south: the fertile Maritime Plain, the central mountains of Israel, the deep rift through which the Jordan River flows into the Dead Sea, and, rising beyond this deepest valley in the world, the high plateau and the mountains of the Eastern Range. Beyond stretches an infinity of desert. In early Bible times, before the trees growing on the ancient forested slopes were cut down or burned, before cities and towns were built, fields cultivated, and swamps drained, this land must have sheltered some species of birds not seen here today.

Near the majestic summit of Mount Hermon live small flocks of the graceful Alpine chough, a handsome bird with black feathers, crimson legs, and a yellow bill. Here among the melting snows of the barren mountaintop another Alpine bird, the snow finch, nests. Only a few miles to the south amid the semitropical foliage of the Jordan Valley, the lovely Palestine sunbird flits restlessly from twig to twig, resplendent in plumage of green, brown, red, and yellow, all shining with metallic luster. When this minute tropical bird hovers delicately over blossoms it is often mistaken for a hummingbird. On rocky hillsides surrounding the Dead Sea, numerous ground-dwelling sand partridges run with incredible rapidity or rest in the shadow of boulders during the noonday heat. Flocks of such birds as pelicans, flamingos, cormorants, herons, and ducks inhabit the swamps around the Sea of Galilee and Lake Huleh and catch fish in the teeming waters. The little Kentish plover patrols the tide line of the Mediterranean, keeping its feet dry just beyond the reach of the waves, while overhead the common tern hovers and flies on narrow wings. Griffon vultures nest in Palestine's rocky ravines, and here too are veritable clouds of rock doves which flutter down on every stony ledge. Until recently the swift-running Syrian ostrich, largest of living birds, roamed the eastern desert. These are only a few of the birds the early Hebrews watched with wonder and admiration, rejoicing in the variety of winged creatures God has made and finding in them an expression of the marvelous fullness of life.

But Palestine is more than a home for many species of birds; it is also a highway for vast hordes of migrants. Long before men used this country as a convenient land bridge between Africa and Asia, birds flew on its aerial highways in their annual journeys north and south. They continued to fly serenely above armies spreading destruction, traders with the products of new civilizations in their packs, and tribes on the march—today they share the sky with man-made "birds" of peace and war. In spring innumerable birds travel along the Nile Valley and the western shores of the Red Sea from the lakes and jungles of Africa and some come even from its southern extremity. Crossing over near Suez they continue northward, the large soaring birds flying overland by day, for the heated air of desert regions rises in strong updrafts and helps them accomplish their journey with slight effort. Small birds usually migrate unseen during the night, resting and feeding on Palestine's abundance during the day. Some birds of the huge migrating flocks remain in this richly-varied country to build nests and rear young, but the majority merely pause for rest and refreshment before continuing their northward journey to breeding grounds in Europe or Asia. Both migrants and nesters take their toll of the swarming insects and small animals which are their natural food and which they help to keep in check.

In the fall the aerial highways are again thronged with multitudes of feathered creatures and their young returning from the north to seek a more favorable environment for the winter. Some come from the cold steppes of Asia or from the fields and forests of Europe, some move in from the east or from the west. Birds are true internationalists, freely crossing perhaps half a dozen boundaries in a day, needing no passport, for the world is theirs. They have wings and can go anywhere. It can be said of those that arrive in Palestine: "And they shall come from the east, and from the west, and from the north, and from the south, and shall sit down in the kingdom of God."

A complete list of all the birds found in this region would be only part of Adam's great list, but it would be long and varied. It would include residents, summer breeders wintering elsewhere, winter visitors nesting elsewhere, migrants passing through the country on regular routes, stragglers, and accidentals. Adam's list of bird names is only a hint in an ancient story and, as far as we know, the attempt to compile a systematic list of Palestinian birds was not made until the eighteenth century.

The first modern study by a qualified observer was undertaken some two hundred years ago by a young Swedish naturalist, Frederick Hasselquist, a pupil of Carl Linnaeus. Though in delicate health, Hasselquist spent four years in this region exploring plant and animal life, collecting specimens, and taking extensive notes. His exertions in the hot climate proved too much for him and on his way home he died in Smyrna in 1752 at the age of thirty-one, "wasting away," Linnaeus said, "like a lamp whose oil is spent."

Linnaeus published his notes in a posthumous volume entitled *Iter Palaestinum* which contains the chapter, "Animals Which I Saw in the Holy Land." Hasselquist lists fifteen kinds of birds and the places where he found them. He saw a falcon, possibly a peregrine, trained by the Arabs for hunting. In Galilee he saw a vulture, a kestrel in the mountains, many jackdaws and green woodspites (woodpeckers) in the oaks, bee-catchers in the plains, goldfinches in the gardens, and many turtle-doves and ring doves. Among the willows of the Jordan and the olive trees of Judea he saw nightingales. In the deserts he found red partridges and quails. He said there were larks "everywhere." Near Jerusalem he saw an Egyptian vulture whose appearance seemed to him "as horrid as can well be imagined." After describing the naked wrinkled face, large eyes, hooked black beak and talons extended for prey, he remarked that here were "qualities enough to make the beholder shudder with horror." But after this outburst Hasselquist writes that "the inhabitants of Egypt cannot be enough thankful to Providence for this bird. All places around Cairo are filled with the dead bodies of asses and camels; and thousands of these birds fly about and devour the carcasses before they putrify and fill the air with noxious exhalations."

More than a century after Hasselquist, Archduke Rudolph of Hapsburg on a shooting expedition in the Jordan Valley saw many of the birds of prey of this region and published his observations of them.

In 1884 the Committee of the Palestine Exploration Fund published in London the first comprehensive list of Palestinian birds, compiled by Canon Henry B. Tristram of Durham, a well-informed observer of nature. His *Flora and Fauna of Palestine* and *The Survey of Western Palestine* were based upon four extended visits to the country between 1858 and 1881. Tristram listed 348 species of birds in this region.

Bird studies continued to be made there. As Egypt and Palestine have many of the same birds, almost all of the Palestinian species are described in Colonel Richard Meinertzhagen's two large illustrated volumes on Egyptian birds published in 1930 under the authority of the Egyptian government. His work was based on bird collections and notes of J. M. Nicoll and is entitled *Nicoll's Birds of Egypt*. In 1954 Colonel Meinertzhagen's *Birds of Arabia* was published and it, too, contains detailed information about the birds of Palestine.

Though on active service in World War II, soldier naturalists in the British Middle East Forces recorded 364 species, 68 subspecies, and 37 others in this area and from these records Captain Eric Hardy compiled *A Handlist of the Birds of Palestine,* a mimeographed booklet issued by the British Middle East Forces in 1946.

Professor Fritz S. Bodenheimer of the Hebrew University in Jerusalem listed 413 species and subspecies in *Animal Life in Palestine,* published in Jerusalem in 1953. He stated that this figure is not final.

Victor Howells in *A Naturalist in Palestine,* published in 1956, vividly described the birds and other creatures he saw there during the months from August to June. He noted that bird environments are being altered: swamps, especially the vast ones around Lake Huleh with its astonishingly rich bird life, are being drained; cities built; fields cultivated; orchards and vineyards planted; water piped into deserts like the Negeb; and millions of seedling trees planted on bare, eroded slopes where once the ancient forests grew. Such changes inevitably affect bird populations: some birds are pushed out while others move in.

As ornithologists continue Adam's task of observing, naming, and classifying birds, many surely pause in the midst of their labors to say:

> O Lord, how manifold are thy works!
> In wisdom hast thou made them all;
> the earth is full of thy creatures.
>
> Psalm 104:24, RSV

CHAPTER 3 ⚜

The Raven and the Dove

IT HAD rained and rained. There had been forty days of incessant downpour beating upon the wooden roof, filling the Ark with a frightening roar. Inside everyone was damp, weary, discouraged. They were a small group, Noah and his wife, their three sons Shem, Ham, and Japheth, together with their wives. But the eight people were not alone, for around them were the animals, hundreds of them patiently enduring the pitching and tossing of the Ark as it floated on the swirling waters of the great flood which now engulfed the earth.

In the beginning it had been a magnificent adventure. Noah's sons had been lighthearted as they cut and planed the gopher wood and built the Ark watertight according to exact specifications. Noah did everything "according to all that God commanded him," for he was that sort of man. Onlookers might jeer at him while he built the huge ship on dry land, far from any river, but Noah kept steadily at the task the Lord had laid upon him until the strange vessel was finished. Then God commanded him:

And of every living thing of all flesh, two of every sort shalt thou bring into the ark, to keep them alive with thee. They shall be male and female. Of fowls after their kind, and of cattle after their kind, of every creeping thing of the earth after his kind, two of every sort shall come unto thee, to keep them alive.

Genesis 6:19-20

Above the procession of creatures into the Ark flew the birds. They are prominent in Noah's story and all eighteen references to them are quoted in this book except Genesis 6:7; 7:3, 8, 14; 8:19, 20. The perching birds found places for themselves along the rafters, while others stood about in uneasy groups. Outside "the windows of heaven were opened," the rains began, and the waters rose and prevailed until even the mountains were covered "and all flesh died that moved upon the earth, both of fowl and of cattle and of beast and of every creeping thing . . . and every man" (Genesis 7:21).

Only at the last could the flood destroy such birds as sea gulls, petrels, and albatrosses, for these can sleep on the water and live for months at a time far out at sea. Eventually even these birds of the lonely ocean wastes must find some shore on which to lay their eggs and rear their young, or their kind, too, would perish, joining "all in whose nostrils was the breath of life, of all that was in the dry land . . . both man and cattle and the creeping things and the fowl of the heaven" (Genesis 7:22-23).

Then after many days God remembered Noah. Within the Ark to ears long accustomed to the drumming of rain came a new and welcome sound. It was the wind. The roar of the downpour diminished and finally ceased altogether. Day after day the waters subsided and at the end of a hundred and fifty days we are told that the vessel at last came to rest upon the mountains of Ararat. Noah opened a window and saw outside a vast expanse of water broken only by mountaintops. The sight dismayed him. In some direction far beyond the horizon there might be dry land, but only creatures of the air could find it.

Noah now proceeded to follow the custom of ancient navigators lost at sea. When their ships were blown off course and out of sight of land, they released doves kept aboard in cages for such contingencies. The direction in which the doves flew off indicated where the nearest land lay. Centuries later Columbus, changing course to follow the direction of flying birds, made his famous landfall. Noah, perhaps because his situation was somewhat different from that of other navigators, decided first to release one of his ravens: "and he sent forth a raven" (Genesis 8:7). In the Ark's dark interior the raven had been croaking dismally its repeated *"prruk," "cruck," "whow,"* or *"glog."* Noah brought it to the window and launched the great bird into the air. Its glossy black feathers shone with steel blue and purple iridescence as it took off and flew with strong and measured flaps into a threatening and desolate world.

In selecting the raven as his first scout Noah made an excellent choice, for this "black dweller of the mountain crags" is a powerful and unusually astute and resourceful bird, possibly the most highly developed of birds, and it can even be taught to utter a few words. With a wingspread of four feet and great strength and endurance, ravens survive where smaller, weaker birds perish. With their vigorous, steady wing-beats they can fly without rest for long periods of time, covering immense distances. Storms do not frighten them and they seem to enjoy soaring high in the face of an approaching gale and opposing its fury. As they circle higher and higher their keen eyes enable them to see for miles around. Because they have heavy beaks and can eat almost anything including carrion, Noah's raven would have found enough to eat in the floating wreckage of a flooded world.

Until the waters disappeared, the raven flew to and fro, like Poe's raven, "desolate yet all undaunted." If it returned to rest upon the Ark at night, as may be implied in the words "went to and fro until the waters were dried up from the earth" (Genesis 8:7, RSV), the bird did not re-enter the sheltering interior and the story indicates that Noah received no help from his great black bird. The raven has been blamed for its disregard of Noah's plight. A legend says that its feathers, which were originally pure white, turned inky black as its punishment for failing Noah. But the raven can hardly be blamed for behaving in its own characteristic manner. Did the raven really abandon Noah in his predicament or was its failure to reappear and seek shelter within the Ark the very sign Noah needed? Noah undoubtedly understood the habits of ravens and the bird's absence must have indicated to him that the flood was receding.

Next he "sent forth a dove from him, to see if the waters were abated from off the face of the ground" (Genesis 8:8). His gentle gray bird with glossy green and lilac neck feathers perched on his hand for a moment and then with a quick flapping of its wings flew out over the water. This bird might have been one of Palestine's abundant rock doves which are believed to be the ancestors of our common domestic pigeon and of the homing pigeons so often employed as message carriers. A dove was well-suited to this task, for when it flies it attains remarkable speed in its first moments and can cover long distances very rapidly. It nests in cliffs and on ledges, preferring pleasant valleys to barren wastes or wind-swept mountaintops.

The dove or pigeon, which is the bird most often mentioned in the Bible, became the chief sacrificial bird, but it was also a creature whose beauty people greatly admired. A psalm whose meaning is somewhat obscure describes the iridescent sheen of dove feathers:

> the wings of a dove covered with silver,
> its pinions with green gold.
> Psalm 68:13, RSV

The Song of Solomon compares the loved one's beauty to that of doves:

> How fair you are, my dear,
> how fair with dove-like eyes!
>
> Song of Solomon 1:15, Moffatt; cf. 4:1

The loved one herself is called "my love, my dove" (5:2; 6:9).

But Noah's dove, in this first bird story of the Bible, had an important mission to accomplish. When Noah saw his dove returning he knew the waters must still lie deep in the valleys.

> But the dove found no rest for the sole of her foot, and she returned unto him into the ark, for the waters were on the face of the whole earth.
>
> Genesis 8:9

She had served him well and deserved protection, so Noah "put forth his hand and took her and pulled her in unto him into the ark."

Seven days passed before Noah again "sent forth the dove." All day while his gentle bird was absent Noah must have scanned the empty horizon for her return, anxiously wondering how much longer his family and the creatures with them could endure confinement in the dark interior of the Ark. Were the waters still deep everywhere? Had his dove found dry land? As darkness approached and he feared she had perished, a spot on the horizon grew larger and more distinct and out of the dusk emerged the small and valiant form of his dove carrying something in her beak.

> And the dove came in to him in the evening. And, lo, in her mouth was an olive leaf plucked off!
>
> Genesis 8:11

Here was proof that in valleys where the olive trees grow the flood waters were subsiding. The earth was drying out and returning to her appointed seasons. God had made peace with man.

Some legends say that it was at this time that the dove, alighting on the moist earth, stained her feet red in the brightly colored mud.

Another week passed and again Noah "sent forth the dove" (Genesis 8:12). This time she found a home for herself and abundant food in the lowlands and "returned not again unto him any more." Needing no further proof that the earth was habitable, Noah removed the covering of the Ark and "behold, the face of the ground was dry." Then he heard God speaking to him:

> Go forth of the ark, thou and thy wife and thy sons and thy sons' wives with thee. Bring forth with thee every living thing that is with thee, of all flesh, both of fowl and of cattle and of every creeping thing that creepeth

upon the earth, that they may breed abundantly in the earth and be fruitful and multiply upon the earth.

Genesis 8:16-17

Led by all the birds of heaven there issued from the dark interior of the Ark a motley throng of living beings. The birds soared and wheeled and glided through the air on wings long deprived of their own element. As Noah watched them fly away he marveled at their skill in the air. Within the Ark they had seemed frail and insignificant, but now even the smallest of these feathered creatures mounted fearlessly into the vast spaces of sky where man could not follow.

With solid ground once more beneath his feet, Noah took stones and built an altar to the Lord and there offered his sacrifices. As smoke rose from the altar there came the sound of God's voice blessing Noah and his sons. God had pardoned men for their evil thoughts and wicked deeds and was about to make His first covenant of love and protection. Surely all fell silent and every wing was folded as God uttered His promise:

And I, behold I establish my covenant with you and with your seed after you, and with every living creature that is with you, of the fowl, of the cattle, and of every beast of the earth. . . . The waters shall no more become a flood to destroy all flesh.

Genesis 9:9-10, 15

Looking up Noah saw a rainbow shining in the receding storm clouds and he believed it was a heavenly symbol of God's mercy and goodness. In the light of the rainbow he knew that henceforth God would guide nature's orderly changes upon which bird and beast and man depend and that "while the earth remaineth, seedtime and harvest, and cold and heat, and summer and winter, and day and night shall not cease." The rainbow arching the heavens was the emblem of God's everlasting covenant not only with Noah and his descendants, but with the whole human race "and every living creature of all flesh that is upon the earth."

> "For a small moment have I forsaken thee,
>   but with great mercies will I gather thee.
> In a little wrath I hid my face from thee for a moment,
>   but with everlasting kindness will I have mercy on thee,"
>   saith the Lord thy Redeemer.

> "For this is as the waters of Noah unto me;
>   for as I have sworn that the waters of Noah
>   should no more go over the earth,

so have I sworn that I would not be wroth with thee,
nor rebuke thee.

"For the mountains shall depart
and the hills be removed,
but my kindness shall not depart from thee
neither shall the covenant of my peace be removed,"
saith the Lord that hath mercy on thee.

Isaiah 54:7-10

PART II

The People of God

CHAPTER 4 ❧
Abraham's Birds

OUT of the distant past towers the figure of Abraham, the father of an extraordinary people and a monumental symbol of faith and obedience. The Bible depicts him as the willing agent of God's purpose for mankind. "By faith Abraham, when he was called . . . obeyed and he went out not knowing whither he went." It shows him as a man inspired by a vision and with the ability and the steadiness of purpose to translate it into reality. Abraham became a great traveler, always undertaking his journeys at the command of the Lord who said to him:

Get thee out of thy country and from thy kindred and from thy father's house, unto a land that I will show thee. And I will make of thee a great nation and I will bless thee and make thy name great, and thou shalt be a blessing. . . . And in thee shall all families of the earth be blessed.

Genesis 12:1-3

Abraham is the first man in the Bible whose journeys can be traced on a map. Unlike his ancestor Noah, he did not go by ship, but proceeded slowly overland from Ur of the Chaldeans, near the head of the Persian Gulf, along the arch of the Fertile Crescent and thence southward, traversing the length of Palestine and continuing on to Egypt before he finally returned to the Promised Land.

Wherever Abraham pitched his tents he was surrounded by birds, for all the lands through which he traveled are on the main migration routes of countless feathered creatures. His own journeys have about them certain aspects of migration. In the Tigris - Euphrates region he would have encountered the typical birds of these broad valleys: partridges, magpies, francolins, ducks, geese, snipe, woodcock —all abounding a century ago when Lady Anne Blunt and her husband journeyed there. If Abraham skirted the Arabian Desert in spring, the area may have appeared to him as they describe it in *Bedouin Tribes of the Euphrates*—

a vast undulating plain of grass and flowers. The purple stock which predominates on the better soils gives its color to the whole country. . . . The hollows are filled with the richest meadow grass, wild barley, wild oats, and wild rye, the haunts of quails. . . . On the poorer soils the flowers are not less gay—tulips, marigolds, asters, irises, and certain pink wallflowers, the most beautiful of all, cousins each of them, to our garden plants; for it was from the desert, doubtless, that the Crusaders brought us many of those we now consider essentially English flowers.

Here Abraham found desert birds: sand grouse, desert and red-legged partridges, larks, kestrels, and many more. Continuing on through deep ravines, past mountains, and across the plains of Palestine he must have seen the birds mentioned in the Bible. His flocks and herds spread out for miles along the rough caravan trails, grazing as they went, and they were watched by eagles and vultures circling overhead and waiting for some hapless creature to fall by the wayside. When Abraham came to the shores of the ancient Nile he found it teeming with bird life and its waters a veritable paradise for waterfowl. The Bible has no record of these birds which flew through eastern skies so long ago.

There is, however, one bird story in the Abraham cycle. It concerns the two commonest groups of Bible birds: those offered as sacrifices and the fearsome birds of prey. The story began one night in the darkness of Abraham's tent where he sat alone remembering all the dangers and difficulties met and overcome in obeying the Lord's command to leave his native country and journey toward the Promised Land. Years had passed since he set out with his wife Sarah, believing that they were to be the parents of a nation destined to bring blessing to all mankind. The years brought him prosperity—his flocks became large and his tents numerous. Yet in none of them dwelt a son born to him and his wife Sarah and they were now an old and childless couple. What of God's promise that Sarah would be the mother of kings and Abraham the father of a great nation?

Suddenly he was roused from his thoughts by a voice saying: "Fear not, Abram, I am thy shield and thy exceeding great reward!"

The Lord repeated His promise of a son and brought Abraham out of his tent to show him the stars, hundreds and hundreds of them shining above his encampment on the plain of Mamre and forming a vault of light over the whole land of Canaan. Abraham heard the Lord's promise that his descendants would become as many in number as the stars and that he would inherit the Promised Land. Contrary to all appearances, Abraham "believed in the Lord, and he counted it to him for righteousness."

The next morning Abraham prepared a sacrifice to seal the covenant between God and himself. He believed that the poured-out blood of a heifer, a she-goat, and a ram would bring him into the very presence of God, and he slaughtered his animals, divided their bodies, and laid them upon the ground. He completed his sacrifice by offering "a turtledove and a young pigeon" (Genesis 15:9).

Abraham may have searched the sky to assure himself that no vulture or eagle saw him lay out the carcasses. There must have been a dark speck, too far away to be identified as a bird, but it was a watchful bird of prey hungrily circling high in the sky. Within minutes Abraham heard the rush of powerful wings as "the fowls came down upon the carcases" (Genesis 15:11). These were the *ayit* or "screamers," the ravenous birds of prey that constantly soar above Palestine scanning the land below with powerful telescopic eyes. When one of them spots carrion it swoops down upon it: the sudden dive is a signal to other birds that can see the first bird, but are too far away to see the carcass for themselves. In turn they also swoop down, transmitting the signal in ever-widening circles until hungry birds for miles around gather at the feast.

Birds of prey were well known to Abraham, for he lived where they were exceedingly plentiful. To feed his many dependents he constantly slaughtered animals from his flocks and herds and threw the offal to the birds. He frequently saw huge carrion birds fighting over scraps of food and perhaps he learned to value them for keeping the land around his tents clean. But Abraham's sacrifice was an offering to God and he would not allow carrion birds to consume it, so all day long he guarded the sacrifice and as fast as birds swooped down upon it he "drove them away." The violence of the words suggests large birds and a hard-fought battle. It lasted until sunset when darkness brought an end to the arrival of hungry birds. This behavior agrees with the results of a number of recent experiments in which carrion birds located their food by sight rather than by smell.

Birds were not the victims in the next sacrifice recorded in Abraham's story. This time he believed the Lord desired him to offer his only son Isaac born to him and to Sarah in their old age. But when his knife was upraised ready to slay the son on whom all his hopes centered, he heard a voice bidding him stop and in a thicket nearby he saw the ram which God had sent for the sacrifice. Abraham had proved his complete obedience and again he heard the voice of God saying: "In thy seed shall all the nations of the earth be blessed, because thou hast obeyed my voice."

Abraham's son Isaac and his grandson Jacob became the fathers of a mighty people who, like Abraham and like Noah (Genesis 8:20), often sacrificed turtledoves and young pigeons. Leviticus states that if a person is too poor to sacrifice a sheep or goat he may offer instead turtledoves or young pigeons as a burnt sacrifice (Leviticus 1:14-17; 14:22, 30), as a sin offering and trespass offering (Leviticus 5:7, 11; 14:22, 30), and for ordinary purifications (Leviticus 12:6, 8; 15:14, 29; Numbers 6:10). This concession to poverty showed that the Law was mindful of the many poor in Israel.

In giving a choice of birds, turtledoves or young pigeons, those who framed the Law revealed considerable ornithological knowledge. Why were these two species named? Was it necessary to give a choice? And why were the pigeons to be young? Answers to these questions lie in the nature and habits of the two species.

The turtledove is a wild bird, never domesticated like its cousin, the common pigeon, for it has strong migratory habits. Its arrival in Palestine every spring when "the voice of the turtle [dove] is heard in our land" (Song of Solomon 2:12), is one of the most striking events of the bird year. The turtledove is smaller and slenderer than the pigeon from whom it can be distinguished by its rounded black tail edged with white. There are reddish feathers in the turtledove's blue-gray head, its mantle is yellowish-brown, and on the sides of the neck it has a black and white striped patch. Rapid fliers, they can hurtle from a perch at full speed. They feed on the ground on grain, seeds, and clover. When approached they flutter away, but can easily be captured on the ground by snares. Only from April to October can turtledoves be obtained, for they spend the winter in Africa. This is the reason another bird had to be authorized for the winter sacrifices.

Commonest of all the pigeons of Palestine is the rock pigeon or rock dove, the second sacrificial bird in Leviticus. Deep in rocky fissures they are safe from hawks and roost in myriads. So abundant are they in the wadies that several are named for them, like the Wadi Hamam, i.e., "Ravine of Pigeons." The rock pigeon's plumage is blue-gray, but the greenish and lilac feathers of its neck have a metallic luster. Its wings and tail are dark gray above, white beneath. Like the turtledove, it is a very fast flier and attains a remarkable speed in a few yards. Rock pigeons do not migrate, but remain in Palestine, build nests, and rear young throughout the year. Adult wild birds are extremely wary and, unlike the turtledove, cannot easily be trapped, but at any time of year a search among the rocks discovers nests with helpless young. The Law, recognizing the habits of these birds, specified that young pigeons are as acceptable a sacrifice as turtledoves.

Besides the exceedingly numerous turtledoves and rock pigeons there are at least four other species of pigeons in Palestine. The Hebrews had only two words: *tor,* translated "turtledove," and *yonah,* translated "dove" or "pigeon," for all species of this large family designated as *Columbidae.* Members of this family occur throughout the world, more than three hundred living species being known. The much-lamented American passenger pigeon, the last member of whose immense flocks died in 1914, belonged to this family and the huge, flightless dodo bird, now extinct, was a relative.

Though members of the *Columbidae* family were the chief sacrificial birds both in Old and New Testament times, the Law provided for the use of others in two special cases. These were in the very ancient rituals of cleansing a leper and cleansing a house. The Law said that two birds were to be used (Leviticus 14:4-7, 49-53), but, instead of designating these birds as *tor* or *yonah,* it used the word *tsippor,* generally translated "sparrow." *Tsippor* really indicates any little bird, even Abraham's turtledove and pigeon of Genesis 15:9 being called *tsippor* in the next verse, probably because they are fairly small birds.

A cured leper brought two birds to the priest who killed one of them "in an earthen vessel over running water." With a scarlet thread the priest tied together a bundle of twigs from the great cedar tree and sprigs of the lowly hyssop. This bundle and the living bird he dipped in the blood of the sacrificed bird. After the leper was sprinkled with blood he was pronounced clean and the priest "let the living bird loose into the open field" (Leviticus 14:7), believing that it carried away all uncleanness. We welcome the picture of one bird escaping from these bloody sacrifices and rejoicing in its airborne body as it flies "out of the city into the open fields" (Leviticus 14:53).

For centuries Abraham's descendants slaughtered birds and other creatures for their sacrifices until men began to suspect that there is really no connection between the blood of a bird and a man's sin. Finally, belief in the efficacy of the ancient sacrifices began to wane as a new understanding of man's relations with God was taught by the great prophets of Israel.

Purge me with hyssop, and I shall be clean,
   wash me, and I shall be whiter than snow. . . .
Create in me a clean heart, O God,
   and renew a right spirit within me.
Cast me not away from thy presence,
   and take not thy holy spirit from me. . . .
For thou desirest not sacrifice, else would I give it,
   thou delightest not in burnt offering.
The sacrifices of God are a broken spirit,
   a broken and a contrite heart, O God, thou wilt not despise.

                                        Psalm 51:7, 10-11, 16-17

CHAPTER 5 ~~~

Birds of Egypt

WHILE the pharaohs ruled Egypt and sailed in their royal barges on the reed-bordered Nile, some of the men and women of the Bible lived in this ancient land. The pyramids were already centuries old when Abraham journeyed there from famine-stricken Canaan. He arrived as a powerful nomad chief with flocks and herds, but it was far otherwise with his great-grandson Joseph who, when only a lad, was brought to Egypt as a slave. His brothers could no longer endure Joseph's proud manner nor the sight of his coat of many colors, so one day they sold him to traders bound for Egypt. He would be lost to them forever in Egypt, or so they supposed.

It was bad enough to be a slave, but Joseph found it far worse to be a prisoner thrown into an Egyptian prison on a false charge. He derived little comfort from the fact that his two fellow prisoners were men of consequence—the pharaoh's chief butler and his chief baker. One night both men dreamed dreams, but only Joseph could interpret them. Joseph predicted that the pharaoh would release his butler from prison and restore him to his exalted post in the palace. When this good fortune came to pass, the butler proved ungrateful to Joseph and forgot him for a long time.

Far different was the fate of the baker. He dreamed that on his head were three white baskets, one upon another, the uppermost containing "all manner of bakemeats for Pharaoh, and the birds did eat them out of the basket upon my head" (Genesis 40:17). Joseph knew that this dream contained a grim warning that the mighty ruler of Egypt was about to hang his baker. Informing the baker of his fate, Joseph added: "the birds shall eat thy flesh from off thee" (Genesis 40:19).

While the birds the unfortunate baker saw in his sleep were only dream birds they must have resembled actual creatures he had seen, perhaps as he plied his trade at the royal bakeries. Were the pastries baked for the pharaoh's table sometimes burned and thrown out for the birds? What kinds of birds gather around such food? As the Hebrew word used in this passage is the general term *oph*, used for any bird, it provides no clue to the species. Today in city parks pigeons and sparrows gather in fluttering, noisy flocks to peck at crumbs from sandwiches and at pieces of stale bread thrown to them. These might well be the birds mentioned by the pharaoh's baker, for many sparrows and pigeons lived in ancient Egypt, as wall paintings and sculptured reliefs show.

If the wretched baker saw dream pigeons and sparrows pecking at his pastries, they were different from the birds that Joseph predicted would feed upon the baker's hanged body, for these would have been flesh eaters: vultures, eagles, and kites, which are still the scavengers in Egypt. Many are represented in Egyptian hieroglyphics, wall paintings, statues, and jewelry. We can even see some of the actual birds themselves, mummified and thus strangely preserved in all their plumage, while their fellows, with whom they flew through the ancient skies so long ago, have been dust for millenniums. Five hundred bird mummies from the twentieth dynasty were unwrapped not long ago and found to include such carrion eaters as: griffon and Egyptian vultures; imperial, short-toed, and spotted eagles; red, and black kites.

The story of how the fortunate butler, who had been restored to his post at the palace, finally remembered Joseph in prison and brought about his release is well known. There followed Joseph's meteoric rise to power over the whole land, his reunion with his brothers who came to Egypt for corn, and finally his father Jacob's arrival with eleven sons and all his household to join Joseph in the land of the Nile. The twelve tribes of Jacob, or Israel as he was often called, flourished in Egypt in the rich land of Goshen where they found good pastures for their flocks and herds.

In the Nile Delta at Lake Menzaleh, near the traditional site of the Israelite sojourn in Egypt, water birds are especially abundant. On his canoe trip in this region almost a hundred years ago, J. MacGregor saw innumerable birds and described, in his *Rob Roy on the Jordan and Nile,* a sight the people of Israel may have seen:

We had been told of the enormous flocks of wild fowl to be seen on this lake . . . but I never expected to see birds so numerous and so close together that their compact mass formed living islands upon the water, and when the wind now took me swiftly to these, and the island rose up with a loud and thrilling din to become a feathered cloud in the air, the impression was one of vastness and innumerable teeming life, which it is entirely impossible to convey in words. The larger geese and pelicans and swans floated like ships at anchor. The long-legged flamingoes and other waders traced out the shape of the shallows by their standing in the water. Smaller ducks were scattered in whole regiments of skirmishers about the grand army, but every battalion of the gabbling, shrieking host seemed to be disciplined, orderly, and distinct.

Some thirty-five hundred years earlier than this account the birds of the Delta were probably no less abundant. The Israelites surely learned from the Egyptians how to hunt ducks in the marshes, how to domesticate geese for their poultry yards, and how to trap quails on migration. Scenes such as these are depicted on the walls of Egyptian tombs. The Egyptians evidently enjoyed nature, for they observed birds and other creatures carefully and their artists rendered the small, lively details of bird life with great skill and accuracy. Forty-five identifiable species have been discovered in Egyptian tomb decorations.

When a new pharaoh came to power who had not known Joseph, the people of Israel were oppressed and enslaved. The pharaoh forced them to build for him two great cities, and, lest these foreigners become "more and mightier" than the Egyptians, he ordered every one of their boy babies thrown into the river. One infant escaped this cruel edict by being hidden in a woven bulrush basket made watertight with pitch. His mother floated the basket among the reeds growing at the river's edge and posted the baby's sister nearby to guard him. In ancient times, as Egyptian wall paintings show, the papyrus reed grew abundantly along the Nile, while on its higher banks lively birds flitted in the palms, acacias, and sycamores. The baby was far too young to notice the birds and his small sister too frightened by her responsibility to delight in the bright-colored, feathered creatures.

The tall papyrus which hid the baby's basket also concealed the nests of waterfowl—herons, ibises, swans, and geese. Perhaps a sacred ibis, disturbed by a tiny wail from the strange, nestlike object among the reeds, shook out its white feathers and lacy black tail plumes and, holding high its bare black head and neck, waded cautiously over to the bulrush ark. The sacred ibis is a fairly large bird, twenty-eight inches from bill-tip to tail-tip, and stands on long thin legs. With its slender, arched bill it probes in the mud for crustaceans, mollusks, small reptiles, and worms. In ancient times the Nile provided plentiful food for these birds and in its dense papyrus thickets they reared their young. Through the centuries the papyrus gradually disappeared from the lower reaches of the Nile, and the sacred ibis, like the hippopotamus, became extinct in Egypt. Today one journeys a thousand miles upstream into central Africa before finding both the hippopotamus and the sacred ibis.

On that far-off day when the great white bird looked inside the bulrush ark it would have seen merely a human baby, fretful and crying like any other infant. A baby was all the pharaoh's daughter and her maidens saw when they came down to the river to bathe. But the princess had compassion on the child and drew him from the water and brought him up as her own son. She named him Moses.

Moses became "learned in all the wisdom of the Egyptians" and was undoubtedly taught to read hieroglyphics which contained so many picture signs of birds that it required something of a bird watcher's skill to become a proficient reader. One had to recognize such details as the bare head and curved neck of the Egyptian vulture, the hooked beak of the peregrine falcon, the flat facial disk of the eagle owl, the crest of the hoopoe, the long neck of the cormorant, the sharp tail of the pintail duck, and the down-curved beak of the sacred ibis. Alan H. Gardiner's *Egyptian Grammar* contains a section listing bird signs which include twenty-two different kinds of birds, eight symbols showing a part of a bird such as a wing or a feather, and more than a dozen miscellaneous avian symbols. Some experts believe that sixteen of these hieroglyphics can be positively identified as to species. One section of hieroglyphic, then, was a veritable bird alphabet, the figures often carefully drawn or carved by artists who had observed the characteristics of birds. Moses must have learned to recognize them all, even the very common "chick" hieroglyphic whose identity is disputed today. If it were a young quail, as many believe, it is strange that adult, domesticated quails are never portrayed in the poultry-yard scenes. Perhaps the "chick" is not a quail at all, but some flightless bird well known in ancient Egypt but now extinct. Many flightless birds that are known to have existed at the dawn of history soon became extinct, for these were among the first to vanish when man became a hunter.

As a young Egyptian prince, Moses saw men venerating three birds: the sacred ibis of Thoth, god of learning, science, and art; the falcon of Horus, chief god of united Egypt; and the vulture of Nekhebt. The bird gods of Egypt must have fascinated Moses until one day, as a weary fugitive, far out in the desert of Sinai at the holy mountain, the reality of all the Egyptian deities shriveled in the heat of a burning bush. As he watched the extraordinary sight of a bush that burned yet was not consumed, Moses' ancestral faith was rekindled. God came to him and spoke to him and in this theophany Moses heard his Lord saying:

I am the God of thy father, the God of Abraham, the God of Isaac, and the God of Jacob. . . . I have surely seen the affliction of my people . . . and I am come down to deliver them out of the hand of the Egyptians and to bring them . . . unto a good land and a large, unto a land flowing with milk and honey.

Exodus 3:6-8

Moses' heart leaped up in thankfulness. His people were to be saved from intolerable oppression. He gave no thought to the means by which liberation would be accomplished until he heard the Lord say to him:

Come now therefore and I will send thee unto Pharaoh, that *thou* mayest bring forth my people, the children of Israel, out of Egypt.

Exodus 3:10

"Who am I?" asked Moses in dismay, convinced that he was too weak and unworthy for this immense task. But with divine help Moses returned to his wretched countrymen in Egypt and began his long struggle with the pharaoh to free the people of Israel.

Before the pharaoh consented to their departure from Egypt ten plagues fell on that unhappy land. No birds are mentioned in this story, though all the birds of Egypt must have been involved in these catastrophes. When the waters became polluted and "turned to blood," fish in the Nile surely died. Did fish-eating birds such as kingfishers, ospreys, cormorants, gulls, pelicans, and herons die also? This must have been the case, for many of these birds eat tadpoles and frogs and the next "plague" was a plague of frogs. Not enough birds had survived the polluted waters to keep the frogs in check and they covered the land. Then lice and flies appeared in such immense swarms that all the insect-eating birds of Egypt, the sparrows, flycatchers, larks, swallows, pipits, wagtails, warblers, wrens, and starlings must have flourished on the abundant insect banquet. Next, the sickness that attacked both man and beast caused many to die and covered the land with carrion on which birds of prey feast. Then hail beat down seed-bearing plants on which finches and other birds feed and swarms of locusts consumed any green thing left. Where were the storks that usually keep the locusts in check? The balance of nature was grievously upset during the ten plagues while the pharaoh pitted his stubborn self-will against Moses and Israel and Israel's God.

At length Egypt's ruler relented and let the people of Israel leave the country where they had lived since the time of Joseph. They celebrated their first passover and followed Moses out of the land of the Nile, while above them soared and circled hosts of migrating birds on their ancestral flyway. The Israelites were now as free from Egyptian bondage as the birds themselves, but four hundred years of living in the fruitful valley of the Nile had not prepared them for the hardships and dangers of the dry and stony Wilderness through which their road now led. Like the birds they needed guidance and protection if they were to survive. What happened to the people of Israel is a well-known story and the hymn they sang in later years still rings with the faith they forged during the terrible years in the Wilderness:

> I will say of the Lord, "He is my refuge and my fortress,
>   my God, in him will I trust."
> Surely he shall deliver thee from the snare of the fowler,
>   and from the noisome pestilence.
> He shall cover thee with his feathers,
>   and under his wings shalt thou trust.
> His truth shall be thy shield and buckler.
>
>   Psalm 91:2-4

CHAPTER 6 ～

Quails in the Wilderness

FREEDOM from Egyptian bondage became a hollow victory to the people of Israel when they encamped in the Wilderness, for over them hung the specter of starvation like an evil vulture. Lack of food made the children silent and hollow-eyed. Their parents began to lose all zest for their great adventure of freedom under God and they began to murmur against Moses. The food they had managed to bring out of Egypt was now gone and they despaired of finding anything to eat in the barren deserts through which they journeyed.

Desperation was not a new experience for Israel. Departing from Egypt they had been pursued by the pharaoh's horsemen and chariots and trapped between the oncoming army and the sea. In this hopeless predicament they cried: "It had been better for us to serve the Egyptians, than that we should die in the wilderness!"

Moses rallied the panic-stricken people. Their impulse to scatter and run blindly in every direction he checked with his heroic shout: "Fear ye not, stand still!" With incandescent faith he promised them the seemingly impossible: "See the salvation of the Lord which he will show you today!"

On that very day they had indeed seen the impossible take place. An east wind divided the waters of the sea and made a dry path over which the people of Israel escaped to the opposite shore. The Egyptians, following close behind, attempted to cross the exposed sea bottom, but their chariot wheels stuck in the soft, moist sand and when the wind shifted and the waters surged back, the mighty Egyptian army was engulfed. Safe on the far shore the people of Israel watched their salvation achieved and began to sing their first hymn of praise:

> Sing ye to the Lord, for he hath triumphed gloriously.
> The horse and his rider hath he thrown into the sea.
>
> Exodus 15:21

In that hour a faith was born which would always sustain them and their spiritual descendants. But their new-found faith was soon tested as they journeyed forward into the Wilderness. At Marah they encountered an enemy more implacable than the Egyptian host, for they were thirsty and could find no pure, sweet water. Forgetting God's mighty act for them at the sea, they cried out from parched throats: "What shall we drink?" Then the Lord taught Moses how to purify the bitter water at Marah and their second great peril was overcome.

Now they were hungry. Forgetting the pure water gushing from a rock and the dry pathway through the sea, their thoughts dwelt on the fatted geese and tasty ducks, the fish and meat so plentiful in Egypt. As they gathered in groups to bewail their fate and criticize Moses, their discontent grew until the whole heroic enterprise was endangered. Wailing, they cried:

> Would to God we had died by the hand of the Lord in the land of Egypt, when we sat by the flesh pots and when we did eat bread to the full! For ye have brought us forth into this wilderness to kill this whole assembly with hunger.
>
> Exodus 16:3

Once again Moses spoke, but his promise that they would eat meat and bread in the morning fell on unbelieving ears and the people endured another miserable night of hunger. During the night, however, the wind shifted and the weather changed.

> And there went forth a wind from the Lord and brought quails from the sea, and let them fall by the camp, as it were a day's journey on this side and . . . on the other side round about the camp, and as it were two cubits high upon the face of the earth.
>
> Numbers 11:31

The little sandy-colored quails which "came up and covered the camp" (Exodus 16:13) were no new delicacy to the Israelites as was the manna that appeared at this time and proved to be a substitute for bread. In Egypt quails had been captured in nets for centuries, as is shown in a wall painting of the twenty-third century b.c. from the tomb of Mera at Saqqara. Undoubtedly the Israelites had often tasted the succulent flesh of these game birds. Hasselquist describes them arriving in March as they have done for thousands of years:

An amazing number of these birds come to Egypt at this time; for in this month the wheat ripens. They conceal themselves amongst the corn, but the Egyptians know extremely well that there are thieves in their grounds; and when they imagine the field to be full of them, they spread a net over the corn, and surround the field, at the same time making a noise, by which the birds are frightened, and endeavouring to rise, are caught in the net in great numbers and make a most delicate and agreeable dish.

In Israel's extremity any food was acceptable, but to be provided with quails in such vast numbers and at just the right moment seemed a miracle indeed. "All that day and all that night and all the next day . . . they gathered the quails" (Numbers 11:32), until it seemed as though the Lord had indeed "rained flesh also upon them as dust, and feathered fowl like as the sand of the sea" (Psalm 78:27). There were bushels and bushels of birds, nine million according to William Gladstone's calculation made on the basis of a thirty-six-hour period and the numbers of Israelites given in the Bible. Though this number is now believed to be exaggerated, it is certain that a vast number of birds appeared. There were far more than the Israelites could eat at one time, so "they spread them all abroad for themselves round about the camp" (Numbers 11:32) to dry and so preserve the flesh for future use.

The quails in this story are depicted according to the true facts of their natural history. Enormous flocks of them migrate north during March and April, reappearing on their way south in August and September. Traveling at night in compact groups they always fly with the wind, for their wings are weak and do not have sufficient lifting power to propel their plump bodies against the wind. They generally select overland routes, but flocks that must cross the Mediterranean choose the shortest sea passage and stop off to rest at Sicily, Malta, or the Greek Islands. Aristotle watched quails collect near the coast waiting for a following wind to help them cross the sea. If the wind shifts while they are over the sea, they are generally blown off course and will eventually fall exhausted into the water. Though the quails of the Bible were wind-driven, they managed to reach land, but they were so fatigued by their struggle against the wind that when they settled on the ground they were unable to fly or run away from the Israelites.

The statement that the birds appeared "as it were two cubits high upon the face of the earth" (Numbers 11:31), can be interpreted in three ways. If the story means that these birds were two cubits or about forty inches tall, they were obviously not quails, for quails are only seven inches from bill to tail-tip. It has been suggested that the birds of this story may have been white storks which migrate through this region in such immense flocks that they sometimes darken the sky. Though storks are large enough for this description, their flesh is inedible, and they can hardly be the birds mentioned. The Douay Version, stemming from St. Jerome's Vulgate, removes the ambiguity of this passage by translating it, "and they flew in the air two cubits high above the ground." Migrating quails fly very low, "two cubits" or three to four feet above ground. Colonel Meinertzhagen describes how, during the second week of September, old men sipping coffee in the streets of Port Said use butterfly nets to catch quails as they fly down the streets at dawn.

While quails do fly low, many scholars interpret the Hebrew text to mean that the birds landed in such great numbers that they covered the ground to a depth of more than three feet. Though undoubtedly an overstatement, it indicates how immense the flock appeared to the people of Israel. It also provides additional confirmation of the identity of these birds, for a vast migratory movement is characteristic of quails. Pliny told the story of a boat crossing the Mediterranean on which so many quails alighted that it sank. Today migrating quails often arrive in such numbers on the Sinai Peninsula that, according to Colonel Meinertzhagen, they literally cover the ground, leaving no room for more birds, unless they alight on the backs of others.

In recent times these very edible birds formed an important export from Egypt and in 1884 some three hundred thousand of them were sold to foreign markets. The trade expanded so rapidly that by 1920 more than three million birds were exported annually. Even the fecund quails with their clutches of six to twenty eggs could not keep pace with this huge slaughter and in six years the export of birds fell to half a million. Then the vast flocks began to disappear. Finally in 1939 the Egyptian government placed restrictions on the netting of quails.

Quails are smaller than the American robin and beautifully marked with black, reddish brown, buff, and white feathers. The female lays her eggs in a nest scooped out of the ground and lined with dry grass or clover. She does all the incubating, though her mate helps her raise the downy chicks that resemble domestic chickens. Their value to man is not alone in their eggs and tasty flesh, for the living birds consume enormous quantities of weed seeds and harmful insects.

Quails on their spring migration through Egypt and Palestine fly low in groups of from ten to forty birds. Though they arrive, as in the Bible story, during the night, they announce their presence early in the morning with a shrill, whistle call, *"peek-whit-whit,"* or a liquid-sounding *"wet-mi-lips."* They repeat this call rapidly throughout the day. When anyone approaches them, they run away, flying up only at the last moment to escape capture. Then they rise very suddenly, uttering a scream, and fly fast, straight, and low. Some quails remain in Palestine to breed, but the greater part of the vast flocks continue north. Their range is immense for they breed throughout Europe, Asia, North Africa, Asia Minor, and Iran east to northern India and they winter in India, Arabia, and Africa north of the equator, and some even continue south to the Cape of Good Hope.

The quails of our story are the migratory quail, *Coturnix coturnix,* sometimes known as the European or Egyptian quail. Their Hebrew name, *selav,* was formerly thought to mean "was at rest" or "grow fat" and was taken to be a reference to their rotund appearance and their reluctance to fly away when flushed, but Dr. G. R. Driver points out that the liquid sound of *selav* is probably an attempt to reproduce their "very liquid" call.

The migratory quail is an Old World bird whose nearest American relatives are the bob-white and the California quail. During the last century the migratory quail was introduced into the northeastern states as a game bird. Thousands were imported and they settled down in their new surroundings, building nests and raising young before flying south in the autumn according to the immemorial custom of their kind. The next spring sportsmen eagerly awaited their reappearance, but not one bird returned. What had happened to them? The fate of the quails remained a mystery until someone remembered that the previous November a ship had reported that while it was sailing hundreds of miles southeast of Cape Hatteras some quails appeared and fell exhausted on deck. Were these the quails introduced into America but still valiantly attempting to migrate in the southeasterly direction their ancestors had used for millenniums from Europe to Africa? If so, the mysterious direction-finders in their tiny brains served them ill in a strange part of the world, for a southeasterly course from New England leads farther and farther into the boundless wastes of the Atlantic where the little migratory quails must have perished in an alien sea.

The wind-blown and exhausted quails of the Exodus story seemed to the people of Israel to be God's bountiful provision for their needs. "The quails were a sign to you" (II Esdras 1:15, RSV).

> Afterwards they saw also a new kind of birds, . . .
> for to give them relief, quails came up from the sea.
> Wisdom 19:11, 12, RSV

> Instead of this punishment thou didst show
>   kindness to thy people,
> and thou didst prepare quails to eat,
> a delicacy to satisfy the desire of appetite.
>   Wisdom 16:2, RSV

Their interpretation of the event also found expression in the Psalms.

> The people asked and he brought quails,
>   and satisfied them with the bread of heaven.
> He opened the rock, and the waters gushed out;
>   they ran in the dry places like a river.
>
> For he remembered his holy promise,
>   and Abraham his servant.
> He brought forth his people with joy,
>   and his chosen with gladness.
>
> And gave them the lands of the heathen;
>   and they inherited the labour of the people,
> that they might observe his statutes
>   and keep his laws.
>
> Praise ye the Lord!
>   Psalm 105:40-45

CHAPTER 7 ~~

On Eagles' Wings

In the third month, when the children of Israel were gone forth out of
the land of Egypt, the same day came they into the wilderness of Sinai . . .
and there Israel camped before the mount.

Exodus 19:1-2

AWED by the rugged splendor of the holy mountain towering
above them, the people of Israel began to pitch their camp on the flat
desert floor at its base. Moses had successfully led his people to this
remote place of silent grandeur in obedience to the Lord's command
to him at Sinai: "When thou hast brought forth the people out of
Egypt, ye shall serve God upon this mountain." What did the Lord
now have in store for Israel?

Moses left the confusion and noise of the camp and went apart to
view the well-remembered scene. Nothing had changed since he stood
there before. High in the sky soared the eagles borne on motionless,
outspread wings far above the gigantic mountain. Sinai, a solid block
of reddish-brown granite, roughly carved into jagged crags and deeply
slashed by gullies, rose abruptly three thousand feet above the level
plain and was so huge and majestic that it appeared to be a suitable
dwelling place for God Himself. It was here that the Lord had once
spoken to Moses. Then while pasturing his father-in-law's sheep among
the scrubby bushes and sparse desert grass at the foot of this mountain
he had seen the incredible sight of a bush aflame yet not burned up.
Today as Moses looked about he saw the bush again and observed that

it was still growing. Here was the place where he once stooped to unfasten his sandals. This was indeed holy ground.

Moses remembered the awe with which he had once heard the Lord speaking to him. The task that the Lord laid upon him had seemed impossible then, but now the well-nigh impossible was accomplished. In the Lord's strength Moses had brought the people of Israel out of Egypt to this holy place. All obstacles had been overcome—his own unwillingness to be Israel's leader, the people's discontent with his leadership, the pharaoh's stubbornness, the hour of peril at the sea, thirst hunger, and the weary miles of rough desert trails. But always there was the sound of the Lord's voice or the pillar of cloud by day and the pillar of fire by night.

What was the meaning of these wonders? All the mighty acts which the Lord had wrought in their behalf were surely for some greater purpose than mere relief from the task of brick-making. What did the Lord want of Israel? Disciplined and matured by failure and difficulty and danger, Moses and his people now expected new commandments and a deeper revelation from God.

Moses walked along the familiar desert path to the huge mass of the mountain and found a path up its almost perpendicular rock wall. From the cool shadows of the lower slope he ascended into blazing sunlight near the summit. "And Moses went up unto God."

Since that day many others have stood where Moses stood and, looking out upon the stupendous spectacle of mountains beyond mountains stretching far into the distance, it has appeared to them, as H. V. Morton described it in *Through Lands of the Bible,* like "a storm at sea turned into stone." Except for a few evidences of life it seems to be a landscape on the moon. The evidences of life are the birds, great eagles and lammergeiers, well-suited in all their ferocity and wild majesty to the savage desolation of this mountain scene.

Moses stood alone on Mount Sinai and as the wind howled around the desolate, rocky summit he heard another sound. It was a voice speaking in the awesome tones he had learned to understand. It was the Lord's voice. The words Moses heard were as swift and rhythmical as a bird in flight and they bore a tremendous message. After all the intervening centuries with their interpreters, editors, copyists, and translators, and after all the misunderstanding and disobedience of men, we believe that the message Moses heard on the holy mount is still preserved in an ancient fragment in the Book of Exodus. No other Bible passage expresses as dramatically as this one God's love and protection of His people and His high purpose for them. In this manner God made His momentous announcement to Moses on Sinai:

Birds in a Tree 3800 Years Ago

Birds such as these flitted through the trees when Joseph and his brothers were in Egypt. They found that the Egyptians enjoyed birds and that their artists had been painting birds with great care and exactness for centuries. Some species can be identified today. In this detail of the fowling scene from the tomb at Beni Hasan, a red-backed shrike with characteristic bill and black "spectacles" is depicted. At the lower left is a hoopoe with curved bill and proudly raised crest. [Page 68]

The Oldest Egyptian Painting of Birds

Long before the time of Joseph, these six geese were painted on the wall of Ra-hotpe's tomb at Meidum. The artist worked confidently, using stylized forms and symmetrical composition. His colors appear as bright as the day they were painted five thousand years ago. James Fisher in *A History of Birds* identifies the species as: two bean-geese feeding on the ground, two white-fronted geese facing left, and two red-breasted geese patterned in chestnut, gray, black, and white. Only the white-front is common in Egypt today. This is a tempera copy of the original painting on stucco which is in the Cairo Museum. [Page 69]

The Red-Breasted Goose of Bible Times and Today

Posing like his ancestors in the Meidum frieze of five thousand years ago, this rare and handsome red-breasted goose was photographed on Martha's Vineyard, Mass., in October 1958. His presence in the Western Hemisphere is something of a mystery, for these geese usually breed in arctic Siberia and winter around the Caspian and Aral Seas and in the lower Tigris-Euphrates Valley. Here Abraham may have seen them near his old home at Ur and later he would have encountered them in Egypt where they were well known in ancient times. Today some are imported and bred in captivity in New York, Connecticut, and Massachusetts. [Page 69]

The Sacred Ibis of Ancient Egypt

This votive figure of a sacred ibis represents a bird believed to have nested in papyrus thickets which, in the time of Moses, grew along the lower Nile. Here it waded on long legs and with its slender arched bill probed in the mud for food. Egyptian artists often depicted the bird. Made of wood covered with painted linen, this figure has inlaid eyes of glass, and a head, neck, and legs of bronze. [Page 69]

A Falcon, Swallow, and Chick

In his youth Moses "was instructed in all the wisdom of the Egyptians" (Acts 7:22, RSV) and he doubtless learned to read hieroglyphic bird signs such as these. The three birds are among the beautifully painted symbols and scenes decorating a wooden coffin made about 2000 B.C. for Prince Dehuti-Nekht and his wife. A blue-green falcon has white underparts, a black eye, and a vivid orange bill. The swallow's pale blue-green plumage is marked with dark blue and its eye and bill are black. Contrasting with the chick's intricately marked, yellowish body are its red eye, bill, and legs. Among the incised hieroglyphics above the painted birds one can see about twenty tiny bird forms. [Page 70]

The Egyptian Goddess Nekhebt

With the star-spangled heaven of which she is mistress depicted in a band above her, a flying griffon vulture decorates a wall of Queen Hat-shepsut's temple at Der-el-bahri near Thebes. The original from which this copy was painted dates from about 1485 B.C., not long before the time of Moses. He would have recognized the bird as the vulture goddess Nekhebt and the signet ring in her talons as the symbol of "countless years." [Page 70]

"All That Day . . . They Gathered the Quails"

Enormous flocks of migrating quails fell into the Israelites' desert encampment and saved them from starvation. Moses' confidence that the Lord would provide for His people is here rewarded. Aaron and the elders express their amazement, while the people of Israel busily catch the quails as they fall. The birds are gathered by the basketful, cooked in pots, or strung up to dry. The engraving is from *Historien des Ouden en Nieuwen Testaments*, published in Amsterdam in 1700. [Page 75]

Migratory Quails

These rotund birds only seven inches in length are smaller than an American robin and look somewhat like diminutive partridges. They are beautifully marked, their general sandy color being streaked with buff and black above, and lighter buff on the flanks. A narrow yellowish line extends through the center of their dark crowns and there is a long pale stripe over each eye. This colored lithograph was designed by the celebrated English bird artist, John Gould, for his large five-volume series, *Birds of Europe*, 1832-1837. [Page 77]

A Golden Eagle on Its Nest

Alertly guarding its nest on a high rocky ledge, a golden eagle is roused by the click of Eric Hosking's concealed camera. The well-camouflaged young eagle at the left has some dark feathers among its white down, but it is still a nestling. Golden eagles are found in Palestine and they nest among the mountains of Sinai. [Page 98]

A King among Flying Creatures

Even in captivity a griffon vulture is every inch a king. His lordly head is covered with thin white down and around his neck he wears a striking white ruff. Keen of eye, strong of beak, and with huge dark wings to carry him far, he is a splendid creature. When he soars on motionless wings, as on page 21, he displays his nine-foot wing span. [Page 107]

The Egyptian Vulture

In a beautifully executed lithograph John Gould portrays, against a background of pyramids, an adult Egyptian vulture with one of its young. Often called "Pharaoh's hen," the bird is found not only in Egypt but in many neighboring countries. H. B. Tristram says that in Palestine the Egyptian vulture is "equally abundant in the plains of Sharon and the naked hill districts to the south. It breeds in great numbers in the valley of the Kedron, heaping up its enormous nest of sticks, rubbish, and old rags on every convenient ledge." [Page 107]

One of the Eagles of Palestine

A tawny eagle expresses the fitness, pride, ferocity, and invincible spirit of all of the eagles of the Bible. "Is not the curve of an eagle's beak a synonym for the countenance of a conqueror?" asked Sacheverell Sitwell. The widely-traveled bird artist, Louis Agassiz Fuertes, painted this tawny eagle from a living bird captured in Ethiopia. Keenly observant of the personalities of birds, and fascinated by the color and texture of their feathers, Fuertes accurately transcribed what he saw. [Page 109]

The Kite

A magnificent bird found in North Africa, western Asia, and Europe, the kite is identified by a long, forked tail and chestnut plumage. Its flight is soaring, buoyant, and graceful. Usually it lays two or three eggs in a nest built of sticks in the fork of a large tree. The nest is lined with dry grass or pieces of cloth. Shakespeare warned that where kites build "look to lesser linen." John Gould designed this plate for one of his handsome bird books. [Page 109]

Largest and Fiercest of the Owls of Palestine   W. COLLINS AND SONS, LTD.

Huge eyes, a strong beak, and cruel claws typify the eagle owl or "daughter of howling." This engraving by Johann L. Frisch is reproduced in *Fine Bird Books 1700-1900,* published by Collins, London. [Page 110]

Hey's Sand Partridge

Found in the wilderness of Judea, where Saul pursued David, Hey's sand partridge is a great runner, speeding along the ground on its olive-yellow feet. The female's plumage is sandy buff, beautifully penciled and barred with brown and chestnut. The male has white lores and a white stripe behind each eye giving him an alert expression. His under-surface is chestnut and white, each feather margined with black. The photograph is from one of John Gould's hand-colored plates in Part III of his folio volumes entitled *Birds of Asia*, published in 1851. [Page 117]

Black-Tipped Cinnamon Feathers Form the Hoopoe's Crest

According to legend, Solomon gave the hoopoes these handsome crests in place of his previous gift of little gold crowns. John Gould included this picture of a male and a female hoopoe at their nest in a hollow tree in *Birds of Europe*. The male stands on guard, his crest erect. The female sits on her eggs with her crest lowered. Hoopoes clearly have not changed their feathers in the 3700 years since the bird in the Egyptian fowling scene (page 81) was painted. [Page 121]

Ye have seen what I did unto the Egyptians,
   and how I bare you on eagles' wings,
   and brought you unto myself.
Now therefore, if ye will obey my voice indeed
   and keep my covenant,
then ye shall be a peculiar treasure unto me. . . .
And ye shall be unto me a kingdom of priests,
   and an holy nation.

Exodus 19:4-6

This message was the revelation for which Moses and all the people of Israel waited. It explained the travails that lay behind them and it pointed to their glorious future under God. The promise was all that really mattered. Tablets engraved with the Decalogue would be given to them later, with the Law, the priesthood, the Ark, the Temple, and the sacred Scriptures. But here was the kernel of their religion in the amazing promise of God, guaranteed by what He had already done for them, and offered now to the people of Israel for their acceptance. This Covenant lies at the heart of the Old Testament story of a people whose ancestor Abraham was chosen to carry out God's vast design and who at Sinai accepted for themselves the role of a holy nation, the people of God. It was with one voice that the people, assembled at Sinai to hear God's Word from Moses, ratified this Covenant. All their dedication to God and their willing obedience echoed and re-echoed amid the rocky crags as they shouted: "All that the Lord hath spoken we will do!"

They were to try and fail and try again, for they did not find it easy to obey the Lord's commands. When they lapsed into pride and congratulated themselves on their favored status as the Lord's own people, their prophets reminded them that they were not chosen because of any virtue they themselves possessed, nor did the Covenant grant them special privileges. In accepting the Covenant at Sinai they undertook a holy calling as God's agents for the salvation of mankind. As the Lord said:

The beast of the field shall honour me,
   the dragons and the owls,
because I give waters in the wilderness
   and rivers in the desert
to give drink to my people, my chosen.
   This people have I formed for myself.
They shall show forth my praise.

Isaiah 43:20-21

In the fullness of time, upon the foundation of this ancient Covenant, Christ proclaimed the New Covenant and the Kingdom of God. As Paul declared in Galatians: "If ye be Christ's, then are ye Abraham's seed and heirs according to the promise." The early Christian Church is described in I Peter as "a chosen generation, a royal priesthood, an holy nation, a peculiar people," called and chosen, as was Israel of old, in order "that ye should show forth the praises of him who hath called you out of darkness into his marvellous light."

The ancient Israelites to whom the Covenant was offered at Sinai had already experienced the weariness of plodding day after day through the rough and burning Wilderness, often thirsty and hungry, sometimes beset by enemies, always uncertain of the way. To them the sight of an eagle or vulture flying overhead brought a sudden lift of spirit. They were in eagle country and while the great birds wheeled majestically on effortless wings in the cool spaces of sky, men watched them with a sense of exaltation akin to their feeling of joy when God was with them. The people of Israel believed He caused them to soar confidently above all trouble and peril and brought them safely to their goal, bearing them, as it were, on eagles' wings. In the poetry of the original Covenant message, "I bare you on eagles' wings," Israel recognized her experience of God.

The eagles mentioned in the Sinai Covenant were as real as the mustard seed or the lost sheep of Jesus' parables. To the people camped below Sinai the message conveyed by the eagles was vivid and immediate. Lest there be any misunderstanding about the holy character of God, and lest the people falsely imagine that He vaunted His own might when He spoke of the king of birds, a poetic commentary on the eagle story was later added in the Song of Moses. In this poem it became abundantly clear that God was to be regarded not so much as a mighty king, but as a loving parent Who defended and trained His people and bore them on His wings.

> As an eagle stirreth up her nest,
>   fluttereth over her young,
> spreadeth abroad her wings, and taketh them,
>   beareth them on her wings,
> so the Lord alone did lead him [Israel]. . . .
>   He made him ride on the high places of the earth.
>   Deuteronomy 32:11-13

On one of the inaccessible ledges of Sinai an eagle's nest may have been visible from the camp below. Surely one of the Hebrew lads would have been curious about the nest and he may have climbed up for a closer view. He soon learned to watch from a distance because of the ferocity with which these birds sometimes use their talons and beaks to defend their young. The nest might look like a careless heap of sticks, but it did not blow away in the wind nor fill with water in a downpour and was soft inside. Its construction must have required great skill. Who taught eagles how to build so well? The parent birds guarded the nest, incubating the eggs, shielding the nestlings from too much sun, warming them when a cold wind blew, and feeding them until they were large enough to fly. Then the parents stirred up the nest and lured the young ones out of it for their awkward first flight. Sometimes the adult birds hovered over their fledglings and fluttered encouragingly around and under them. At a distance the eaglets appeared to be carried at times on a parent's wings, but this is not the case. Although grebes, swans, and some other birds paddle through the water with their young ones nestled on their backs, there is no reliable report of any bird actually flying with a smaller bird on its back. In the main, however, the ancient observations made at the eagle's nest were amazingly accurate.

Lammergeiers as well as eagles breed among the rocky ledges of the mountains of Sinai and may well be the birds described in Exodus and Deuteronomy. Largest and most magnificent of the vultures, the lammergeiers of Sinai and Palestine have a wingspread of nine feet or more and fly with extraordinary ease and grace. Their heads are covered with white feathers like an eagle's and they have long blackish beards which give them their other name, bearded vulture. Their upper plumage is finely penciled, their under plumage tawny, and they have large, ferocious-looking eyes. In the air they can be recognized by their long, pointed wings and wedge-shaped tail.

About thirty years ago Colonel Richard Meinertzhagen spent a snowy night alone on Mount Sinai and recorded this story in *Birds of Arabia:*

And when the sun rose over the deserts of Arabia the mist began to clear, revealing a crystal-clear ruby blaze over the eastern skies, and I looked down on one of the most beautiful sights I have ever witnessed: to the east I could see the Gulf of Aqaba and on the west I could see parts of the Gulf of Suez. On this holy mountain I felt very near to God. I turned to look at the chapel. On the small wooden cross sat a lammergeier, all hunched up in the cold but gloriously golden in the sunlight; and as I watched him, but a few yards off, his great wings spread out and he sailed forth into the gorges of those barren mountains searching for his breakfast, as his kind have done since the days of Moses.

From the day when Moses descended from the holy mountain with the eagle message in his heart, the people of Israel saw in the wings of these majestic birds a symbol of God's redeeming activity and of His care and protection of His people. "Hide me under the shadow of thy wings" (Psalm 17:8), they prayed. Again and again they confessed their faith in God who "shall cover thee with his feathers and under his wings shalt thou trust" (Psalm 91:4; also 36:7; 57:1; 61:4; 63:7). In a day of peril as great as any their ancestors had encountered centuries earlier, the threatened people heard the prophet Isaiah strengthen their wavering faith in words that echo the Song of Moses:

> Like birds hovering, so the Lord of hosts
>   will protect Jerusalem;
> he will protect and deliver it,
>   he will spare and rescue it.
>
> Isaiah 31:5, RSV

The wings of God became more than a figure of speech to the people of Israel. Neighboring peoples pictured their kings sitting on thrones that were supported and guarded by winged beings. Because God was Israel's King, they built Him a throne guarded by cherubim with wings of beaten gold. These winged figures were placed above the chest, called the Ark of the Covenant, containing the stone tablets of the Law.

During the Wilderness years Levi's sons carried the Ark of the Covenant. It went with the Israelites when they crossed the Jordan into the Promised Land. While the "judges" ruled Israel it remained at Shiloh in a sacred room of the Temple where the child Samuel heard the voice of God. Though the Ark fell into the hands of the enemy during the Philistine war, David recovered it and brought it into Jerusalem where his son Solomon built for it the Holy of Holies in his new Temple.

There is a tender scene in the Book of Ruth in which Boaz of Bethlehem says to Ruth, the foreign girl from Moab who had so faithfully cared for her mother-in-law:

> The Lord recompense thy work, and a full reward be given thee of the Lord God of Israel, under whose wings thou art come to trust.
>
> Ruth 2:12

The words of Boaz evoke a picture of the Ark with the golden wings of the cherubim protecting the dwelling place of the Lord. Boaz did not mean that God actually has wings, for this would be to confuse symbol with reality. Turning away from the bird gods of other peoples, Israel acknowledged only God and He was not a bird. The strict injunction of the Second Commandment prohibited idolatry: "Thou shalt not make unto thee any graven image. . . . Thou shalt not bow down thyself to them, nor serve them." Any image, whether it was "the likeness of any beast that is on the earth, the likeness of any winged fowl that flieth in the air" (Deuteronomy 4:17)—all these Israel was forbidden to worship.

Time and again the people of Israel, looking longingly at the power and good fortune of the Egyptians, Assyrians, or Babylonians, were tempted to worship their heathen images which seemed to grant many desirable things. But the prophets of Israel continued to denounce all man-made gods for their worthlessness. From the Apocrypha come two derisive outbursts against heathen idols:

> Bats, swallows, and birds light on their bodies and heads; and so do cats. From this you will know that they are not gods; so do not fear them.
> Letter of Jeremiah 6:22, RSV

> In the same way, their gods of wood, overlaid with gold and silver, are like a thorn bush in a garden, on which every bird sits.
> Letter of Jeremiah 6:71, RSV

Paul saw the folly of Greek and Roman idolatry which substituted a lower, created being for the ineffable perfection of the eternal Creator. Those who did not honor God and give Him thanks and worship Him were not wise but foolish and their minds were darkened. In order to have something to worship, they

> changed the glory of the uncorruptible God into an image made like to corruptible man, and to birds, and four-footed beasts, and creeping things.
> Romans 1:23

But it is to the eternal credit of Israel that her people declined to worship idols and remained, on the whole, faithful to the Lord. The majesty of eagles, the power of vultures, the far-seeing vision of hawks, the loving protection of any parent bird for its young might remind men of some aspect of their Lord, but God Himself was to them neither eagle, vulture, hawk, nor any bird whatever.

As their experience of Him deepened, they no longer thought of Him as remaining in the confined space between the cherubim in the Holy of Holies, but they sang that He was "enthroned on the praises of Israel" and "righteousness and justice are the foundation of his throne." The shadow cast by His "wings" lengthened beyond the borders of Israel until, in the fullness of time, it included all of Christ's redeemed community "out of every kindred and tongue and people and nation."

The eagles of Sinai continued to fly through the consciousness of Israel. It was, perhaps, the great nameless prophet of the Exile who wrote most stirringly of them after the bitter years of national defeat and captivity:

> Hast thou not known? Hast thou not heard
> that the everlasting God, the Lord,
>   the Creator of the ends of the earth,
> fainteth not, neither is weary?
>   There is no searching of his understanding.
> He giveth power to the faint,
>   and to them that have no might he increaseth strength.
> Even the youths shall faint and be weary,
>   and the young men shall utterly fall.
> But they that wait upon the Lord shall renew their strength;
>   they shall mount up with wings as eagles;
> they shall run and not be weary;
>   and they shall walk and not faint.
>
> Isaiah 40:28-31

God's chosen people continued to suffer affliction, but in His love and pity "he redeemed them and he bare them and carried them all the days of old." In the last book of the Bible, the eagles of Exodus fly again, for once more the Church of God is in danger and in the symbolical guise of a woman is rescued from the dragon.

> And to the woman were given two wings of a great eagle,
> that she might fly into the wilderness.
>
> Revelation 12:14

CHAPTER 8 ⚮
The Bird List of the Bible

THE famous bird list of the Bible is in Leviticus 11:13-19 and also in Deuteronomy 14:11-18. Both versions are practically identical and serve the same purpose: to catalogue the birds whose flesh the Israelites were forbidden to eat. A stern "thou-shalt-not" hangs over this list, making it more like a state law protecting certain species of birds than like a modern bird watcher's "life-list," or his field notes of species seen during a day or a season. Few of the birds often appearing on our lists are mentioned in the Bible list. It contains no cheerful winter chickadees, nor the first robin of spring, no small shore-birds of lonely beaches, nor the gay throng of warblers flitting northward through the spring woods. It is, nevertheless, fascinating, for many of its creatures are the swift, bold, fearless birds of prey which were so well-adapted to life in ancient times but are fast disappearing today as civilization covers more of the earth. The list indicates to us what creatures swooped and dived and flitted through the air above Palestine, made nests on its inaccessible cliffs, or hooted in the night three thousand or more years ago. Many of these birds soared in huge circles, patrolling the sky as the Israelites crossed the Jordan and entered the Promised Land; they hovered hungrily on outspread wings above the battle when Deborah's army met Sisera's; and they watched from a safe distance while David guarded his father's sheep on the hillsides near Bethlehem, for David's aim was deadly.

Only twenty items appear in the Bible bird list, but, as we shall see, it includes more than twenty species. In the Authorized Version it is translated as follows:

Of all clean birds ye shall eat.

But these are they of which ye shall not eat: the eagle, and the ossifrage, and the osprey, and the glede, and the kite, and the vulture after his kind, and every raven after his kind, and the owl, and the night hawk, and the cuckoo, and the hawk after his kind, the little owl, and the great owl, and the swan, and the pelican, and the gier eagle, and the cormorant, and the stork, and the heron after her kind, and the lapwing, and the bat.

Deuteronomy 14:11-18

The Revised Standard Version, Moffatt's translation, the Douay Bible, or any one of a number of other translations gives a slightly different list. Concerning the chief names, however, there is considerable agreement, for this is a list of so-called "unclean" birds the eating of whose flesh could defile the holiness of God's people. As we have a fairly clear idea of the meaning of "uncleanness" we know what birds would probably be considered ritually contaminated.

Ritual uncleanness was an idea that sprang from deep sources. The people of Israel believed that all life, both of men and of animals, belongs to God who created it and from this primitive "reverence for life" came the ancient commandment, "Thou shalt not kill." People noticed that when a great amount of blood is lost the strange and wonderful thing we call life comes to an end. Because in some mysterious way blood seemed to be the very essence of life, they said: "The blood is the life." Believing as they did that life belonged to God, they declared that to eat blood was an offense against God and made one ritually "unclean" and unfit to approach the Lord in His holiness. The Hebrew law stated: "Ye shall eat no manner of blood, whether it be of fowl or of beast" (Leviticus 7:26). Though they ate the flesh of many "clean" birds and animals, they never ate their blood. The "law of the beasts, and of the fowl, and of every living creature" (Leviticus 11:46) made a distinction between the "clean" and "unclean" and gave explicit directions for eating "clean" creatures.

And whatsoever man . . . which hunteth and catcheth any beast or fowl that may be eaten, he shall even pour out the blood thereof . . . for it is the life of all flesh. . . . Whosoever eateth it shall be cut off.

Leviticus 17:13-14

Birds of prey, and others whose food consists almost entirely of carrion or flesh, eat blood and hence these creatures were considered "unclean" and held in "abomination." They were thought to be capable of infecting with their own impurity anyone who partook of their flesh. "Uncleanness" was a complex matter and probably other considerations besides blood entered into it. Birds seen around dead bodies, birds associated with strange foreign gods, birds of desolate places where it was feared that demons dwelt, or birds found torn and dead (Ezekiel 44:31)—all these were doubtless considered "unclean."

With the idea of "uncleanness" as one of the clues, Dr. G. R. Driver in the *Palestine Exploration Quarterly,* April 1955, and in some of his later studies, proposed some new identifications for the birds of the Bible list. His expert knowledge of the ancient Hebrew language and the help he received from the well-known ornithologist, Dr. David L. Lack, make Dr. Driver's list exceptionally interesting. His proposals pay tribute to the care and intelligence of those who originally compiled the list, for he finds it divided into three parts: the first contains fifteen land birds; the second, three water birds; and the last, two miscellaneous creatures. The land birds are subdivided into families in a descending scale of sizes, beginning with large birds of prey, followed by the crow tribe, the larger owls, the smaller birds of prey, and finally the smaller owls. As the approximate length in inches of all these birds is an important factor in Dr. Driver's identifications, these figures are given in the accompanying bird list. From the griffon vulture, measuring as much as forty-five inches from hooked beak to tailtip and having an enormous wingspread, sometimes as wide as eight or nine feet, the birds shrink in size down to the eight-inch scops owl.

In the second part of the list the osprey is followed by lake and river birds. The last part contains the hoopoe with its attractive crest of reddish feathers tipped with black and white. Though not a bird of prey, the hoopoe probes in filth for insects and worms and this habit doubtless earned for it an "unclean" classification. Finally, there is the bat which, as we know and the Hebrews undoubtedly realized, is not a true bird but a flying mammal whose flesh is reported to be inedible.

First on the list comes the griffon vulture, a superb creature when it flashes down out of the sky like dark lightning. Wheeling majestically on motionless wings at great heights, it is a veritable king among flying creatures. The Egyptians, Assyrians, and Persians perceived this creature as one who was omnipresent, far-seeing, and demanding. As these were aspects of royal power, these ancient peoples carried the image of a griffon vulture on their battle standards as a grim embodiment of their rulers.

Among the highest and most inaccessible rocks griffon vultures find their favorite nesting places. There are records of famous eyries near Jericho, under Mount Nebo, in the ravine of the Jabbok, in the gorge of the Litani River, in the ravines of Mount Carmel, and amid the

THE BIRD LIST IN LEVITICUS

Hebrew Name transliterated (as in Young's *Analytical Concordance*)	Dr. G. R. Driver's suggestions	Approximate length in inches	Revised Standard Version	Authorized Version
1 nesher	griffon vulture (sometimes the golden eagle)	45	eagle	eagle
2 peres	bearded vulture	45	ossifrage	ossifrage
3 ozniyyah	short-toed eagle	27	osprey	osprey
4 daah	(black) kite	23	kite	vulture
5 ayyah	saker falcon	22	falcon	kite
"after its kind"	common buzzard	17		
6 oreb	raven	22	raven	raven
"after its kind"	rook	18		
7 bath yaanah	eagle owl	18	ostrich	owl
8 tachmas	short-eared owl	14	nighthawk	nighthawk
9 shachaph	long-eared owl	14	sea gull	cuckoo
10 nets	kestrel	14	hawk	hawk
"after its kind"	sparrow hawk	12		
11 kos	tawny owl	16	owl	little owl
12 shalak	fisher owl		cormorant	cormorant
13 yanshuph	screech owl	13	ibis	great owl
14 tishemeth	little owl	10	water hen	swan
15 qaath	scops owl	8	pelican	pelican
16 racham	osprey	33	vulture	gier eagle
17 chasidah	stork	40	stork	stork
	heron	38		
18 anaphah	cormorant	33	heron	heron
19 dukiphath	hoopoe	12	hoopoe	lapwing
20 atalleph	bat		bat	bat

eight-hundred-foot cliffs of Wadi Hamam on the west side of the Sea of Galilee. The soft limestone precipices of this deep chasm are honeycombed with innumerable holes, passages, and caverns where griffon vultures have nested undisturbed since the time of the Romans. Recently the "griffonry" on Mount Carmel has suffered from depredations by Arabs who prize vulture fat as a medicine for rheumatism.

At daybreak griffon vultures soar high above the earth, sweeping the horizon with their keen eyes for a sight of food. The Talmud says they can see carrion in Palestine even when they are flying over Babylon! Be this as it may, their vision is remarkable, as Job says in 39:29. After several hours aloft they return to their high ledges where they perch motionless until evening. Though they can consume a great amount of food at one time and will gorge themselves when carrion is available, they are able to exist for long periods without it. Thus they are well adapted to their special function in the economy of nature.

Deprived of the element in which it reigns and sitting in a zoo cage, a griffon vulture is still a splendid creature with gray-brown plumage, blackish wings and tail feathers, and a ruff of soft white down encircling its neck. Its talons and feet are weaker than an eagle's because it does not hunt live creatures, but its beak is large, hooked, and powerful. When perching it appears gloomy and sullen as if resentfully brooding over its ancient classification of "unclean." Actually a griffon vulture has clean habits, bathing frequently and keeping its plumage in excellent condition. It is intelligent, sociable, good-tempered, and does not snarl or quarrel with other birds over food. But no one can forget of what its food consists.

The lammergeier, or bearded vulture, resembles the griffon vulture in its huge wingspread and its ability to soar for hours on motionless wings. It has a habit of dropping its victims from a great height in order to shatter their bones. Aeschylus is said to have been killed when a lammergeier, mistaking his bald head for a stone, dropped a tortoise upon it from high in the air. The Hebrew word *peres* meaning "smasher" applies quite accurately to this bird. Lammergeiers have become uncommon in Palestine and they are disappearing from the remote mountain ranges of Europe and Asia. A caged lammergeier used to sit like a dispossessed king in the New York Zoological Park, its head sunk disconsolately on its chest, its large melancholy eyes staring vacantly as though longing for space in which to exercise its surpassing powers of flight. The huge bird seemed to be mourning the threatened extinction of its kind which has lived on earth for uncounted ages.

In addition to the two vultures already described, the small Egyptian vulture, or pharaoh's hen, is common in Palestine. Near at hand it is an ugly, almost repulsive creature, but like the other vultures, its grace of flight and superb mastery of the air give it great beauty. It has white plumage, black wings, and a fringe of long feathers around its head. Besides carrion it eats garbage and filth which the larger vultures will not touch. It must have been considered "unclean," for it is the foulest, though most useful scavenger of the East. As it wanders unmolested around village streets it wears an intelligent, almost cunning expression and it searches for rats, mice, lizards, or refuse of all kinds in the performance of its valuable sanitary services.

The third bird, the *ozniyyah*, is probably the short-toed eagle, which is the commonest eagle in Palestine. In the Targums *ozniyyah* is translated *'ar*, meaning "watcher," a name that fits the short-toed eagle perfectly, for it often sits all day on a rock or tree watching for the snakes, lizards, and frogs on which it feeds. The biblical town of Ar, set among the hills of Moab, may be named for the short-toed eagles which haunt the cliffs of this desolate region.

The vultures and eagle already described are found only in the Old World and with the kites, hawks, eagles, and harriers belong to a family named *Accipitridae*. New World vultures including the turkey vulture, the black vulture, and, among the largest of flying birds, the California condor and the Andean condor, belong to a different family called *Cathartidae*.

Vultures of both families, however, have heads that are either naked or covered with thin down. An old legend tries to account for this fact. One day, so the story runs, the sun beat so fiercely upon King Solomon's head that he cried: "O vultures, fly between me and the sun and protect me from its burning rays!" Paying no attention to the royal command the vultures flew away. Solomon became so enraged that he cursed them and decreed: "The feathers of your head and neck shall fall off and you shall feel the heat of the sun, the bite of the wind, and the beating of the rain. Your food shall be carrion and you shall be unclean to the end of time!"

Though the Hebrews listed only two or three vultures, they undoubtedly considered all the vultures and eagles of Palestine "unclean." To them any vulture meant all vultures and possibly all eagles as well. In a few contexts the Bible clearly uses *nesher* for an eagle, which is its translation in the Authorized Version. *Nesher*, however, should usually be translated vulture. It is not strange that the ancient Hebrews often failed to identify and name these birds precisely. Gliding far overhead in the Palestinian sky the five kinds of vultures and the nine eagles of this region look so much alike that even a trained observer needs binoculars and a field guide to identify at a distance such eagles as the short-toed, the golden, the imperial, the tawny, the spotted, and Bonelli's. Recently while Victor Howells was traveling in Palestine he discovered far up on a steep hillside what he supposed to be an Arab boy standing on a rock. To his horror he saw the figure go to the very edge of the rock, lean far out over the abyss and jump off. Instead of plunging down, however, the "boy" opened two brown wings and sailed up into the sky. It was undoubtedly an eagle, probably an imperial eagle, but having failed to distinguish a bird from a boy, Victor Howells was reluctant to make a definite identification.

An outstanding feature of Palestine's bird life is the immense number and great variety of its birds of prey of which Tristram in one year found forty-three species. He said that

over the deep valley of the Jordan kestrels hover and kites and short-toed eagles soar throughout the year; harriers and buzzards perpetually sweep across the marshes and maritime plains; the traveller can never mount a hill without being watched by parties of griffons and eagles circling far above him.

Besides the abundant eagles and vultures there is a bewildering variety of buzzards, hawks, kestrels, kites, harriers, and falcons. Captain Eric Hardy recently listed some twenty species of smaller carrion and flesh eaters, for which the compilers of the two Bible lists had only four or five names: *raah, ayyah, daah* or *dayyah,* and *nets.* These may have been the only names in common use, but the compilers had evidently observed the strikingly different birds in this group and knew that these names were not enough for so many distinct species. They solved this difficulty by adding the phrase "after its kind" to *ayyah* and *nets.*

When the vultures have eaten to satiety, flocks of kites, the Hebrew *daah* or *dayyah,* gather to consume the remnants of carrion. However repulsive their eating habits, in the air kites are noble birds. Far up in the sky they remain suspended on apparently motionless wings, their tails widely expanded. When they wheel and turn they use their tails as a rudder, inclining them so as to steer their light bodies through the curve. It was the kite's tail, Pliny said, that first showed men how to steer their ships with a rudder.

Not all the birds in this group eat carrion, for many buzzards, falcons, hawks, kestrels, and harriers prefer to catch their own game and eat fresh food. Some of these birds are magnificent hunters, so outstanding in fact that the sakker falcon, lanner falcon, and the extremely swift peregrine falcon have been used by men for hunting small game. As they consume a variety of flesh including insects and their larvae, snakes, frogs, lizards, rats, mice, rabbits, birds, and many other small animals, their presence in a neighborhood insures it against plagues of these creatures.

The Bible list continues with the *oreb* or "the raven after its kind," including under one name all members of the numerous *Corvidae* or crow family of the East. This family qualifies for the "unclean" list because its members feed on carrion, refuse, reptiles, fish, insects, worms, in fact anything alive or dead. In Palestine, the largest, most powerful, and most intelligent member of this family is the common raven. The brown-necked raven is more of a desert bird and nests in Wadi Qelt and at Jericho, while the small fan-tailed raven nests in colonies on inaccessible cliffs near the Dead Sea. Ravens are gregarious, roosting by the hundreds on Jerusalem's Old City walls and about the Mosque of Omar during winter nights. In the morning they fly in croaking black flocks to the slaughterhouses for their daily rations. Among them can be found other members of their family: hooded crows, jackdaws, and rooks. These birds sometimes served as a sort of clock, for on murky days when sunset, which marks the beginning of the Sabbath, could not be seen, it was assumed to be the time when ravens and crows returned to their roosts.

A feature of Dr. Driver's list is its eight different owls. It is not surprising that they form the best-identified group among the birds of prey, for the Hebrews were able to see owls at close range. Unlike vultures and eagles, owls frequently nest near buildings, and fly very close to the ground. They are nocturnal hunters and their weird cries and hooting in the night make their presence known even when they cannot be seen. Their bodies are adapted for night hunting, for they have large eyes, extremely sensitive ears, hooked bills, and claws powerful enough to kill whatever prey they pounce upon. Their forward-facing eyes are set in their flattened faces and give them binocular vision. As their eyes are more or less fixed in their sockets and virtually immovable, the owl must turn its head to see anything not directly ahead. It can, however, rotate its head through 270 degrees or more, and it thus has the widest binocular field of vision among birds. If a person walks around and around a perching owl, the bird appears to screw its head continuously in one direction, keeping the person in constant focus. Alexander Wetmore, the well-known ornithologist, said that when he was a small boy he ran around and around an owl expecting, perhaps even hoping, to see the bird twist its head completely off. But the owl kept its head, for after rotating it through 270 degrees the bird was able to snap its head back to the starting point with a lightning motion, too swift for the dizzy little boy to see.

The largest and fiercest owl of Palestine is appropriately named the eagle owl, *Bubo bubo,* while its Hebrew name, *bath yaanah,* means "daughter of howling." It is one of the commonest owls, haunting caves and ruins as Isaiah (13:21) and Jeremiah (50:39) describe and roosting during the day among scrubby bushes of semidesert places. This owl is akin to the great horned owl of North America, the "tiger of the air." Tristram found many eagle owls in the rock tombs of Petra, chief city of ancient Edom, and recognized in them a literal fulfillment of Isaiah's prophecy: "And thorns shall come up in her palaces, nettles and brambles in the fortresses thereof; and it shall be an habitation of dragons and a court of owls" (Isaiah 34:13). The cry of this night monster is a loud, prolonged, powerful hoot which sounds like a cry of desolation or, as Micah observed in 1:8, a note of mourning. Eagle owls prey upon lambs, hares, partridges, and rodents, and have even been known to attack men. A captive bird in a zoo or even a stuffed specimen in a museum case can be an alarming sight with its long ear tufts, curved, cruel beak, and huge eyes which to the naturalist W. H. Hudson seemed to kindle "into great globes of quivering yellow flame." A live eagle owl appearing suddenly in the night can be really terrifying. Victor Howells tells of encountering one whose three-foot-long body and immense wings blotted out the moon and frightened the camels and their riders with its loud, high-pitched *"boo-hoo, boo-hooo."*

The owls, according to Dr. Driver's translation, begin with the largest and become smaller and less fearsome as the list proceeds. Their order is interrupted at one point by the *nets,* indicating hawks, kestrels, and other small birds of prey. The smallest owl is probably the *qaath,* the scops owl, which is smaller than a robin, and feeds on insects. It haunts old ruins, crying monotonously *"yu-hŭ"* or *"kiu-kiu."* Only slightly larger than the scops owl is the little owl, *tishemeth,* the most abundant of all Palestinian owls. Little owls wail among the ruins of buried cities or haunt olive groves and thickets. They are comical-looking creatures when perched in an upright position, for they twist their flat heads to see what is going on. When disturbed they bob and bow grotesquely. This is the owl associated with Athena and often depicted on Greek coins. It became the symbol of wisdom and it is the creature made famous by the phrase "wise as an owl."

Following the nocturnal birds of prey come birds that hunt in the water. Ospreys are spectacular fishing hawks and are found near most of the large bodies of water in the world. When an osprey sights a fish swimming far below, it hovers for a moment, then closes its wings and dives swiftly and accurately upon its prey. It strikes the water with great force feet first. There is a splash and the bird often disappears beneath the surface. In a moment it rises with the fish, spreads its broad wings, shakes the water from its plumage, and flies away to devour its catch. It always adjusts the grip of its talons to carry the fish head foremost and thus reduce air resistance to a minimum.

Storks and herons wade into shallow water on their long legs and probe in the mud with long bills for small reptiles and fish. Cormorants dive into deep water and actually swim beneath the surface in pursuit of prey.

Such were the birds the people of Israel might not eat. But the list is far more than a collection of ancient food taboos. Not only does it show that these people carefully observed the feathered creatures around them, but it remains a monument to their deep regard for the sacredness of life and their desire to obey God in every area of their lives.

Ye shall therefore put difference between . . . unclean fowls and clean, and ye shall not make your souls abominable by beast or by fowl. . . . And ye shall be holy unto me, for I the Lord am holy and have severed you from other people that ye should be mine.

Leviticus 20:25-26

PART III

When the Kings
Reigned

CHAPTER 9

Swifter than Eagles

Young David fingered the five smooth stones in his shepherd's bag. They would do. He had chosen them carefully from the brook. Even if the Philistine giant were as large as the soldiers reported him to be, David was not afraid. Had he not killed a lion and a bear that preyed upon his father's sheep? Day after day guarding the flock on remote pastures and watching lest eagles pounce on the newborn lambs and make off with them, he had practiced hurling stones from his sling. His accuracy had become so great that he could place the stones where he aimed them. Warned about the giant's huge shield and sharp sword, David remained undaunted. He was only a shepherd boy from Bethlehem, too young to serve with his three older brothers in King Saul's army. If his father had not sent him with bread, cheese, and parched grain for his soldier brothers, he would not have been in the Israelite camp at all. Why was he going forth alone to do what no man of Israel dared?

Every soldier had heard the shout of the Philistine giant: "I defy the armies of Israel this day. Give me a man that we may fight together!" But not a man had stepped forward to accept the challenge. King Saul and his army trembled in their tents and became demoralized by inaction until David arrived and offered to fight Goliath.

David stepped into the open space between the two armies, and at the sight of this slim lad with a ruddy face and fair countenance standing alone and unarmed, Goliath laughed. He had asked for a man to fight with and they had sent him a mere child! "Come to me," he roared, "and I will give thy flesh unto the fowls of the air, and to the beasts of the field" (I Samuel 17:44).

The threat of death without decent burial did not frighten David. He had heard these grim words before and they had no power to move him now. He felt vividly alive, every faculty awake, every muscle quivering. But he carefully eyed Goliath's heavy equipment and assessed it for what it was worth. "Thou comest to me with a sword, and with a spear, and with a shield," he shouted, "but I come to thee in the name of the Lord of hosts, the God of the armies of Israel whom thou hast defied!"

Then he hurled back Goliath's threat, crying: "I will give the carcases of the host of the Philistines this day unto the fowls of the air and to the wild beasts of the earth!" (I Samuel 17:46).

David, feeling courage surge within him, believed he could not fail. In a flash he knew why, and his voice became deep with emotion as he declared: "All this assembly shall know that the Lord saveth not with sword and spear, for the battle is the Lord's, and he will give you into our hands."

Swiftly he darted toward the giant. Just out of range of Goliath's spear David took careful aim and hurled one of his smooth stones at the giant's forehead. The stone hit its mark and Goliath fell, stunned by the sudden blow. David rushed forward and, seizing the giant's own sword, cut off his head. With their champion dead the Philistines fled and that day King Saul and the Israelites prevailed over their enemy.

There was a greatness about David from the beginning and he became a hero whom all Israel loved, except King Saul. Finally, growing jealous of David's fame, the king tried to harm him. With Jonathan's help David fled from the court, but Saul pursued him relentlessly, deep into the wilderness near the Dead Sea. One night, David slipped cautiously into Saul's camp. He entered the king's tent and, finding that no guards had been posted to watch over the sleeping king and all his men, he silently and quickly grabbed the king's spear and water jar. But he did not harm Saul, for he had deep respect for the man who, however unworthy, was "the Lord's anointed." David crept safely out of the camp and gained the top of a neighboring hill. From there he awakened the king with his shout: "Wherefore doth my lord thus pursue after his servant, for what have I done and what evil is in mine hand?"

He waved the king's spear in token that he intended no harm against Saul, for he could easily have killed the king with it while he slept. David was a harmless fugitive and he taunted the king with the irony of their situation. "The king of Israel is come out to seek a flea, as when one doth hunt a partridge in the mountains!" (I Samuel 26:20).

David's words roll away thirty centuries and we can almost hear a young man panting as he runs from his pursuers. He is hot and weary and knows that someday he may be run to exhaustion like a partridge, for the chase which he has done nothing to merit is relentless. "Mine enemies chased me sore, like a bird, without cause" (Lamentations 3:52).

The bird David mentioned must have been Hey's sand partridge, sometimes called the Palestine partridge, for this is the only partridge found in the wilderness region west of the Dead Sea where Saul was pursuing David. The range of this bird in Palestine is confined to the Jordan Valley, the Dead Sea Depression, and the Wadi Arabah, but it is also found in rocky, desolate regions of Sinai, northwestern Arabia, and Persia.

Whoever hunts a partridge in the mountains is out for a game bird that makes excellent eating. Outstanding himself, David would surely have appreciated the qualities of the *qore*. Hey's sand partridge is a great runner, and when chased it speeds along the ground for a considerable distance on its olive-yellow feet, jumping, if necessary, from rock to rock or even ascending almost perpendicular cliffs. It often runs so far that it becomes exhausted and can be overtaken and knocked down with a stick. During the heat of the day it rests in the shadow of a rock or bush. It is related to the quail and pheasant, though it is larger than a quail and without the long tail of a pheasant. Like these birds, it lives on the ground and in April lays its clutch of five to seven eggs in a shallow depression scratched in the ground.

Hey's sand partridge is a medium-sized bird. The plumage of the male is sandy buff, its upper tail coverts are penciled and barred with brown, and its undersurface is chestnut and white, each feather margined with black. It has a white stripe behind its eye and white lores. The female is entirely grayish-buff, delicately marked.

As a shepherd boy in the hills around Bethlehem David must have seen many partridges, but here he would have found a different species —the handsome chukar partridge with red legs and bill, white throat edged with a black line, and heavily barred flanks. When David heard the ringing call notes of these partridges in the early morning, he would have prepared for a day of chase among the low bushes and tufted grass of the stony uplands around Bethlehem.

The range of this bird extends from the Alps to the Himalayas and on into China. The Indian form of the chukar partridge was introduced into the United States where it failed to establish itself in the eastern and central parts of the country, but it found a suitable habitat in the bleak mountain ranges of Nevada.

David's magnanimity in sparing his life touched King Saul and he ceased pursuing his "partridge." But David dared not trust the king and fled to a safe refuge in the land of the Philistines. David was, consequently, far away when the Philistines attacked Saul's army at Mount Gilboa. The Israelites fled, three of Saul's sons were slain and he himself was wounded by Philistine arrows. Standing on the great promontory of Gilboa the tall king knew he had lost the battle and, rather than be captured, he fell upon his own sword.

When news of the disaster reached David he fasted and mourned until sunset, for he had loved Saul's son Jonathan and he honored the king. David poured out his grief in a noble lament:

The beauty of Israel is slain upon thy high places.
  How are the mighty fallen! . . .
Ye mountains of Gilboa
  let there be no dew, neither let there be rain upon you. . . .
For there the shield of the mighty is vilely cast away,
  the shield of Saul, as though he had not been anointed with oil. . .
Saul and Jonathan were lovely and pleasant in their lives,
  and in their death they were not divided.
They were swifter than eagles,
  they were stronger than lions. . . .

II Samuel 1:19, 21, 23

In the king of birds and the king of beasts David found fitting symbols for the speed and might and majesty of Israel's tall king and his son Jonathan. The bird David named was the *nesher,* but he may have seen in his mind's eye not a vulture nor even the imperial eagle described as somewhat "heavy and slow on the wing," but the magnificent golden eagle, *Aquila chrysaëtos,* named for the golden tinge on its head and nape and one of the best-known eagles in the world. Golden eagles are found during the winter all over Palestine, but in summer they retire to the mountain ranges of Hermon and Lebanon. They seem to embody the majesty of Palestine's mountains, the ruggedness of her wild and rocky valleys, the freedom of her skies, and the speedy might of Israel's first king.

The golden eagle is a large, dark-brown bird that glides and soars on widespread wings watching for prey from great heights. From there, pressing its wings against its sides, it power dives upon its victim usually taking it by surprise and striking it dead in an instant with its powerful, sharp talons. Hares and rabbits are its usual victims though it takes prey as large as a lamb. One eagle is said to have snatched a puppy from inside a Bedouin tent. On the ground the golden eagle loses its dignity and runs with a comic, mincing gait that any fleet-footed partridge could outstrip, but in the air this eagle reigns supreme, a veritable monarch of the sky. As William Blake said: "When thou seest an eagle, thou seest a portion of genius; lift up thy head!"

The speed of this eagle is remarkable. In 1929 an English airman flying down the east coast of Greece at four thousand feet found himself on a course parallel to that of a golden eagle. As the eagle passed it turned its head to look back at the plane going steadily at eighty miles an hour. When stooping on prey these eagles are believed to go much faster. The Mongols of Central Asia train these swift birds to hunt, and in Turkestan a twelve year old golden eagle named Alagym is reported to have taken fourteen wolves in one day. No wonder men admire this splendid bird. In Scotland a Highland chief wears in his bonnet three flight feathers of a golden eagle.

"Swifter than eagles," sang David, remembering many a battlefield where Saul faced the dreaded Philistines and struck them with lightning speed. Despite his failings and his last bitter defeat, Israel's first king was to David a veritable eagle among men.

CHAPTER 10 ❧

The King Who Talked About Birds

WHEN Solomon, the son of David and his beautiful wife Bath-sheba, succeeded to his father's throne, he inherited a kingdom established by Saul's valor and David's greatness. Solomon's reign was to be memorable for its grandeur which sometimes bordered on the fabulous. As a young king he asked the Lord for an understanding mind and heart so that he could choose between good and evil and govern the people wisely. Solomon was no doubt sincere at first in his request for wisdom, but later he seemed to desire it mainly to enhance his reputation. If he became the wisest man in the world, people would greatly admire him. Solomon's dream of personal glory was largely fulfilled, for according to the Bible record "he was wiser than all men . . . and his fame was in all nations round about." The distilled wisdom of three thousand proverbs was attributed to him. He seemed to know everything.

Was Solomon our earliest-known lecturer on natural history? That is one interpretation of the famous sentence:

And he spake of trees, from the cedar tree that is in Lebanon even unto the hyssop that springeth out of the wall. He spake also of beasts and of fowl, and of creeping things, and of fishes.

I Kings 4:33

An even more intriguing interpretation of this verse depends upon the alteration of one word and declares that Solomon spoke not of but

to beasts, to birds, and to reptiles and fishes. As Kipling wrote in one of
his *Just So Stories:*

> There was never a king like Solomon,
> Not since the world began;
> But Solomon talked to a butterfly
> As a man would talk to a man.

There is a legend that Solomon possessed a magic ring which enabled
him to understand animal language. Such a ring would have been useful to him, especially in the case of birds, for, according to ancient
beliefs, birds acquired wisdom from soaring in the air and they were
able to foresee future events. Birds were also believed capable of understanding and reporting what men said; hence the advice: "Curse not the
king, no not in thy thought . . . for a bird of the air shall carry the
voice, and that which hath wings shall tell the matter" (Ecclesiastes
10:20). A similar idea is expressed in the phrase, "a little bird told me."

An entertaining legend tells how one day, while he was journeying
across the desert, Solomon noticed a hoopoe flying above him and protecting his head from the sun's rays with the shade of its outspread
wings. "What can I give you as a reward for this?" the grateful king
asked of the bird. "A crown of gold like yours," replied the hoopoe who
had been much impressed by Solomon's grandeur. The bird's request
was granted and a little gold crown appeared on its head. Immediately
the hoopoe began to have trouble, for everyone tried to steal its crown.
In desperation the poor bird finally went to Solomon. "What do you
want this time?" asked the king, not unkindly, for he had foreseen what
would happen. "It is my crown," sighed the bird, "please take it from
me." So Solomon took back his golden gift and gave the bird a crest
of black-tipped cinnamon feathers instead. The hoopoe never forgot
the former splendor of its golden crown. Today all these lovely, strange
birds wear their crests proudly, like the headdress of an American
Indian, and they are forever bending and bowing as if to admire their
reflection in every puddle. They raise and lower their handsome crests
like a fan that is alternately opened and closed.

Though the suggestions that Solomon was an authority on nature and
understood animal language cannot be taken seriously, the proverbs attributed to him, or perhaps only dedicated to him, show considerable
knowledge of natural history. They contain detailed knowledge of such
things as "the way of an eagle in the air" (Proverbs 30:19), a sparrow's
flitting (Proverbs 26:2, RSV), and the wariness of a bird when it sees a
net spread to catch it (Proverbs 1:17).

Impressive as Solomon's wisdom was reported to be, it was all but overshadowed by his magnificence. When the Queen of Sheba came to test his wisdom she brought a camel train laden with spices, gold, and precious stones, but even she was overwhelmed by "Solomon in all his glory." In Jerusalem she saw Solomon's elaborately decorated Temple and the imposing new palaces he was building for his foreign wives. He had so many horses, horsemen, and chariots that she could not even count them. The Queen of Sheba admired all the splendor of his court with the many courtiers, gorgeously-attired servants, and cup-bearers. She was amazed at the amount of food necessary to feed this great retinue in a single day: thirty measures of flour, sixty measures of meal, ten fat oxen, twenty pasture-fed oxen, one hundred sheep besides harts, roebucks, fallowdeer and, most surprising of all, "fatted fowl" (I Kings 4:22-23). No wonder that when the Queen of Sheba had seen all these things she was completely overwhelmed and "there was no more spirit in her."

The *barburim,* translated "fatted fowl," eaten at Solomon's table are mentioned only here in the Bible. Years later when Nehemiah listed his much less lavish daily provisions of "one ox and six choice sheep, also fowls . . . and all sorts of wine" (Nehemiah 5:18), he calls his fowls *tsippor* rather than *barburim.* What sort of birds were Solomon's "fatted fowl"? Possibly they were ducks or geese imported from Egypt to satisfy the whim of one of his queens, or guinea hens, or cuckoos which were often stuffed and considered a great delicacy in ancient times. The best suggestion seems to be that they were chickens, whose Arabic name, *birbir,* may be derived from *barburim.*

Our common barnyard fowl, said to be the most valuable bird in the world, is a descendant of the wild red jungle fowl native to the forests, thickets, and bamboo jungles of India, Burma, and Malaya. This bird is believed to have been domesticated before 2700 B.C. and carried from its original home to all parts of the world. The prolific hens were valuable for their eggs, the chickens for their tender meat, while the aggressive cocks provided amusement in the popular sport of cock-fighting. As long ago as the fifteenth century B.C. the Annals of Thut-mose III, one of Egypt's conquering pharaohs, mention birds that "bear every day" among the tribute brought back from Babylonia. Could these be hens? There is a Chinese tradition that in this same century poultry was introduced into China from Burma. Beginning then probably in the fifteenth century B.C. the red jungle fowl began to move slowly both west and east by overland routes doubtless in the caravans of merchants. In the ninth century B.C. Homer mentioned a cock in the *Odyssey.* Eighth-century coins from Ephesus depict a cock. Aristophanes called it the "Persian bird" in reference, no doubt, to the land from which the Greeks obtained it.

When did these birds reach Palestine and how did they come? An onyx seal, recently unearthed near ancient Mizpah in Palestine, is engraved with the figure of a fighting cock. Its inscription, "Belonging to Jaazaniah, servant of the king," and the place where the gem was found, point to the Jaazaniah mentioned in II Kings 25:23 as its original owner. He was one of Zedekiah's "captains of the armies" who came to Mizpah after the king's defeat by Nebuchadnezzar. If the seal belonged to this Jaazaniah, the fighting cock it portrays dates from about 587 B.C.

Though the Old Testament is silent about these birds, except for Solomon's "fatted fowl" and two other possible references, by New Testament times the crowing of cocks was a familiar sound in Jerusalem. But this period was a thousand years after Solomon's reign and if *barburim* were indeed chickens served at the royal table, Solomon and his guests must have eaten them as a great luxury especially imported from the East.

When King Solomon built his famous Tarshish ships at Ezion-geber on the Gulf of Aqabah and sent them south into the Red Sea with the fleet of Hiram king of Tyre, they sailed on to the mysterious "land of Ophir." Was this the coast of Zanzibar in Africa, or a region in southern Arabia, or Malabar in India? The fabulous cargoes brought back in the ships might have come from any one of these distant places.

And they went to Ophir, and brought from there gold, to the amount of four hundred and twenty talents; and they brought it to King Solomon. . . . For the king had a fleet of ships of Tarshish at sea with the fleet of Hiram. Once every three years the fleet of ships of Tarshish used to come bringing gold, silver, ivory, apes, and peacocks.

I Kings 9:28; 10:22, RSV

Wherever they landed, whether it was Africa, Arabia, or India, Solomon's sailors found traders with strange, exotic wares, ivory and apes from Africa, chickens and gorgeously-colored peacocks from India or Ceylon. "Peacocks" is the translation of *tukkiyyim* which ocurs in the Bible only in I Kings 10:22 and the parallel passage in II Chronicles 9:21. Scholars tell us it is not a Hebrew word and Dr. Albright believes it is derived from the Egyptian *ky*, meaning "ape." If this is so, the famous peacocks of Solomon must be dropped from the Bible and baboons substituted for them. Other scholars, however, find the word closely akin to *tokei*, the Tamil name for "peacocks," and believe it may be the name Solomon's mariners learned for this most gorgeous of birds from the Indian dealers. The cargoes of gold, silver, and ivory were probably ordered for the decoration of Solomon's Temple and his new palaces in Jerusalem. The king could desire no more splendid ornament for his terraces and courtyards than peacocks proudly wearing their feathered crests and spreading their huge fan-shaped and very decorative upper tail coverts. If it is true that Solomon really talked about birds and was interested in nature, what more suitable presents could his sailors bring him than apes and peacocks?

Though Phoenician traders brought peacocks from India to the pharaohs of Egypt long before Solomon's time, the two Bible references to these birds are believed to be the oldest written records of them outside India. Centuries later Aristotle said that Alexander the Great introduced peacocks into Greece. They are often mentioned by Greek and Latin authors. Suetonius reported that cooked peacock brains were among the exotic dishes served to that great eater and drinker, the Emperor Vitellius. Peacocks were believed to be Juno's favorite bird, as eagles were the favorites of her husband Jupiter. When a Roman empress died a peacock was released from her funeral pyre as a sign that she had become a goddess and was now immortal. The peacock of the dead empress was equivalent to the eagle set free when an emperor died.

From the curious notion that peacock flesh does not decay came the use of peacocks as emblems of immortality. Christian artists drew, painted, or carved many a gorgeous peacock to represent this idea. Today when a pope is carried in his processional chair, two chamberlains on either side of him bear *flabelli*—great fans of ostrich plumes tipped with peacock feathers and mounted on long poles. Derived, no doubt, from the fans waved to keep insects from the ancient sacrifices, the *flabelli* became a mark of honor for Church dignitaries. The ostrich plumes suggest power, as they did in ancient empires, while the peacock feathers represent immortality.

For a nonmigratory bird whose original home was the East, peacocks have traveled far, their beauty being their passport to foreign lands. Fortunately they are hardy birds and thrive in many climates and under various conditions. Only two wild varieties of this bird are known: the Indian peafowl which is the familiar royal blue bird seen in zoos, and the green peafowl which is seldom seen outside its native habitat. White peafowls sometimes appear in domestication, but these are a mutant race of the Indian peafowl. If this bird strutted and displayed and uttered its raucous cries in the courtyards of Solomon's palace long ago, it would have typified all the pride and grandeur of Israel's most magnificent king.

CHAPTER 11 ⚞

Vultures and Bible History

DAVID was still a young king and Solomon had not yet been born when a famine gripped the kingdom for three years. The rains ceased, crops failed, grass withered in the pastures, and grapevines and olive trees bore no fruit. In towns and throughout the countryside people were hungry and they feared that the Lord was angry with them. When David took their plight to God he learned that the famine was the punishment for a cruel deed of the previous reign when King Saul had brutally murdered the neighboring Gibeonites.

"What shall I do for you?" asked King David of the Gibeonites who had survived the massacre. "And wherewith shall I make the atonement?" Refusing blood money for the outrage, the Gibeonites demanded seven princes, Saul's sons and grandsons, to be handed over to them for execution. Such was the temper of those rude times that David replied: "I will give them." But he spared the little lame prince Mephibosheth, for he was Jonathan's son.

It was April. A good barley crop was ripening in the fields, the first reaping had begun, and people looked forward hopefully to the end of the long famine, now that David had placated the Gibeonites by surrendering to them the seven princes. But on the hill at Gibeon a mother sat on sackcloth spread upon the rock and endured a terrible vigil. She was Rizpah whom King Saul had loved and who had borne him two sons. Their dead bodies now hung from gallows above their mother and with them hung the bodies of five of Saul's grandsons. All through the summer Rizpah guarded them and in her epic devotion she "suffered neither the birds of the air to rest on them by day, nor the beasts of the field by night" (II Samuel 21:10). Her ordeal lasted five months and during that time she drove away jackals and hordes of ravenous vultures, ravens, and kites.

Finally, after the meager crops were harvested, the autumn rains began and men knew that the famine was finally ended. No one had ever before witnessed such devoted love nor such heroic endurance as that of Rizpah. David recognized greatness when he saw it and the news of this mother moved him to make amends to her. He ordered the seven bodies hanging at Gibeon to be taken down and the bodies of King Saul and Jonathan to be rescued from the Philistines so that he could give proper burial to all these men of the royal house of Saul in their own family tomb.

In those days when men feared not so much death, which comes to all, as lack of proper burial, they believed that during the time a man's body remained unburied he could not be "gathered to his fathers" and find rest among the departed in Sheol. To have one's body consumed by birds and beasts was the ultimate horror, for then one would never rest. Goliath had threatened young David with this fate only to have the threat hurled back at him. The curses that followed the blessings in Deuteronomy warned that "thy carcase shall be meat unto all the fowls of the air" (Deuteronomy 28:26). Again and again throughout the Old Testament and on into the New, whenever the terrifying words are spoken they evoke a grim picture of warfare, death, desolation, and unburied corpses. Above every battlefield the dark shapes of vultures appear and swiftly tear down out of the sky and one must cease to look. No blame can be attached to birds who merely carry out the repulsive task assigned to them. Nature has equipped them for this role. The eye of the vulture is keen to spot carrion, his beak strong to tear it, and his head unfeathered lest it become soiled. He has strong wings to take him wherever carrion is, but his feet and talons are weak, for his prey is already dead.

When Solomon's son Rehoboam came to the throne, the united kingdom ruled over by Saul, David, and Solomon was fatally split into north and south. Only the Southern Kingdom of Judah remained faithful to Rehoboam, while the Northern Kingdom of Israel chose Jeroboam as king. One day Jeroboam's wife went to Shiloh to consult the prophet Ahijah about her sick child. The prophet gave the queen "heavy tidings" for he predicted the death of her son and disaster for her husband.

Go, tell Jeroboam, thus saith the Lord God of Israel: . . . "Thou hast not been as my servant David who kept my commandments and who followed me with all his heart. . . . But thou hast done evil. . . . Therefore, behold, I will bring evil upon the house of Jeroboam. . . . Him that dieth of Jeroboam in the city shall the dogs eat and him that dieth in the field shall the fowls of the air eat."

I Kings 14:7-11

In succeeding reigns the grim words were repeated. King Baasha heard them from the prophet Jehu (I Kings 16:4). The gaunt and fiery prophet Elijah pronounced them against King Ahab, husband of the notorious Jezebel (I Kings 21:22-24).

While conspiracies, assassinations, and slaughter marked the reigns of Israel's kings, a foreign danger threatened. As the mighty Assyrian army, intent on conquest, advanced steadily toward their country, the people of Israel felt like helpless prey upon which a vulture swoops. The prophet Hosea saw the threat and vainly warned his countrymen:

> Set the trumpet to your lips,
> for a vulture is over the house of the Lord,
> because they have broken my covenant,
> and transgressed my law.

Hosea 8:1, RSV

But the Northern Kingdom of Israel failed to heed its prophets and the warning trumpets were not sounded. When the Assyrians came against the beautiful capital city of Samaria in 722 B.C. the last king of Israel was captured, the city was destroyed, and the ten tribes of Israel were deported.

Meanwhile the Southern Kingdom of Judah braced itself against the conquering Assyrians. As the enemy advanced nearer and nearer there was consternation among King Hezekiah's counselors in Jerusalem. Alarm was felt even in far-off Egypt. One day ambassadors from Egypt arrived in Jerusalem to make a defensive alliance with Hezekiah's little Kingdom of Judah against the common enemy. The official spokesman for Judah was the prophet Isaiah. He greeted the Egyptian emissaries but very courteously requested them to return home. Judah, he told them, did not need an alliance with Egypt, for the Lord was protecting the country and when the time was ripe He would destroy the Assyrian army. The vultures would feast, not upon Judah, but upon the terrible army of Assyria. Isaiah predicted that the dead army would be left "unto the fowls of the mountains" and so numerous would the corpses be that the birds of prey "shall summer upon them and all the beasts of the earth shall winter upon them" (Isaiah 18:6).

Unfortunately Isaiah's advice was not heeded. King Hezekiah and his people, hoping "to strengthen themselves in the strength of Pharaoh and to trust in the shadow of Egypt," made an alliance with Egypt, unmindful of the Lord's strength and their safety under the shadow of His wings. Isaiah continued to warn his countrymen:

> Woe to those who go down to Egypt for help
>   and rely on horses,
> who trust in chariots because they are many
>   and in horsemen because they are very strong,
> but do not look to the Holy One of Israel
>   or consult the Lord! . . .
> The Egyptians are men, and not God;
>   and their horses are flesh, and not spirit.
>
> Isaiah 31:1, 3, RSV

Isaiah knew that the chariots and horsemen engaged in this ancient struggle between Assyria, on the one hand, and Egypt and her ally, Judah, on the other, were of less importance than the spiritual forces involved. He believed that the spiritual forces were paramount and that the purposes of God, who controls both men and nations, would prevail. If Judah would put away her evil-doings and calmly trust in the Lord, she would be delivered from this great peril and gain a security the Egyptian alliance was powerless to provide. Isaiah's words rang out above the fear and tumult of those days:

> In returning and rest ye shall be saved;
>   in quietness and in confidence shall be your strength.
>
> Isaiah 30:15

But fear was in control and Isaiah's words were brushed aside.

Relentlessly the Assyrian invasion swept southward until King Sennacherib's army closed in upon Jerusalem. His official record of the campaign boasts: "As for Hezekiah, the Judean king who had not submitted to my yoke . . . himself I shut up like a caged bird in Jerusalem."

Isaiah noted the arrogance and haughty pride of the Assyrian conqueror. Sennacherib seemed to him like the one who steals eggs, scaring away the parent birds and leaving a desolate and silent nest behind. In the stirring events of this time (as narrated in II Kings 18-19; Isaiah 10:5-19; and chapters 36-39) attention is focused on the Assyrian conqueror, the "caged" king of Judah, and the indomitable prophet Isaiah who in the dark days of 701 B.C. proclaimed God's unfailing care of His people and said:

The Fighting Cock on Jaazaniah's Seal

The onyx seal on the right was used to stamp documents and jars of produce. It was found at Tell en-Nasbeh eight miles north of Jerusalem near ancient Mizpah. Two lines of Phoenician letters state: "Belonging to Jaazaniah, servant of the king." The fighting cock, which shows up clearly in the seal's impression in soft wax at the left, indicates that these birds were known in Palestine as early as 587 B.C., when the Jaazaniah of II Kings 25:23 lived. [Page 123]

Peacocks May Have Ornamented Solomon's Palace

Brought by the ships of Solomon's Red Sea fleet from some eastern port, these most gorgeous of birds were surely a match for "Solomon in all his glory." The peacock is a symbol of immortality in this detail from Carlo Crivelli's "Annunciation" painted in 1486. Represented here is the loggia above the Virgin's house where everything is richly ornamented. The goldfinch in the cage and the dove on the perch have, like the peacock, symbolic meaning—the dove typifying purity and the goldfinch foreshadowing the Passion. [Page 124]

The Peacock Emblem of Immortality

When Archbishop Theodore was laid to rest in this richly decorated sarcophagus, his mourners saw the peacocks as symbols of immortality. Two others birds feeding on grapes probably represent the souls of the faithful, while the vine signifies the Church, in an allusion to Christ's words: "I am the vine, ye are the branches" (John 15:5). The sarcophagus, dated 688 A.D., is in the Church of St. Apollinare in Ravenna. [Page 124]

"I Have Commanded the Ravens to Feed Thee There"

Wearily the strong prophet turns his head toward a raven bringing him food. By a rocky cave beside the Brook Cherith, here merely implied by the lush foliage at his feet, Elijah hides from the wrath of King Ahab. The final scene of the fiery old prophet's life takes place in the distance. On the near side of the Jordan a company of prophets waits while Elisha, who has accompanied his master to the end, watches the chariot and horses of fire carry Elijah to heaven. The picture, with its insight into character, its keen observation of nature, and its pleasing simplicity, was painted by Girolamo Savoldo (1488-1548). [Page 148]

"The Swallow Flits"

The Egyptian sculptor, who long ago modeled this swallow in plaster, portrayed its characteristically long tail streamers and short bill. He even indicated the swallow's wide gape that aids it in scooping insects from the air. Beautifully executed are the wings which take this bird through the air in swooping, graceful flight. These were the birds the Psalmist saw nesting in the Temple and darting swiftly about that sacred place. [Page 157]

133

Trees Shelter Innumerable Nests

Bible lands are the home of many sparrow hawks such as this mother bringing food to her downy young. Hawks build their nests in the tops of tall trees, as pictured here, or in rock crannies. In ancient times they were one of the species included in the Hebrew name *nets.* The abundant sparrows of the Jordan Valley are their chief prey. The long tail and barred under-parts are characteristic of sparrow hawks. A white "eyebrow" identifies this bird as the female. [Page 165]

Nebuchadnezzar's Dream Tree

While the mad king eats grass like an ox, many kinds of birds dwell in the boughs of the great tree above him. This parchment page from the oldest known copy of St. Beatus of Liebana's *Commentary on the Apocalypse and Daniel* was illuminated and written by the ancient Spanish artist, Maius, in 922 A.D. His composition is vigorous and his drawing rudely spontaneous. The artist was clearly not a bird watcher, for his decorative and lively birds portray no identifiable species. [Page 166]

The Turtledove—The Feathered Harbinger of Spring

When "the voice of the turtle [dove] is heard in our land" the people of Palestine knew that spring had arrived. Throughout Bible times turtledoves were one of the commonest sacrifices offered by poor people in the Temple. Though John Gould designed the plate for *Birds of Europe,* his wife executed the drawing and colored it. She conveyed the iridescence of the plumage and the gentleness of the bird. [Page 172]

Eric Hosking

"The Stork in the Heaven Knoweth Her Appointed Times"

Jeremiah praised these birds for obeying their "appointed times" of migration through Palestine. Here a stork, flying with neck outstretched and legs extended behind, has fingered out its outermost primaries to form slots. These control the air-flow over the upper surface of the wings, thereby increasing their lift. Characteristic of soaring birds is the great breadth and span of these wings. [Page 181]

The White Stork Is Well Known in Palestine

Long red legs for wading in shallow water and a long red bill for catching fish are the stork's most colorful features. Many of these great white birds travel through Palestine each year on their northward journey and some remain there for several months to breed. The oldest record of migration (Jeremiah 8:7) mentions the stork. This hand-colored lithograph of a striking creature is from John Gould's *Birds of Europe*. [Page 182]

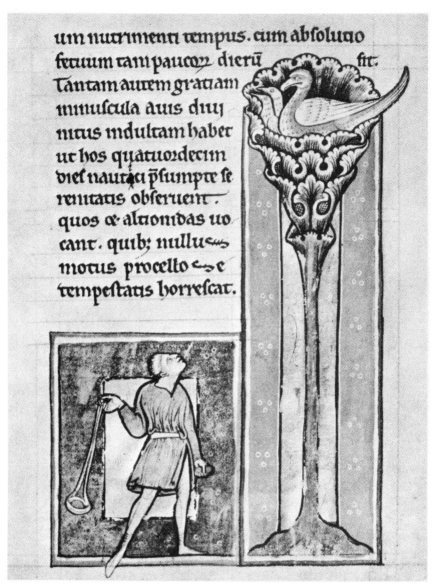

um nutrimenti tempus. cum absoluto
fetuum tam paucoz dierū fit.
Tantam autem gratiam
minuscula auis diui
nitus indultam habet
ut hos quatuordecim
dies nautici psumpte se
renitatis obseruent.
quos & alcionidas uo
cant. quib; nullus
motus procello
tempestatis horrescat.

"One Who Throws a Stone at Birds"

A bird hunter uses a stone and sling reminiscent of David's weapon in his contest with
Goliath. Peering over the edge of their ornamental nest two young birds watch the
enemy, while their parent seems to be calculating the degree of danger before flying
away. The nest's great height together with the bird's hooked beak, long wings, and two
nestlings seem to identify these birds as eagles. The illumination is from a twelfth-century
English bestiary. [Page 196]

An Ostrich Family

Largest of living birds, ostriches inhabit open, sandy plains as depicted in this habitat group in The American Museum of Natural History. A shallow nest has been scooped in the foreground for the huge eggs. Protectively colored chicks have bristly feathers and the long legs and necks of their parents. The male on the right raises his wings and displays his white plumes. The female holds her head high to spot distant danger. Ostriches sometimes act as lookouts and give the alarm to smaller creatures such as gazelles which like to feed in their neighborhood. [Page 205]

Ostriches Have Been Hunted for Millenniums

Ostriches can outrun the fastest horses and were it not that the hero is a god and has his own wings, he would be unable to overtake the bounding bird. This Assyrian cylinder seal made from gray marble in the eighth century B.C. is now in the Pierpont Morgan Library. During photography the seal was rotated so that the young or distant bird appears twice, as does part of the winged hero. A comparison of this ostrich with the mounted birds opposite shows how accurately the Assyrian sculptor rendered a huge bird on a tiny seal. [Page 207]

From His Birth Jesus Was Surrounded by the Humble Creatures

Folchetto da Saginesio in this "Nativity," painted about 1485, added a rabbit munching foliage to the customary ox, ass, and sheep. But the notable feature here is the great variety of birds. A pair of mallard ducks with three ducklings swim in the pond. A guinea fowl, partridge, and stork (or egret) pose in the foreground. On a branch over the stream a kingfisher watches for his dinner. A dove drinks from the water trough. The owl perched on a dead branch watches an angel. Three goldfinches and a fourth flying bird, which may be a bullfinch, all symbolize sacrifice, while the swallow on the roof is an emblem of the Resurrection. [Page 233]

"They Brought Him to Jerusalem to Present Him to the Lord"

Giotto depicts with simplicity and power the chief elements of the story. Joseph holds the two gentle pigeons for Mary's sacrifice. Mary, dressed in a blue mantle, stretches out her arms across the altar to receive her Son. The "just and devout" Simeon has blessed the Child and spoken his thanksgiving. Anna is entering to give "thanks likewise unto the Lord." Despite much restoration, the figures in this tempera panel have reality and their significant gestures give animation to the scene. Even the birds are somehow not mere feathered lumps, but quivering creatures intently watching the stately drama. [Page 234]

143

Child and Goldfinch

The curious Child and the friendly goldfinch are oblivious of adoring angels and all the jeweled splendors with which they are surrounded in Spinello Aretino's "Madonna Enthroned." In this detail, Boy and bird are interested only in becoming acquainted with each other. Besides the appealingly human response of the Child to the goldfinch, the picture also contains symbolic meaning, for the goldfinch was a sign of the Passion. Aretino, an Italian painter (1330-1410), was influenced by Giotto's style and by the painters of Siena. [Page 235]

> Like a bird fluttering above its nest,
>   shall the Eternal ward Jerusalem,
>   shielding her and saving her,
>   sparing and preserving her.
>   Isaiah 31:5, Moffatt

History records that in 701 B.C. Jerusalem was indeed saved and the Assyrian army, whether destroyed by disease or recalled to deal with uprisings at home, raised the siege of the city and withdrew. Isaiah's faith was vindicated. The Lord had protected His city.

Evils continued to corrode the nation's life and less than a hundred years later, the prophet Jeremiah saw new dangers threatening from abroad. The vultures were flying again. Jeremiah prophesied during years fraught with terror, ruin, and death when the mighty Assyrian Empire was overthrown and the new Babylonian Empire rose to power and spread westward under the leadership of Nebuchadnezzar. In prophecy after prophecy, Jeremiah denounced the evils of his own people and warned them of coming destruction. Jerusalem was finally destroyed in 587 B.C., its king and people exiled to Babylonia, and the vultures, which Jeremiah had mentioned, feasted upon the slain (Jeremiah 15:3; 16:4; 19:7; 34:20). "And the carcases of this people shall be meat for the fowls of the heaven, and for the beasts of the earth; and none shall fray [frighten] them away" (Jeremiah 7:33).

When Jerusalem fell, death and destruction were everywhere.

> O God, the heathen are come into thine inheritance;
>   thy holy temple have they defiled;
>   they have laid Jerusalem on heaps.
> The dead bodies of thy servants have they given
>   to be meat unto the fowls of the heaven,
>   the flesh of thy saints unto the beasts of the earth.
>   Psalm 79:1-2

The horror of these events reached those who had already been exiled to Babylonia. Among them was the prophet Ezekiel who painted grim pictures of birds of prey and their repulsive feasts (Ezekiel 29:5; 32:4; 39:4, 17-20). He wrote a parable of eagles to warn his people against Nebuchadnezzar of Babylon who, like "a great eagle with great wings, longwinged, full of feathers which had divers colors, came unto Lebanon and took the highest branch of the cedar" (Ezekiel 17:3). Egypt, he said, was like a second eagle with "great wings and many feathers" (17:7), though it lacked the colored plumage representing Babylonian royalty.

In the Book of Daniel, Nebuchadnezzar (or possibly a later ruler) was again seen as an eagle, but some personal calamity had befallen him for "his hairs were grown like eagles' feathers and his nails like birds' claws" (Daniel 4:33). Nebuchadnezzar became a bedraggled caricature of the eagle symbol of royal power.

When Cyrus appeared in the middle of the sixth century B.C. and led his Persian army to victory over Babylon, an unnamed prophet hailed him as the instrument of God's purposes to deliver Israel from exile and restore her to her own land. Once again an emperor was likened to a bird. The speed of Cyrus' conquests seemed like that of a vulture hastening to its prey, an idea reinforced by the vulture emblem depicted on the standards of the Persian army. Inevitably the great nameless prophet of the Exile saw Cyrus as the "ravenous bird from the east, the man that executeth my [the Lord's] counsel from a far country" (Isaiah 46:11).

The two references to vultures in the Apocrypha (II Maccabees 9:15; 15:33) come from the period when the Greek dynasty of the Seleucids controlled Palestine.

Finally, in New Testament times when Rome became the oppressor of the Lord's people, the author of Revelation used the idea of vultures, and especially Ezekiel's picture of the horrible feast, to portray the overthrow of evil preparatory to the reign of Christ. "All the fowls that fly in the midst of heaven" are summoned to gather at a feast of the slain and "the fowls were filled with their flesh" (Revelation 19:17, 21).

CHAPTER 12 ～⁄⁅

Elijah's Ravens

I⁀ ᴡᴀꜱ as desolate a place as one can imagine. The sun-baked walls of the ravine rose bare and stony out of the tangle of underbrush. No one ever came here and Elijah felt safe. Ever since he had prophesied drought in Israel and had seen fear and savage anger darken King Ahab's face, Elijah had been on the run. A hunted man cannot rest. Only after he had crossed the Jordan River and, continuing on past Jabesh-Gilead, had come to the edge of the desert where he had hidden himself in dense thickets, did he loosen his leather girdle and stretch out his tall, rugged body on the ground. As a youth shepherding flocks in the rough pasture lands through which he had just fled, he had grown strong and hardy, able to run long distances and endure on the scantiest of food. It was the training a prophet needed in the ninth century ʙ.ᴄ. when Ahab ruled the Northern Kingdom of Israel and no prophet of God was safe. But after his long flight even Elijah's iron strength was exhausted, his throat parched, his tongue swollen, and he lay panting on the ground.

Elijah closed his eyes but he could still see Ahab's sumptuous palace on the hill at Samaria from which he had just escaped. He had stood before Ahab and his fanatical Queen Jezebel and with incredible daring had spoken the Lord's words which burned like a fire within him. The four hundred and fifty prophets of Baal that ate at Jezebel's table crowded around and stared insolently at him, seeing him only as an uncouth prophet of the unpopular God of Israel. They were confident of their own power at court and feared nothing Elijah might say, for their Canaanite cult was well-established in Israel and their altars and sacred groves were everywhere. With his piercing prophet's eyes Elijah looked at the heathen altars, the priests of Baal, Jezebel, and the people she ruled. Could these men and women indeed be Israel, the people God had chosen to be His own? Then Elijah raised his voice and flung out his message: "As the Lord God of Israel liveth, before whom I stand, there shall not be dew nor rain these years, but according to my word!"

His stark words compelled attention and everyone in Ahab's council chamber saw only too plainly the grim specter of drought when wells and cisterns become dry, fields and pastures burn brown, cattle die, and people cry for food. King Ahab trembled. The prophets of Baal buzzed around Jezebel and in the confusion Elijah made good his escape.

Now as he lay with every muscle aching he knew the terrible price a man pays for being a prophet of the Lord. People had murmured against Moses; Samuel was disobeyed. "Which of the prophets have not your fathers persecuted?" Stephen was to say in later years.

From nearby came the delicate tinkling of a tiny stream pouring over pebbles. The Lord had not abandoned His prophet to die of thirst in a dry wadi. The Brook Cherith still ran in its hidden bed among thick bushes at the bottom of the ravine. Already there was drought in Israel, but here where God had directed him to flee, there was flowing water which Elijah could drink.

Elijah knelt beside a clear pool from which he scooped handfuls of refreshing water. His thirst quenched, he lay down again, but hunger kept him awake. Then came a rushing sound of great wings and he remembered all that the Lord had promised.

Get thee hence, and turn thee eastward, and hide thyself by the brook Cherith, that is before Jordan. And it shall be that thou shalt drink of the brook; and I have commanded the ravens to feed thee there.

I Kings 17:3-4

Incredibly it was happening—great black birds flew into the ravine and each one carried in its massive beak a piece of food for Elijah.

And the ravens brought him bread and flesh in the morning, and bread and flesh in the evening, and he drank of the brook.

I Kings 17:6

In the days that followed, the ravens became Elijah's friends. However far they roamed for food during the day they always returned to the deep rocky glen where they raised their young. They were indeed "ravens of the valley" (Proverbs 30:17). Twice a day Elijah watched them flying toward him in their characteristic way, alternately flapping and gliding on horizontal wings. They sailed and soared in updrafts of warm air high above the ravine, diving and rolling and tumbling, hovering and playing about in the sky on huge wings, carrying out the purposes of their Creator. Their deep, raucous croak, *"pruck-pruck,"* seemed part of the wilderness. Elijah must have admired their glossy black plumage, and their stout bills. It has been noted that ravens and other members of the crow family often store surplus food in rocky crevices or beneath a covering of leaves and this habit may explain the action of the ravens in the Elijah story.

Until the Brook Cherith dried up in the great drought, Elijah remained safely hidden there. He believed that both drought and ravens were sent by God—the former, to awaken Israel to her sin so that the Lord might bless her again, the ravens, to sustain him whose mission of turning the hearts of the people back to their God was not yet accomplished. Daily when he heard the whir of ravens' wings, he knew that the Lord watched over him and that in God's mighty sovereignty over nature there exists the quality of love.

Notwithstanding Elijah's story, ravens have usually been regarded as birds of evil omen and their uncanny sagacity has been attributed to Satan. Men have shuddered at their weird croak believing it to be the voice of doom. Some of the Hebrews, it is true, perceived in the raven's ebony plumage a beauty like that of the dark hair of a loved one.

> His head is as the most fine gold,
>   his locks are bushy,
>   and black as a raven.
> His eyes are as the eyes of doves.
>   Song of Solomon 5:11-12

The Hebrews knew the raven as an "unclean" bird with a reputation for plucking out the eyes of its victims. "The eye that mocketh at his father and despiseth to obey his mother, the ravens of the valley shall pick it out, and the young eagles shall eat it" (Proverbs 30:17).

Ravens have a nobility all their own. Two of them were said to attend the Norse god Odin and whisper advice in his ear. Danish vikings depicted a raven on their flag, and Indians of Alaska often carved a raven figure on their totem poles. These birds of mountains, rocky cliffs, semideserts, and virgin forests are widely distributed over Europe, northern Asia, and North America. They are quick-sighted, intelligent, and the largest of the order of perching birds. Sailing and soaring on black wings against a background of forests, cliffs, and sky, these creatures appear worthy of being agents of their Creator.

PART IV

Birds of the Prophets,
Priests, Psalmists,
Writers

CHAPTER 13 ⟅⟆
The Way of an Eagle in the Air

AGUR was a very wise man whose quick, observant eyes saw many curious and remarkable things that other people seldom noticed. He also had a knack of writing pithy sentences and proverbs which have delighted and instructed people for the past two thousand or more years. He saw that "ants are a frail folk, but they store up food in summer" and that "the locusts have no king to lead them, but they advance in order." He compared a king marching with dignified bearing at the head of his army to a lion with stately tread and a proudly "strutting cock" (Proverbs 30:31, Moffatt). He made the gruesome discovery that ravens finding a corpse first pick out its eyes. But with all his knowledge and sophistication this wise man of antiquity admitted that he could not understand "the way of an eagle in the air" (Proverbs 30:19). When he saw a great bird sail through the sky he could only marvel.

Perhaps as a small child Agur flapped his arms, as children sometimes do, trying to fly, but he learned his lesson quickly—no amount of arm-flailing ever lifted a person even a fraction of an inch off the ground. The wonder of bird flight remained a mystery for centuries. Even today, though we have learned how to fly in machines, and though we know the properties of air and the structure of a bird's wing, we still do not completely understand how a bird flies. Men were earthbound for thousands of years, for we learned to fly only a half century or so ago. Birds, however, took to the air some 125 million years ago and their descendants have been flying ever since. No wonder they are consummate aerial artists!

For the thousands of years birds kept their secret of flying men could only dream about imitating them. During the Renaissance, when nothing seemed impossible to men, Leonardo da Vinci believed that he had discovered the way to fly and he constructed two very ingenious wing-flapping machines to be strapped onto a man's back. They were useless, of course, but men had begun to try. In the last century Orville Wright spent hours on his back watching buzzards soar overhead, but he admitted that all he got from watching them was "plenty of flying fever." The birds still possessed their secret. When the Wright brothers finally built an airplane that could fly, they examined a picture of a gliding sea gull and realized that it was using the same principles of flight and balance and the same equipment they used for their plane. The Wrights constructed airfoils, flaps, slots, and a propeller, but they saw that the single structure of a bird's wing performed all the functions of their own complicated equipment and was at the same time a handsome outer garment, a raincoat, and a perfect overcoat against the bitterest cold! Year by year airplane makers improved their navigation instruments, but a bird can find its way in darkness over trackless oceans and the mysterious faculty it uses is far more perfectly developed than anything man has yet devised. The wonder of an eagle in the air remains.

The marvelous ease of gravity-defying flight, the sheer grandeur and grace of an eagle mounting the sky reminded the Hebrews of their spiritual experience. When they trusted in God, they discovered the enormous lifting power of faith and hope. The great prophet of the Exile expressed this unforgettably:

> But they that wait upon the Lord shall renew their strength,
>   they shall mount up with wings as eagles;
> they shall run and not be weary;
>   and they shall walk and not faint.
>
>   Isaiah 40:31

It was the Lord who pardoned their sins, healed their sickness, saved them from death, crowned them with His love, and gave them their heart's desire. The Psalmist praises the Lord for this experience of restoration in which "thy youth is renewed like the eagle's" (Psalm 103:5). His phrase is based on an old idea that eagles renew their youth by soaring toward the sun. Eagles live long and there is a record of a golden eagle attaining an age of eighty years in captivity. It was, perhaps, because eagles soar to great altitudes that the legendary Babylonian shepherd Etana chose an eagle for his space flight to the moon. A lammergeier was once observed in the neighborhood of Mount

Everest flying at 25,000 feet. The Psalmist's phrase was well-chosen. How does a bird "fly away as an eagle toward heaven" (Proverbs 23:5)? A soaring bird is borne up so easily on its great wings that it appears to be free from the pull of gravity, but actually, gravity is exerting a constant downward force upon the bird. A greater force opposes it, however, with the result that gravity is counteracted and the bird is pushed upward. This greater upward thrust comes from a rising current of air. Sometimes the upcurrent is produced by a horizontal air current meeting a cliff or some other obstacle and being deflected upward. A more powerful upcurrent is produced when the sun heats the bare earth of fields, sandy plains, or mountaintops and the air above them becomes superheated and rises in warm upcurrents or thermals. When a large bird enters one of these thermals it extends its wings in the soaring position and fingers out the tips of its primaries so that it can take every advantage of the rising current of air to lift it higher and higher. The bird rides, as it were, in an invisible elevator. As soaring occurs only when there is constant forward movement, the bird cannot mount vertically in the thermal, but must either glide forward or circle round and round, higher and higher in the rising current.

The spectacular soaring of thousands of storks, kites, eagles, vultures, buzzards, hawks, and gulls has been graphically described in the *Ibis* by Colonel Meinertzhagen and others who watched these birds on migration through Egypt, Sinai, and Palestine. After ten o'clock in the morning, when the sun has heated the ground, soaring birds locate an ascending column of warm air either by the "dust devils" it stirs up or by the presence of other birds soaring in it. Throngs of them crowd into the thermal and with no effort on their part are carried upward, their wings and tails motionless but spread out to give them the largest possible surface in contact with the rising air. In Palestine an entire flock of white storks was seen to flap its way into a thermal and then, without a wingbeat, spiral rapidly upward to a height of four thousand feet. These bird circuses may be large and varied. When the first birds reach the top of the thermal they peel off and make a long glide down to the base of another. Meanwhile more and more birds are entering the first spiral from below. D. R. Mackintosh reported in the *Ibis* the record number of two hundred and fifty eagles and vultures enjoying the free lift in a single thermal. Glider pilots imitate a bird's technique and are sometimes accepted by the birds as one of themselves. As reported in *The Listener*, February 3, 1937, Philip Wills went aloft in his glider and located an updraft. He entered it only to see all the vultures in the neighborhood follow his lead into the rising column of air and swing up in spirals after him.

Soaring storks look so large and powerful that the prophet Zechariah thought they could fly away with something as heavy as a bushel measure filled to the brim. In his vision he saw an ephah measure filled with all the crime and evil of Israel. There were two women who "had wings like the wings of a stork, and they lifted up the ephah between the earth and the heaven" (Zechariah 5:9), and carried the heavy burden away to Babylon.

Actually, even large birds are able to lift only a little weight in addition to their own. It is believed that if the strongest eagles can lift as much as ten pounds, they cannot carry it far. The persistent stories of eagles snatching up children must therefore be exaggerated, as is the Greek myth of the shepherd boy Ganymede who was seized by an eagle and borne aloft to Mount Olympus where he became cupbearer to the gods.

In order to fly at all, birds must be as light as possible. For this reason their bodies contain large air-filled cavities and their bones, though strong, are usually thin, and exceedingly light. Soaring birds like hawks, vultures, and albatrosses, all of whom need great buoyancy, have hollow air-filled bones, light as paper. Dr. Robert Cushman Murphy found that a frigate bird with a wingspread measuring seven feet, had a skeleton weighing only a quarter of a pound which is actually less than the weight of the bird's feathers.

To "fly away like a bird" (Hosea 9:11) or to "go free like birds" (Ezekiel 13:20, RSV) requires wings. When Jeremiah warned that the country of Moab would be destroyed, he referred to flying:

> Give wings unto Moab,
>   that it may flee and get away,
> for the cities thereof shall be desolate,
>   without any to dwell therein.
>   Jeremiah 48:9

Feathered wings are among the most remarkable and beautiful structures of the animal world. Feathers are believed to have developed from the scales of reptiles. Wings were perfected through the eons until they enable today's birds to flap and flit and flutter, to soar and sail and swoop, to dive and zoom and hover and even, in a few cases, to fly backward. Flight is not produced by random, unco-ordinated movements, but is like a ballet with each wing and tail feather changing its shape and position and executing an intricate movement in a precise and perfectly timed sequence. So swift and complex are the feather, wing, and tail motions that lift a bird into the air, steer it, propel it, and keep it balanced that only slow-motion photography discloses the amazing technique and beauty of flying.

Under a microscope a wing feather reveals its astonishing intricacy and beauty. From the shaft of the feather grow hundreds of barbs which branch into hundreds of thousands of barbules. These in turn have millions of branches called barbicels some of which end in tiny hooks designed to lock the barbicels, barbules, and barbs together into a continuous, flexible web or vane. The vane acts like an oar and makes flying possible. When the microscopic hooks are disarranged the barbicels separate, but a bird can restore the feather's web by preening. Many wing feathers, each of a special size and shape and each with its own function, make up a bird's wing. The wings themselves differ widely from one species to another according to the way of life and type of flight of each bird.

The various flight patterns of birds are recognized in the proverb which states that "the sparrow flutters, the swallow flits" (Proverbs 26:2, Moffatt). Sparrows move their wings rapidly, but swallows dart swiftly enough to catch insects on the wing.

The eagle uses its great wings not only for soaring and gliding, but to brake its immensely swift power dive. Again and again the Bible mentions the swift flight of eagles and vultures. The curses that will come upon Israel if she disobeys God contain a warning: "The Lord shall bring a nation against thee from far, from the end of the earth, as swift as the eagle flieth" (Deuteronomy 28:49). This catastrophe overtook the Northern Kingdom in 722 B.C., and Judah a little more than a hundred years later. Of this latter event Lamentations said:

> Our persecutors are swifter than the eagles of the heaven.
> They pursued us upon the mountains;
> > they laid wait for us in the wilderness.
> > > > Lamentations 4:19

Jeremiah warned of a foe that would approach with an eagle's speed.

> Behold, he comes up like clouds,
> > his chariots like the whirlwind;
> > his horses are swifter than eagles—
> > woe to us, for we are ruined!
> > > > Jeremiah 4:13, RSV

In two other passages Jeremiah said that the approaching enemy would "fly as an eagle" (Jeremiah 48:40; 49:22), though he probably never dreamed that his poetic phrase would become a grim reality in the twentieth century. With his fellow prophet Habakkuk he waited while the enemy rapidly swept nearer and nearer Jerusalem. Habakkuk wrote of the Chaldean conquerors:

> Their horses also are swifter than the leopards,
>   and are more fierce than the evening wolves. . . .
> And their horsemen shall come from far,
>   they shall fly as the eagle that hasteth to eat.
> Habakkuk 1:8

Among the famous Dead Sea Scrolls is the much-discussed Habakkuk Commentary. This ancient scroll, the dating of which is the subject of debate, identifies the enemy horsemen as belonging to the Kittim who, the commentator declares, "devour all peoples like a vulture without being satisfied." But who are the Kittim? If we knew, we might be able to date the scroll accurately. Possibly a bird gives us a clue. As the commentator emphasizes the bird's rapacity rather than its speed, he seems, therefore, to refer to a vulture rather than to an eagle. If the unknown Kittim had been Romans, eagles might have been mentioned, in reference to the eagles on their standards. Vultures, on the other hand, would more likely signify earlier conquerors. All this, however, lacks certainty.

The beauty and speed of winged flight are immortalized in this Psalm:

> If I take the wings of the morning
>   and dwell in the uttermost parts of the sea,
> Even there shall thy hand lead me,
>   and thy right hand shall hold me.
> Psalm 139:9-10

Not only does the dawn have wings, but clouds and snow are likened to birds.

> Therefore the storehouses are opened,
>   and the clouds fly forth like birds. . . .
> He scatters the snow like birds flying down,
>   and its descent is like locusts alighting.
> The eye marvels at the beauty of its whiteness,
>   and the mind is amazed at its falling.
> Ecclesiasticus 43:14, 17-18, RSV

The Confraternity Edition of the Bible expresses these thoughts even more poetically: "like vultures the clouds hurry forth," and God "sprinkles the snow like fluttering birds."

So marvelous is a bird's flight and so impossible is it of human attainment that it seems to have a godlike quality. Again and again the

Bible mentions wings and flying in connection with God (II Samuel 22:11; Psalm 104:3; Isaiah 8:8; Malachi 4:2). Winged beings, "the cherubim of glory," may once have been myths, but they express truth in a poetical form in many a Bible passage (I Kings 6:27; 8:7; I Chronicles 28:18; II Chronicles 3:11-13; 5:7-8; Isaiah 6:6; Ezekiel 10:15-21; 11:22; Hebrews 9:5). The Hebrews praised God and sang of heavenly winged creatures that supported and conveyed His very throne:

> And he rode upon a cherub and did fly.
> Yea, he did fly upon the wings of the wind.
>   Psalm 18:10

CHAPTER 14 ✒

Where Birds Make Their Nests

SEARCHING for birds' nests in the Bible takes the reader almost everywhere. We have found the birds themselves in a great variety of places: riding out a flood on a strange boat, eating pastries from an Egyptian basket, falling exhausted into a desert encampment, running from pursuers on arid hillsides, strutting in a palace courtyard, swooping upon battlefields, and bringing morsels of food into a remote wadi. We shall find nests in as many likely and unlikely places. Palestine offered ideal nesting sites among her limestone cliffs, her ancient trees, her watercourses and barren hills, her fields and swamps.

It was not unusual as one walked along a path, to spot a nest in a tree or on the ground. Every Israelite knew he must not rob the nest and take the parent bird as well, for a law in Deuteronomy forbade this. It was written in a legal way to cover every circumstance of finding a nest.

If you happen to come upon a bird's nest on a tree or on the ground, with young ones or eggs and the mother-bird sitting on the young ones or on the eggs, you must not take away the mother-bird along with her brood; what you must do, is to let the mother-bird go, as you take the brood for yourself, that all may go well with you and that you may have a long life.

Deuteronomy 22:6-7, Moffatt

As this stands among the humanitarian laws and ends, as does the Fifth Commandment which speaks of honoring one's father and mother, with the same promise: "that all may go well with you and

160

that you may have a long life," we can, perhaps, see it as an expression of reverence for motherhood. In those crude, far-off days the people of Israel were moved in certain circumstances by compassion and mercy and it was repugnant to them to take advantage of a bird whose parental instinct to protect its young made it an easy prey to the hunter.

The effect of this law about birds' nests was to preserve the breeding stock and thus help to conserve man's natural heritage. Perhaps some of the species of birds now flying in Palestine owe their survival to these two verses in Deuteronomy. The stories of such birds as the great auk and the passenger pigeon have made us aware that when a living species is destroyed it can never be replaced. Today the principle embodied in this nearly three thousand year old Hebrew law protecting the breeding birds of Palestine is gaining wide acceptance. In the United States, however, it was not until 1918 that the shooting of game birds in their breeding season was abolished.

There was one bird sanctuary in Israel, one place where robbing a nest or molesting parents and their nestlings was forbidden.

> Yea, the sparrow hath found an house,
>   and the swallow a nest for herself
>   where she may lay her young,
> even thine altars, O Lord of hosts,
>   my King and my God.
> Blessed are they that dwell in thy house,
>   they will be still praising thee.
>   Psalm 84:3-4

Birds were quick to notice that nests built within the sacred area of the Temple at Jerusalem were inviolate. Here both man and bird found peace and security in God's house. Even the untamable swallows came here every year to raise their young. Today where the Temple once stood swallows still return to their ancestral nesting places, while swifts breed in the porch of the Mosque of Omar, and palm doves and kestrels nest nearby.

The custom of protecting birds in the Temple was adopted by the Mohammedans, as Charles M. Doughty recorded in his famous *Travels in Arabia Deserta.* As he journeyed toward Mecca,

Doves flitted and alighted in the path before us. The rafiks told me, "It were unlawful to kill any of them, at least within the bounds!" for these are doves of the Haram [Temple], which are daily fed in Mecca of an allowance . . . of wheaten grain. When it is sprinkled to them they flutter down in multitudes, though perhaps but few could be seen a moment before: they will suffer themselves to be taken up in the peoples' hands.

The bird that "found an house" in the Temple was the biblical "sparrow," the *tsippor,* a name denoting such small birds as the Palestine house sparrow and the wren. The house sparrow of Palestine, *Passer domesticus biblicus,* the commonest bird in the Holy Land, is a lively, noisy, prolific creature laying its first eggs in the early spring and sometimes raising as many as four broods a year. In Bible days many young sparrows were hatched in the shadow of the Temple and dwelt secure and blessed in that holy place. When they grew older they came and went in chattering multitudes, stirring up dust in ancient courtyards. Though tunefulness might be lacking in their songs, no one could accuse them of halfheartedness as they raised their twittering, chirping voices in a tumultuous din of praise.

Among the nesting "sparrows" of the Temple may have been wrens, as the University of Chicago Version of the Bible suggests in its translation of Psalm 84. Wrens are half-sociable, half-shy little busybodies, with cocked tails and cheerful, nonstop chatter. The great American ornithologist Dr. Frank Chapman remarked: "Build a house almost anywhere from Patagonia to Canada and a house wren appears." Possibly wrens appeared when Solomon built the Temple and continued to find safe nesting places in its cracks and ledges.

The wren of Bible days might be the subspecies observed in Lebanon by Colonel Meinertzhagen and named *Troglodytes troglodytes syriacus.* Today it is a rare winter visitor to the Jordan Valley and is seen below Jerusalem and in the Wadi Qelt. The wrens of the Temple would have been descendants of birds of the Western Hemisphere, where the wren is believed to have originated during the Pleistocene epoch. The wren family is one of the very few that apparently crossed Bering Strait, successfully invaded Asia, and pushed on westward to the farthest limits of Ireland and Iceland. This feat is a record, even for such "a dynamo in feathers" as the wren.

Wrens often select bizarre nesting sites: a cabbagehead, a coil of rope, a mailbox, a cow skull, a tin can, a pair of trousers hung out on a clothesline, the family automobile, a houseboat traveling on the Nile. They nest in such places as the fold of a church curtain or an "ivied abbey-wall." A legend tells of a wren that laid an egg in St. Malo's cloak while he was pruning the monastery vines. When nesting in the Temple, wrens often had to defend their large broods against sparrows, swallows, and pigeons. As Shakespeare said in *Macbeth:*

> . . . The poor wren,
> The most diminutive of birds, will fight,
> Her young ones in her nest, against the owl.

No Temple pigeon should have disdained its tiny wren neighbor, for the English country rhyme, quoted by Edward A. Armstrong in *The Wren,* proclaims:

> Coo-oo, coo-oo,
> It's as much as a pigeon can do
>   To maintain two;
> But the little wren can maintain ten
> And bring them all up like gentlemen.

An enigmatic verse in the Psalms may refer to an unusual nesting place of doves. In Eastern countries today broken earthenware pots are sometimes used for birdhouses, especially for doves. Does the following passage refer to this custom?

> Though ye have lien among the pots,
>   yet shall ye be as the wings of a dove covered with silver,
>   and her feathers with yellow gold.
>
> Psalm 68:13

When Jeremiah accused the partridge of nest robbing, he was on unsure ground.

> Like a partridge hatching eggs it never laid,
>   so is the man who makes money unfairly;
> it leaves him ere his life is over,
>   and in the end he proves himself a fool.
>
> Jeremiah 17:11, Moffatt

Jeremiah here refers to the ancient belief that a hen partridge steals eggs from other nests and incubates them with her own, only to have the stolen chicks return to their own mothers as soon as they can fly. This strange and erroneous idea undoubtedly stemmed from the large clutch a partridge lays. One nest Tristram discovered in the wilderness of Judea contained twenty-six eggs. The Authorized Version represents Jeremiah's partridge as a disappointed mother who "sitteth on eggs and hatcheth them not," for they are stolen from her. She thus becomes a warning not to count your chickens before they are hatched. In the Revised Standard Version Jeremiah's partridge seems to be so enthusiastic a foster mother or baby sitter that she "gathers a brood which she did not hatch," and attempts to raise them with her own chicks.

Though nests were safe in the Temple, elsewhere they were often robbed. Perhaps as a boy Isaiah went egg-gathering in the hills outside Jerusalem. It was good sport for a boy and quail and partridge eggs were welcome additions to the diet of city dwellers in the spring. Was it the memory of such an expedition that gave Isaiah his idea of Sennacherib as a nest robber? The scene in which Sennacherib insolently boasts of his conquests is an accurately described egg-gathering expedition:

> And my hand hath found as a nest
>   the riches of the people;
> and as one gathereth eggs that are left,
>   have I gathered all the earth;
> and there was none that moved the wing,
>   or opened the mouth, or peeped.
>   Isaiah 10:14

On his egg-gathering expeditions young Isaiah would have been careful to observe the law forbidding the harming of parent birds. The eggs he describes were forsaken, or perhaps merely left, when the brooding bird was scared away. There is an overtone of rueful sadness in the last two lines, as if Isaiah remembered himself as a small boy trudging back to Jerusalem with his basket full of eggs, but with the realization in his heart that these would never become chirping fledglings and flying birds enjoying their freedom in the sky.

Lively young birds are entertaining to watch, but they are easily thrown into a panic and behave like fugitives from conquered Moab.

> And then at the fords of Arnon
>   the folk of Moab shall flutter
> like birds that scatter
>   from a rifled nest.
>   Isaiah 16:2, Moffatt

It is unsafe, as Proverbs noted, for a young bird to stray far from its nest.

> Like a bird that wanders from her nest,
>   so is a man who wanders far from home.
>   Proverbs 27:8, Moffatt

The rocky gorges and ravines where eagles and vultures reared their young and rock doves nested were the most secure places the Israelites knew. It was said of the nomadic Kenites when they lived in Wadi Arabah south of the Dead Sea: "Strong is thy dwellingplace, and thou puttest thy nest in a rock" (Numbers 24:21). In this region surrounding the impregnable, rock-cut city of Petra, lived the Edomites in their mountain villages. But Jeremiah prophesied against them:

> "Thy terribleness hath deceived thee,
>   and the pride of thine heart,

O thou that dwellest in the clefts of the rock,
    that holdest the height of the hill!
Though thou shouldest make thy nest as high as the eagle,
    I will bring thee down from thence,"
        saith the Lord.

Jeremiah 49:16

The third and fourth verses of Obadiah repeat this prophecy and speak of "thy nest among the stars," higher than Habakkuk's "nest on high" (2:9), and far beyond the realms of ornithology.

A more suitable nesting place is that of the dove "in the clefts of the rock, in the covert of the cliff" (Song of Solomon 2:14 RSV) or "in the sides of the mouth of a gorge" (Jeremiah 48:28, RSV). Tristram saw immense flocks of rock doves breeding in the ravines near Jericho, and in the precipitous cliffs of Wadi Hamam. When thousands of doves appeared "with a rush and a whir that could be felt like a gust of wind," Tristram was amused to see a griffon vulture lose both dignity and equilibrium as the rock doves swept past in a sudden rush of wings and wind. Pigeons indeed "fly as a cloud" as Isaiah 60:8 notes. The end of this verse, which says "as doves to their windows [cotes]" may be the only Old Testament reference to man-made nesting places and the keeping of birds.

Trees sheltered innumerable nests, for Palestine was well-wooded in early Bible times.

The trees of the Lord are full of sap,
    the cedars of Lebanon which he hath planted,
where the birds make their nests.
    As for the stork, the fir trees are her house.

Psalm 104:16-17

The cedar of Lebanon, the tallest and most massive tree the Hebrews knew, captured their imagination. High in these great trees eagles nested securely (Jeremiah 22:23). This cedar is a slow-growing evergreen which provides dense shade with its dark-colored leaves shining silvery in the sun. It lives to a great age and sometimes attains a girth of forty feet, a height of ninety feet, while its branches extend out to form a circle two to three hundred feet in circumference. It is a veritable king of the forest, but unfortunately few cedars of Lebanon survive today. Ezekiel pictured an awe-inspiring cedar of Lebanon so large that it shelters "birds of every feather living under it, in the shadow of its branches" (Ezekiel 17:23, Moffatt). In Ezekiel's prophecy the cedar tree represented Assyria under whose sovereignty or within whose boughs "all birds of the air nested," but when it was cut down and fell "the birds all perched upon its ruined trunk" (Ezekiel 31:6, 13, Moffatt).

Birds filled the tree King Nebuchadnezzar saw in his dream, for upon its "branches the fowls of the heaven had their habitation" (Daniel 4:21). Of this colossal tree, typifying the dominion of his mighty kingdom of Babylonia, Nebuchadnezzar said:

> I saw, and behold a tree
>   in the midst of the earth,
>   and the height thereof was great.
> The tree grew, and was strong
>   and the height thereof reached unto heaven,
>   and the sight thereof to the end of all the earth.
> The leaves thereof were fair,
>   and the fruit thereof much,
>   and in it was meat for all.
> The beasts of the field had shadow under it,
>   and the fowls of the heaven dwelt in the boughs thereof,
>   and all flesh was fed of it.
>
>   Daniel 4:10-12

Nebuchadnezzar dreamed that an angel came down from heaven and cried:

> Hew down the tree, and cut off his branches,
>   shake off his leaves, and scatter his fruit;
> Let the beasts get away from under it,
>   and the fowls from his branches.
>
>   Daniel 4:14

Daniel tells that Nebuchadnezzar became mad soon after he had this dream and "he was driven from men, and did eat grass as oxen, and his body was wet with the dew of heaven, till his hairs were grown like eagles' feathers, and his nails like birds' claws" (Daniel 4:33). But after seven years the king's understanding returned and he praised God "whose dominion is an everlasting dominion and his kingdom is from generation to generation."

The dream birds of Nebuchadnezzar's tree lost their nests when the huge tree was cut down, but real birds had been losing their nesting sites among the giant cedars of Lebanon and in the forests of Palestine even before Bible times. In the era of the early pharaohs, before 2000 B.C., the Merikare texts of the ninth and tenth dynasties describe Palestine as a land that is inaccessible by reason of its dense forests! This description is supported by such remains of prehistoric woodland animals as a wild boar's tooth and deer antlers, which archaeologists have unearthed in the now treeless hill country. As Egypt grows no timber, the pharaohs imported cedars and other great trees from the forested slopes of Palestine and the areas to the north. Denudation began early.

When the people of Israel left the dry and barren wilderness behind to enter the Promised Land, its great forests impressed them and they heard, as it were, "the trees of the wood sing out at the presence of the Lord, because he cometh to judge the earth." But when they settled down and began to plant fields, the tribes of Ephraim and Manasseh found that forests covered their lands and they complained that the territory allotted to them was too small. Joshua replied: "Get thee up to the wood country and cut down for thyself there . . . if Mount Ephraim be too narrow for thee" (Joshua 17:15). So while trees were felled and land was cleared, the "beasts of the forest," the lions, leopards, bears, and wolves, as well as forest-dwelling birds became scarcer.

About 1000 B.C. when Hiram king of Tyre felled cedars which were "the glory of Lebanon," he sold their durable, huge timbers to Solomon both for his palace, called "the house of the forest of Lebanon," and for the Temple. Cedar was the most permanent wood he could use, for its oil not only imparts a wonderful fragrance to the wood, but prevents worms and dry rot. The forests of Lebanon were dwindling.

Warfare hastened the destruction of forests. The Israelites themselves practiced a limited conservation for they had a law forbidding soldiers to destroy trees used for food:

> "When you besiege a city for a long time . . . you shall not destroy its trees by wielding an axe against them; for you may eat of them, but you shall not cut them down. Are the trees in the field men that they should be besieged by you? Only the trees which you know are not trees for food you may destroy and cut down that you may build siege-works against the city. . . ."
>
> Deuteronomy 20:19-20, RSV

This law was not binding upon the Assyrians and in their savage destructiveness they cut down many kinds of trees. Their great king Sennacherib boasted gleefully: "I have . . . reached the ravines of Lebanon; I fell its tallest cedars, and its rare cypresses" (Isaiah 37:24, Moffatt).

Besides war's destruction there was always the danger of forest fires and often the cry must have sounded: "The flame hath burned all the trees of the field!" (Joel 1:19).

As the primeval forests of Palestine disappeared, forest-nesting birds disappeared also. The Israelites carefully terraced their deforested hills and, in order to support a large population, they planted grape vines, fig and olive trees, and garden crops. Different birds came to nest in these new environments. But when civil war broke out or foreign invaders tramped across the fields, these flourishing terraced gardens were neglected or destroyed. Retaining walls fell into disrepair, violent rains washed soil from the hillsides, and the bushes, dwarf shrubs, and grasses which succeeded the garden crops struggled for existence against erosion and the constant gnawing of men's flocks. Finally the hillsides became barren and desolate and the rocky skeleton of the earth poked through the thin soil. The farms and orchards and gardens had perished and the great forests which had preceded them were only a memory.

With extraordinary insight the prophets declared that nature suffered because of the wickedness of men. Isaiah said:

> The earth shall be utterly laid waste
>   and utterly despoiled . . .
> for they have transgressed the laws,
>   violated the statutes,
>   broken the everlasting covenant.
>   Isaiah 24:3, 5, RSV

The results of violence, greed, and wastefulness were clear to the prophets. Hosea said that because there were perjury, murder, stealing, debauchery, and bloodshed in Israel, the land shall mourn and the birds "shall be taken away" (4:3). Where God was not known, truth and mercy disappeared and all the moral sanctions. It was in such a situation that Jeremiah saw a desolate land from which "all the birds of the heavens were fled" (Jeremiah 4:25; 9:10; cf. Zephaniah 1:3) and he asked:

> How long shall the land mourn,
>   and the herbs of every field wither
> for the wickedness of them that dwell therein?
> The beasts are consumed and the birds.
>   Jeremiah 12:4

It seemed to Jeremiah that the Lord's heritage had become "as a speckled bird, the birds round about are against her" (Jeremiah 12:9). These words may refer to a bird of unusual coloring or marking which is attacked by other birds, or to a carrion-eating hyena around whose lair the birds of prey hover.

The Bible contains other pictures of desolation in many of which, instead of an absence of birds, there is a whole assemblage of doleful creatures. When the prophets predicted the overthrow of Babylon they said that "owls shall dwell there" (Isaiah 13:21; Jeremiah 50:39) and we can almost hear an owl, often called the "mother of ruins," crying its mournful *"hoo-hoo-hoo"* through the night. From neglected swamps would sound the harsh *"aark, aark"* or the deep *"woomp"* of bitterns, for the once proud city of Babylon had become "a possession for the bittern" (Isaiah 14:23).

When Edom was destroyed the prophet envisaged a whole convention of mourners howling and wailing in its ruins and haunting its waste lands:

> But the cormorant and the bittern shall possess it,
> the owl also and the raven shall dwell in it. . . .
> And thorns shall come up in her palaces,
> nettles and brambles in the fortresses thereof,
> and it shall be an habitation of dragons
> and a court for owls. . . .
> The screech owl also shall rest there,
> and find for herself a place of rest.
> There shall the great owl make her nest and lay,
> and hatch and gather under her shadow.
> There shall the vultures also be gathered,
> every one with her mate.
>
> Isaiah 34:11, 13-15

The identification of the birds assembled in desolate Edom is no easy task and instead of some of those given in the Authorized Version above we find: hawks, ostriches, night hags, and kites, in the Revised Standard Version; a pelican, in Moffatt; an ibis, in the Douay Version; and a jackdaw, in the American Translation.

The author of Revelation was certainly impressed, as we are, with the vividness of these descriptions of ruined cities, for when he prophesied the downfall of Rome, he too mentioned birds and described the imperial city as "a cage of every unclean and hateful bird" (Revelation 18:2).

The pelican and the owl appear again in the wail of the Psalmist:

> I am like a pelican of the wilderness,
> I am like an owl of the desert.
> I watch and am as a sparrow alone upon the house top.
>
> Psalm 102:6-7

The pelican is a magnificent bird in flight, with its huge white wings and long, yellowish bill. When it sits motionless at the edge of a swamp, its head against its breast, digesting the fishes it scooped up in its pouch, it becomes the very image of brooding sorrow. This doleful sight is followed by the melancholy sound of an owl, described by Moffatt as "moping in the ruins" and uttering its long, tremulous "*oo-oo-oo-oo-OO*."

Mournful behavior comes next when the Psalmist mentions "a sparrow alone upon the house top." It would have occasioned no surprise to see a bird on a Palestinian housetop pecking at seeds in the hard-packed earth of which the roof was made. But a lonely sparrow is an anomaly, for where there is one sparrow there are generally more. As the Psalmist's solitary housetop bird is a *tsippor*, we do not necessarily have to translate it "sparrow," but are free to interpret it as some other small bird with shy, unsociable habits. The blue rock thrush, *Monticola solitarius*, has been proposed for this passage. This bird is the size of a robin and is found in Palestine from September to April. The plumage of the male is a dull blue-gray, while that of the female is brown with a faint blue wash. The blue rock thrush haunts lonely cliffs, ravines, and rocky hillsides, sometimes coming into towns and perching on ledges from which the male sings his plaintive, loud, monotonous "*tseec*." Captain Eric Hardy saw blue rock thrushes among the Dead Sea cliffs, on the citadel, and the walls of Jerusalem where the Psalmist may have seen them many centuries ago.

Among all the nesting places and bird habitats described in the Bible the most appealing and certainly the most attractive to us are those in the great nature psalm:

> He sendeth the springs into the valleys
> which run among the hills. . . .
> By them shall the fowls of the heaven have their habitation,
> which sing among the branches.
>
> Psalm 104:10, 12

CHAPTER 15

The Singing of Birds

THE sounds of Bible days have been silenced in the great deeps of history. The music of David's harp, the resonant tones of the prophets, the melody of Temple songs, the harsh shouts of ancient battles—all these no longer echo in any ear, but the bird songs of those far-off days still enliven the Holy Land today. The songs themselves are immeasurably old, some of them possibly having been sung long before there was any human ear to hear them and delight in their sweetness. Adam may have heard these melodies in Eden and they echoed throughout the long history of Israel.

In well-watered valleys guarded by the hills, wherever trees line the banks of rushing streams, birds flit from branch to branch singing their haunting music. Commenting on the lovely description in Psalm 104: 10-12 Tristram said:

In this passage, as the Psalmist is speaking of the trees which overhang the water courses . . . the singing of the different species of warblers (*Turdidae*) is perhaps pointed to, and especially the Bulbul and Nightingale, both of which throng the trees that fringe the Jordan, and abound in all the wooded valleys, filling the air in early spring with the rich cadence of their notes.

Izaac Walton declared that the nightingale "breathes such sweet loud music out of her little instrumental throat, that it might make mankind to think Miracles are not ceased."

Places like these and perhaps the very same bird songs are described in Shakespeare's lines:

> . . . shallow rivers, to whose falls
> Melodious birds sing madrigals.

On the northern limits of Palestine, Henry van Dyke heard "the chant of innumerable birds filling the vault of foliage above our heads." Where semitropical shrubs and trees overhang the stream flowing in the Ravine of Kedron, the Palestine bulbul, the finest songster of the country, sings its rich, flutelike song. This is a bird of gardens, palm groves, and verdant wadis and Tristram called it "the true nightingale of the East."

Many of the bird songs of Palestine are old-world melodies celebrated in the verses of Chaucer, Shakespeare, Wordsworth, Shelley, Keats, and scores of other English poets. A nineteenth-century English traveler wrote from northern Palestine: "The pretty crested larks, 'that *tira lira* chant,' rose into the merry blue sky twittering their song to the sunrise." Surely he remembered Shakespeare's line: "Hark, hark! the lark at heaven's gate sings." Skylarks, nightingales, greenfinches, great tits, chaffinches, goldfinches, and chiffchaffs fill the tree-fringed Jordan and the wooded valley with their songs. They are as worthy as their English relatives of Izaac Walton's exclamation: "Lord, what music hast Thou provided for Thy saints in heaven, when Thou affordest bad men such music on earth!"

When the winter rains with all their cold discomforts ended, the people of Palestine welcomed spring with its flowers and bird songs. Among the harmonies pouring from the throats of myriads of birds one particular melody is noted in the Song of Solomon:

> For lo, the winter is past,
>   the rain is over and gone.
> The flowers appear on the earth,
>   the time of the singing of birds is come,
> And the voice of the turtle [dove]
>   is heard in our land.
>   Song of Solomon 2:11-12

The reason for the turtledove's pre-eminence in this poem is indicated in Tristram's account of their arrival in April. He reported that "while other songsters are heard chiefly in the morning . . . the Turtle immediately on its arrival pours forth from every garden, grove, and wooded hill its melancholy yet soothing ditty, unceasingly from early dawn till sunset." By sheer repetition the turtledove attracts attention to its song. Softer and sleepier than the song of other pigeons, it is described as a purring *"roor-r-r."*

Strangely enough the lines from Psalm 104 and the description of spring in the Song of Solomon are the only references to bird song in the canonical books of the Old Testament, though the apocryphal book of the Wisdom of Solomon contains the line: "a melodious sound of birds in wide-spreading branches" (17:18, RSV).

The first note of the dawn chorus is mentioned in Ecclesiastes, not for its loveliness, but to indicate how early a light sleeper awakes: "he shall rise up at the voice of the bird" (12:4). These words occur in a haunting passage on old age beginning: "Remember now thy Creator in the days of thy youth, while the evil days come not, nor the years draw nigh when thou shalt say, 'I have no pleasure in them.' " But the preacher who speaks so sadly has no ear for the joyful harmonies of morning. To him the day which began with bird song is an evil one in which "all the daughters of music shall be brought low." He has no heart for the sounds of Chaucer's spring when

> . . . smale foweles maken melodye,
> That slepen al the nyght with open eye.

The scarcity of bird song in the Bible is hard to explain. Far from the haunts of singing birds, the Hebrews lived in close-packed towns or villages protected by stone walls. Parks, tree-shaded avenues, and suburban gardens were virtually unknown to them. They did, however, work in fields, orchards, and vineyards and travel along the rough highways. Possibly the songs of spring are not so rich and varied in Palestine as in some other lands. Captain Hardy noted there "the absence of much bird song, particularly thrush song."

To other types of song the Hebrews were neither deaf nor indifferent and many references to song, singers, and singing can be found in Bible concordances. Levites, daughters of Zion, sons of Asaph, singing men and singing women, all these were mentioned. The Hebrews heard the singing of woods and hills, of trees and mountains and the heavens. Their own hearts sang and they themselves were ever raising their voices in the melodies of praise.

If they paid little attention to bird songs, they were very much aware of the ominous or melancholy calls and sounds birds make. When Micah realized that catastrophe was about to overtake Judah he lamented:

> I will make a wailing like the dragons,
> and mourning as the owls.
> Micah 1:8

The puzzling Hebrew word, *bath yaanah,* here translated "owls," may possibly be ostriches. However, as ostriches are said to boom or roar like a lion, the "mourning" or "wailing" mentioned by Micah is more appropriate to the eagle owl with its deep *"boo-hoo, boo-hooo"* sounding like the voice of doom. The bird, whether eagle owl or ostrich, is a companion to the afflicted (Job 30:29), holds court in the waste lands of Edom (Isaiah 34:13), and with the jackals honors the Lord who gives "waters in the wilderness" (Isaiah 43:20). When the *bath yaanah* appears among the ruins of Babylon (Isaiah 13:21; Jeremiah 50:39), it cannot be an ostrich for these birds do not haunt ruined or deserted cities. In these two passages the *bath yaanah* is probably an owl like those Lady Anne Blunt heard crying in a ruined town in the Euphrates Valley.

After the Assyrian army raised the siege of Jerusalem and departed, King Hezekiah was no longer shut up like a caged bird, but he fell grievously ill, "sick unto death," and turned his face to the wall and moaned and wept. When he recovered he composed a thanksgiving psalm in which he compared himself to three birds. "I did mourn as a dove" (Isaiah 38:14) is clear enough, but what does the king mean by: "Like a crane or a swallow, so did I chatter"? Cranes, because of their unusually long windpipes, make a very loud, resonant trumpeting that is not like the voice of swallows. It has, therefore, been suggested that the *agur* of this passage is not a crane but a thrush or wryneck. The latter is a gray-brown bird slightly larger than an English sparrow. It migrates through Palestine, flying in flocks of twenty or more, but some pairs remain there to breed. It runs on trees like a mouse and is related to the woodpeckers. The wryneck is a retiring bird, haunting old orchards and more often heard than seen, for when it is alarmed it remains motionless. Its sharp, penetrating, nasal, whistling cry, *"kew, kew, kew,"* may reproduce the sound of Hezekiah's complainings.

Hezekiah's *sus,* though usually translated "swallow," is probably more accurately translated "swift," as in the University of Chicago Version. The swallow's note is a pleasantly soft twittering and warbling, but the common swift has a shrill, prolonged, piercing, high-pitched scream like a human cry of pain. Furthermore, in Jeremiah 8:7, the *sus* is described as migratory. In Palestine many swallows remain throughout the year, but the swifts are all migrants. The common swift of Palestine is somewhat like the chimney swift. In March 1945 Captain Eric Hardy heard several common swifts on their northward migration screaming their piercing signals to one another as they flew over Jerusalem. Could Hezekiah have heard these shrill cries from the invisible flyway as he lay on his bed in that same city centuries ago?

Hezekiah's great-great-grandson, the seventh-century prophet Zephaniah, predicted the downfall of mighty Assyria and the destruction of Nineveh. Her ruins would be haunted by the birds of desolate places, he said, and their lugubrious voices would intensify the sense of doom:

> The vulture and the hedgehog
> shall lodge in her capitals;
> the owl shall hoot in the window,
> the raven croak on the threshold;
> for her cedar work will be laid bare.
>
> Zephaniah 2:14, RSV

Doves crooning their deep *"oo-roo-coo'* seem to be mourning some sorrow. Tennyson suggested the plaintiveness of their cry in "the moan of doves in immemorial elms," and centuries earlier the Hebrew prophets heard the same lamentations. Before the destruction of Nineveh in 612 B.C. Nahum pictured Huzzab, who was possibly the captive Assyrian queen, "carried off, her ladies mourning like doves" (Nahum 2:7, Moffatt). Several years before the destruction of Jerusalem by the Chaldeans in 587 B.C., Ezekiel wrote of those fortunate enough to survive that holocaust:

> But they that escape . . . shall be on the mountains like doves of the valleys, all of them mourning, every one for his iniquity.
>
> Ezekiel 7:16

After the return from exile in Babylonia, one of the unnamed prophets whose writings were included in the Book of Isaiah, made a confession of the national sin and said:

> We roar all like bears, and mourn sore like doves;
> we look for judgment, but there is none,
> for salvation, but it is far off from us.
>
> Isaiah 59:11

Tristram described the sounds made in Jerusalem by the raven tribe, sounds that must have been familiar in Bible times. Ravens

are present everywhere to eye and ear. . . . The discordant jabber of their evening sittings round the temple area is deafening. The caw of the Rook and the chatter of the Jackdaw unite in attempting to drown the hoarse croak of the old Raven, but clear above the tumult rings out the more musical call-notes of hundreds of the lesser species. We used to watch this great colony as, every morning at day-break, they passed in long lines over our tents to the northward: the rooks in solid phalanx leading the way and the ravens in loose order bringing up the rear, far out of shot. Before retiring for the night, popular assemblies of the most uproarious character were held in the trees of Mount Olivet and the Kedron, and not till after sunset did they withdraw in silence, mingled indiscriminately, to their roosting-places in the sanctuary.

Familiar as the people of Israel were with the "discordant jabber" of the raven family and with the mournful cooing issuing from their dovecotes, they surely preferred happier music. Did they, as is common in the East today, keep tame songbirds in cages for the pleasure of listening to these tiny musicians? One Bible reference indicates that this may have been so:

> Will you play with him like a pet bird,
> or cage him to amuse your maidens?
> Job 41:5, Moffatt

Sennacherib's boast that when he besieged Jerusalem he kept King Hezekiah shut up inside the city "like a caged bird," indicates that as long ago as the eighth century B.C. birds were kept as pets. It was a common thing for Greek houses to have cages hung outside and many Greek vases of the fifth and fourth centuries B.C. depict tall wicker bird cages for sparrows, nightingales, blackbirds, starlings, and other singing or so-called "talking" birds. The most famous pet bird of antiquity was Lesbia's *passer* which Catullus described as a small, tame, loving creature who chirped to its mistress. It may have been a bullfinch, perhaps the trumpeter bullfinch of North Africa and Sinai which has a beautiful, distinctive, piping note. The Romans delighted in the brilliance of the nightingale's song and Pliny reports that Nero's mother, the Empress Agrippina, was presented with a rare white nightingale that cost the purchaser the equivalent of one hundred dollars. The empress was evidently a bird lover for she also kept a thrush that could "talk."

In Bible times many Hebrew homes may have been enlivened by music from songbirds kept in cages outside the door. Then, as today in this region, the bird most frequently seen may have been the brightly-colored goldfinch which is caught on the hills around Jerusalem where it feeds on the abundant thistles. Handsome black bulbuls with their striking white "spectacles" were also familiar pet birds for they were easy to tame and were outstanding singers. The Talmud contains an allegory of two song birds—one is free, the other caged. The free bird comes to the handsome cage and envies the comfortable life and rich food of its friend, never realizing that the caged bird has paid for all this with its freedom.

Lovely as the songs issuing from cages were, surely the Hebrews, who longed for freedom so much for themselves, found keener enjoyment in the songs of free birds: crested larks singing their clear, crisp song as they rise into the sky to greet the sunrise; desert larks whistling their melancholy song as they dive to their perches; Isabelline wheatears cheerfully calling to each other in the air, *"wheet whit, wheet whit"*; or Tristram's grackles making the cliffs ring with their richly musical roll of powerful notes.

In post-biblical days the Jews believed there was singing in heaven from a great cage in which dwelt a vast assemblage of birds. These were the souls of men waiting for God to call them and place them in human bodies. One of the rabbis taught that the Messiah would not appear until every soul had been taken from the heavenly cage to live on earth. When someone died it used to be the custom to open a window so that the soul might fly away as a bird and return to its former home in heaven. There the souls of the righteous, wearing their crowns, were believed to gather on the walls of paradise to sing the praises of God.

CHAPTER 16 ﹏

Their Appointed Seasons

Birds coming and going at their appointed seasons are part of the great pulse of nature beating steadily through the centuries. These heartbeats of nature, these annual migratory journeys, are very conspicuous in Palestine, situated as it is on one of the chief flyways of the world. One spring day while Tristram stood on the bank of a tributary to the Jordan near the northern limits of the Holy Land, he saw around him and overhead the procession of birds that perpetually sweeps northward at this time of year.

The thickets abounded in francolin, while the valley itself seems to be the highway of all the migratory birds returning from their African winter quarters to western Asia and Russia. Bands of storks, masses of starlings, clouds of swallows, long lines of swifts and bee-eaters may be seen hour after hour ceaselessly passing northwards overhead, while the surface of the plain is alive with countless myriads of familiar songsters in loose, scattered order, hopping, feeding, taking short flights, but all pursuing their northward course.

Today migration is a well-known phenomenon, but long ago men did not understand why flocks of birds suddenly appeared and then disappeared. They asked one another why yesterday the hillsides were covered with birds, but today hardly one can be seen. They noted that the same thing happened last year at this season and every year as far back as the oldest person could remember. Why do the birds come? Where do they go? And who taught the birds their timetables of the seasons? Who guides them along the flyways of the world? In attempting to answer such questions men formulated the earliest theories about migration.

The oldest reference to migration in the Bible, and probably in world literature as well, appears in the prophecies of the great seventh-century prophet Jeremiah. This observant, sensitive man from the country village of Anathoth knew many things about birds and mentioned them more frequently in his prophecies than any other Hebrew prophet. In this very fact certain aspects of Jeremiah's personality emerge. Jeremiah might have discovered even more than he did about birds if he had remained in his native village, but when the Lord called him to perform a heartbreaking mission, he left all the fascination, beauty, and tranquillity of the countryside to enter the arena of human passions and politics in the city of Jerusalem. In the years prior to the final destruction of Jerusalem by the Chaldeans, Jeremiah spoke for the Lord in that great city and became His voice, exhorting the people "to root out and to pull down and to destroy" all the evil in the kingdom of Judah and "to build and to plant" all that God ordains.

Only Jeremiah's sermon remains from a certain day long ago, but we can well imagine the scene. Jerusalem is astir and throngs of curious people are gathering in the outer court of the Temple where Jeremiah will deliver an urgent message from the Lord. Already the watchful priests have arrived and are looking about warily. The princes are there, too, and some of King Jehoiakim's counselors. There are crowds of ordinary men and women hoping for something exciting to enliven the drabness of their days. The atmosphere is tense, expectant, and hostile, for everyone recalls Jeremiah's last address in this place. Jeremiah himself arrives and the crowd makes way for him to pass. He looks in vain for a friendly face or a smile of encouragement. Even the fragments of conversation he overhears are charged with enmity.

"Imagine calling our sacred Temple a den of robbers!"

"He isn't even original and I'm bored with the same old line—'obey my voice and I will be your God and you shall be my people.' He just repeats what Moses and the prophets said long ago!"

"Did you hear him threaten that we're to be meat for the fowls of heaven?"

"Ha! Ha! Then I'll see to it that he becomes the first morsel!"

"He will not dare speak so harshly after what happened last time."

When he overhears this statement Jeremiah winces. Will he have enough boldness to speak for the Lord today as he spoke that last time? Then he accused the people of falsehood, theft, murder, adultery, idolatry, and false worship and the priests wrathfully demanded his death. Now as he reaches the Temple gateway Jeremiah turns to face the people. For a moment he stands there silently, waiting for his heart to stop its pounding and for the Lord to give him courage to deliver his message. He knows that his words will fall on this expectant multitude "like a hammer that breaketh the rock in pieces." Only in the Lord's strength will he be able to speak.

Suddenly above the open court Jeremiah sees a flight of storks traversing the sky on huge, outstretched wings. Their white bodies, black flight feathers, red bills, and long red legs stretched out behind are clearly visible from below and the birds make a striking pattern against the blue sky. Jeremiah and the people massed in the Temple square see these great white birds from the mysterious unknown, bound for unimaginable regions of the north, as creatures of vast horizons.

"Storks overhead!" they cry. "They are back again."

They always come when spring returns and the sight of them gives a lift to all hearts. Jeremiah notes that the flock is heading northeast in the direction of Anathoth where many a spring he has watched storks spreading out over the fields, systematically clearing the land of grasshoppers, lizards, frogs, and snakes. For a moment he longs to be in his peaceful country home, far from these unfriendly faces, but the Lord's words are like a fire burning in his bones. As the storks fly out of sight he commences to speak, beginning with the old prophetic announcement: "Thus saith the Lord!" He continues:

> Why then is this people of Jerusalem slidden back
>   by a perpetual backsliding?
> They hold fast deceit,
>   they refuse to return. . . .
> No man repented him of his wickedness,
>   saying, "What have I done?"
>
> Jeremiah 8:5-6

The crowd mutters angrily, well knowing that the charges against them of backsliding, wickedness, and disobedience are true, but they are exasperated to hear this village firebrand say it so plainly and ignore the fact that they are God's own people to whom He gave His Law as their proud possession. Jeremiah is trying to convince them that having the Law is not enough—they must obey it. He must show them, vividly enough to catch their attention, that they are forever breaking the Law. Even the birds which reappear each spring to keep their appointment with the Lord obey His ordinances more faithfully than the Lord's own people. Perhaps the crowd will listen if he mentions birds. Jeremiah speaks slowly and distinctly at first, but his voice rises almost to a shout at the climax:

> Yea, the stork in the heaven
> knoweth her appointed times;
> and the turtle [dove] and the crane and the swallow
> observe the time of their coming;
> but my people know not
> the judgment of the Lord.
>
> Jeremiah 8:7

Are not men better than birds? Yet in their seasonal comings and goings birds seem wiser than men! Jeremiah pours scorn on men:

> How do ye say, "We are wise,
> and the law of the Lord is with us"? . . .
> The wise men are ashamed. . . .
> Lo, they have rejected the word of the Lord,
> and what wisdom is in them?
>
> Jeremiah 8:8-9

The Bible records that these words fell on deaf ears and that Jeremiah was rejected by king and people, but they could not silence him. Even when everything seemed hopeless, with the Covenant broken and the nation apparently abandoned by God, Jeremiah spoke, in words that have echoed through the centuries, of a New Covenant which God would write in each person's heart.

Jeremiah's life was often in danger during the years before Jerusalem fell to the Chaldeans in 587 B.C. A group of survivors from the ruined city carried him off with them to Egypt, where, much against his will, he spent his last years. Perhaps he derived some comfort for his broken heart in the quiet pleasure of watching the birds of Egypt and seeing once more the huge flocks of strong-winged storks fly overhead.

Even if they could not explain it, the people of Jeremiah's day recognized the phenomenon of migration. Did their ancestors journeying out of Egypt some six hundred years earlier realize that the birds that fell into their wilderness camp were part of a migratory wave of quails? After the people of Israel settled in Palestine, did they understand the meaning of the long lines or groups of birds flying north each spring and south each fall? They noticed, as the Song of Solomon indicates, the sudden reappearance of the migratory turtledove and heard its softly repeated spring song. Slowly the facts fitted themselves together and the idea of migration as expressed by Jeremiah finally emerged.

The Bible contains other references to the mysterious currents of winged life that flow through Palestine. The verse in the Book of Hosea mentioning this phenomenon (11:11) is believed to date from the sixth century B.C. or later, long after Hosea's time and Jeremiah's as well, for it describes Israel's return from Babylonian captivity.

The Book of Job, believed to have been written after Jeremiah prophesied, lists migration among the marvels of the world. In 39:26 Job uses the annual journeys of birds to show men the foolishness of imagining themselves equal to God.

Isaiah seems to describe great migrations of African birds in his "Woe to the land shadowing with wings, which is beyond the rivers of Ethiopia" (Isaiah 18:1), but as "shadowing" is more correctly translated "buzzing" or "whirring," this verse must picture, not birds, but swarms of insects that infest the Nile Valley.

The chief birds mentioned in the Bible in connection with migration are the hawk of Job 39:26 and the storks, turtledoves, and cranes of Jeremiah's prophecy. All but the turtledoves are conspicuous daytime migrants, while the turtledoves, though they arrive during the night, are ubiquitous and noisy enough to attract everyone's attention. The least observant person could hardly fail to note white storks overhead. "Grotesque, ungainly, gothic birds," Henry van Dyke described them when he saw them patterned against the morning sky of the Holy Land.

In the following passage from *A Naturalist in Palestine* Victor Howells vividly portrays a white stork migration he observed a few years ago near Gaza:

Over the sea, coming from the direction of Egypt, came a quickly moving grey cloud alone in the clear blue sky. As it came nearer, we could see that it was something other than a cloud. It was a huge flight of birds; storks in their thousands, little ones, parents and old folk. Some flying fresh and sprightly as if they had not come far, no doubt from Egypt. Others flew slowly and laboriously, seemingly very tired, having come, perhaps, from Southern Rhodesia on their northward flight. Some of them had joined the main body of birds as they flew through Africa and all of them, young and old, felt the compelling urge to get on the move and travel to another location for the next season of their lives.

The flight had continued without a break, with more and more birds joining the few who had begun the journey, until eventually there were thousands. From the time they began to migrate until they had reached these shores the storks had been flying for over three months. The journey for some of them, in fact, was not yet over as they would go on across to Turkey. Still others went on to Germany and even to Russia. . . .

The scouts and leaders of these white storks flew over the coastline, some flying so low that their wings almost touched the tops of the highest palms, while others flew high to spy out the land ahead of the main flock. Then the main body of the birds was overhead and all around me. The air was filled with the noise of their big wings and the breeze caused by the passage of their big bodies in the air swept the dust from the trees. The sky was obscured while they passed over, with slowly flapping wings, dangling legs and sharply pointed beaks.

The main body of the flight was a mile or more wide and several miles long, a sight never to be forgotten. Already some of the birds were beginning to glide down in the fields, but most of them flew on to their special feeding ground, the fields around the town of Gaza. There, each year, the storks usually remain for a period of several months. A large number would remain in the fields and make their nest and produce their brood. In the Gaza fields the storks would be able to find ample supplies of snakes, lizards, fish and insects to eat.

The passage of *Ciconia ciconia,* or white storks, was the beginning of the bird migration over and into Palestine. This country can be truly termed the crossroads of bird migrations. There is at this time of the year, the month of April, a constant passage of a great number of various species from most of the countries of the world. Nearly every month throughout the year sees some bird on its passage to the south or to the north, December and January being the only months in which there is very little activity of this kind. The Wadi and the dunes then begin to be filled with birds and their varied songs are heard in the hot air.

The story of another stork migration in this region is narrated by Colonel Meinertzhagen in *Birds of Arabia.* In September 1917 during World War I, he was stationed on the Mediterranean coast south of Gaza at a British camp which enemy planes had been harassing. Soldiers with whistles were posted around the camp to warn of approaching planes. One day at noon all the whistles shrilled at once as thousands of white specks appeared in the sky. Everyone rushed to repel what threatened to be a large-scale attack and antiaircraft guns were fired to keep off the raiders. For ten minutes the air was filled with puffs of bursting shells, but the enemy "planes" kept steadily on their course, coming nearer and nearer. Finally one of them was hit and tumbled to earth, a mass of white feathers. At this the guns were quickly silenced and the great flock of storks flew on.

So dependable are the migration schedules of many birds that primitive people often gave bird names to the months. In the days of Hesiod, the Greeks timed certain farming operations by their arrivals. April in Palestine might well have been called stork or turtledove month. The barley harvest was usually under way when the turtledoves appeared in veritable clouds and settled down to feed on clover and leguminous plants. Tristram said that "they stock every tree and thicket. At every step they flutter up from the herbage in front—they perch on every tree and bush—they overspread the whole face of the land." And they sing from dawn to dark.

Jeremiah's *agur,* usually translated "crane," is also very conspicuous on migration. The crane, with its wingspread of eight feet, is the largest bird using the flyway over Palestine. Flocks of as many as two thousand of these huge, slate-gray birds have been sighted at a time, passing over-head in V-shaped or line formation, each bird flying with its long neck outstretched. Cranes are noisy on passage and sometimes their metallic trumpeting is heard before the birds come into view. Toward evening they coast down for a landing in such numbers that they often darken the sky. Tristram, commenting on a flock that settled down near his camp, said that "their whooping and trumpeting enlivened the watches of the night." From the Wilderness of Sinai observers have seen cranes crossing the Red Sea from Africa in such great numbers that their line appeared to stretch across the whole breadth of the sea. Such massed armies as these could not go unnoticed and may have given the son of Sirach the idea for his saying: "Birds flock with their kind" (Ecclesi-asticus 27:9, RSV).

As a conspicuous migrant clearly obeying the ordinances of God, the crane is suitable in Jeremiah's context, but some translators prefer to render *agur* as "wryneck." Though shy, inconspicuous, and only slightly larger than an English sparrow, the wryneck is a migratory bird that announces its spring arrival with a distinctive laugh or whistling call *"pleid, pleid, ha, ha, ha."* This monotonous cry is the chief reason, as we have already noted, for translating *agur* as "wry-neck" in Isaiah 38:14. Gilbert White in *The Natural History of Sel-borne* remarked that in England the wryneck was the first bird to arrive in spring. As a harbinger of spring the wryneck would have been a likely bird for Jeremiah's list.

The identification of Jeremiah's *sus* or *sis* as a swallow puzzled Tristram when he noticed that in Palestine many swallows remain through the winter. Jeremiah indicates that the *sus* is migratory for he says these birds "observe the time of their coming." Swallows utter a soft note while, as we have already learned, Hezekiah's *sus* (Isaiah 38:14) made a sound like the cry of pain. The mystery of the biblical *sus* was solved for Canon Tristram one April day a hundred years ago when he was encamped under Mount Carmel. Suddenly vast numbers of migrating swifts appeared and passed northward in long streams. Many remained behind to swarm about the towns and countryside and dart with arrowlike speed up and down the streets and fields in pursuit of gnats. Wondering if these dramatically migratory birds with their shrill, piercing cry might not be the biblical *sus,* he shot several and spread them out in front of his tent. "I asked the Arab boys, who crowded around, what the birds were, and they called them *Sis.*" When he pointed to swallows and inquired their name, the Arab boys called them *Sununu.* In the Arabic *sis,* Tristram concluded, "we have the local name handed down unchanged from the Hebrew. . . . The most unobservant Arab must notice the sudden return of the Swift, while its note admirably expresses the cry of pain." Jeremiah's *sus* is now translated "swift" in at least two modern versions of the Bible: Moffatt's and that of the University of Chicago Press.

It is not only in Bible translations that swifts are confused with swallows. Swifts resemble swallows in general appearance and behavior, for both have forked tails, eat insects on the wing, and nest in chimneys or under eaves. To add to the confusion, many people call the American chimney swift a chimney swallow. But swifts and swallows are structurally very different. Swifts with their four forward-pointing toes cannot perch, while swallows perching on telephone wires and television antennae are a familiar sight of late summer. The swallow's flight is swooping and graceful. Swifts are the speed champion among all the small birds of the world, for they fly with extreme rapidity on scythe-shaped wings. As we have already noted, the swallow has a soft voice and utters a cheery, twittering song, sometimes rendered *"feetafeet, feetafeelit,"* while the voice of the swift is a piercing screech.

Swifts are the most aerial of birds and they seem to hurtle through the air for the sheer joy of flying. Their long, thin wings are designed for speed and in flight they embody the perfection of motion through air. As they dash wildly forward, alternately gliding on outspread, motionless wings and then rapidly beating their wings, they scream as if in ecstasy. They have been known to feed one hundred miles from their nearest breeding place, thus flying at least two hundred miles a day merely for food. Their speed is prodigious. A pilot cruising in his plane at sixty-eight miles an hour observed swifts flying in easy circles around him and going at an estimated one hundred miles per hour. The English poet Lord de Tabley described their headlong flight:

> Like a rushing comet sable
> Swings the wide-winged screaming swift.

Swifts spend most of their life in the air. Besides eating flying insects on the wing, they drink by skimming over the surface of the water, mate in mid-air, and even collect nesting materials from the air. Unless they are injured, they never set foot on the ground, for their short legs are useless for walking, and their take-off from a flat surface is very slow. At night they rest by clinging to a crack or crevice in some wall.

Their nests are constructed of straw, feathers, leaves, or other wind-blown flotsam which they carefully glue together with their viscous, quickly hardening saliva. The nests of certain cave-dwelling swifts of Asia are made entirely of hardened saliva which is the chief ingredient of the famous "birds' nest soup."

Various species of swifts have been reported in Palestine. Tristram found white-bellied or Alpine swifts in the wildest and most inaccessible ravines of the Jordan Valley and the gorges of Moab. Captain Hardy found the nest of a common swift in Jerusalem, and reported large summer nesting populations at Haifa and Tel Aviv. Colonel Meinertzhagen wrote of large breeding colonies of the Asiatic swift at Jerusalem, Hebron, and Nazareth.

The behavior of these amazing birds was noted by William M. Thomson when he visited the pool of Solomon near Bethlehem. The birds he describes in the following passage from *The Land and the Book* are probably Alpine swifts, larger and faster than the common swift, and with white underparts:

The atmosphere was suddenly darkened by an immense flock . . . of swifts, that came up like a cloud of locusts. Many thousands gathered above the upper pool, which was nearly full of water. . . . Their flight was so swift that they cut the air with a peculiar noise, like the whizzing of a ball, especially when from on high they darted down upon the surface of the water, which they did with a shrill scream, as though frightened or exultant at their own daring exploit. . . . As the day advanced and the heat increased, they all disappeared, resorting to the cliffs, as I was informed, in the surrounding valleys, where they build their nests.

To Jeremiah's migratory birds—the stork, turtledove, crane, swift, and perhaps wryneck and swallow—must be added the hawk which, during the fall migration, Job saw "stretch her wings toward the south" (Job 39:26). This hawk undoubtedly rode the thermals as do its North American counterparts that pass over Hawk Mountain Sanctuary in Pennsylvania. *Nets,* the Hebrew name for this bird, is believed to be derived from its flashing speed and may denote a kestrel, the commonest of the smaller hawks. Today kestrels by the hundreds fly with rapid wingbeats or hover high in the sky over Palestine. They abound in the desolate regions near the Dead Sea and nest, in company with eagles and griffon vultures, in many rocky gorges, and in Jerusalem near the site of the ancient Temple.

Job's verse mentions the hawk's migratory flight toward the south in the autumn. In Ronald Knox's translation of this verse a marvelous aspect of migration is mentioned: "Is it of thy devising the hawk grows full fledged, in time to spread her wings for the southward journey?" How carefully the life schedules of birds are devised!

The complexity and stir and tremendous vitality of bird life and travel in and through the Holy Land is described by Dr. W. K. Bigger in *Handbook of Palestine*. He says that in December and January the great migration routes through the country are virtually deserted, but in February the impressive migratory pageant begins with the arrival of Alpine swifts. They are followed in ten days by the common swifts. Egyptian vultures appear about the end of the month, and early in March come the hoopoes, cuckoos, redstarts, and warblers. During the final weeks of March and throughout April the day and night skies are alive with traveling birds as the spring migration reaches its peak. Summer visitors arrive, migrants pass through the country, and winter visitors depart for more northern nesting grounds. By May the summer visitors have settled down in Palestine and the rear guard of the northward-bound migrants—the nightingales, golden orioles, rose-colored starlings, and many waders—sweep through the country. For about a month the tide of migration pauses, only to resume its flow in the southward direction about June 20 when common swifts reappear in successive waves from northern breeding grounds. By July the waders invade the beaches and from then until the second week of November the spring procession repeats itself in reverse: summer visitors leave, winter visitors pour in, while a constant stream of migrants use the flyway over this centrally located country.

From early times men tried to discover why birds make long journeys. How do they travel? What is their goal? How do they set their course for distant places? It was noticed that birds generally fly south for the winter and north in the spring. Their chief reasons for traveling seemed to be to reach places with favorable conditions for breeding in the summer and those offering abundant food in the winter.

How birds, especially small ones, travel long distances and cross wide bodies of water, puzzled men until someone proposed an ingenious theory: small birds ride on the backs of larger birds. There were some people who went so far as to say they had seen little birds waiting on the Mediterranean shore for their great winged ferries! Today we know that a three-and-a-half-inch ruby-throated hummingbird can fly five hundred miles nonstop across the Gulf of Mexico and we no longer underestimate the flying endurance of even the smallest birds.

When people asked where the birds go in the fall, Aristotle suggested that some really do not go anywhere, but lie hidden and dormant, hibernating during the winter. Other birds like the European robin, he said, change their plumage and become redstarts in winter. Pliny was certain that swallows turned into frogs. The theory of hibernation has been discarded and the idea of the transmutation of species is untenable, though many birds do change their plumage with the seasons, as any bird watcher knows.

As late as 1703 a "Person of Learning and Piety" wrote a pamphlet entitled "An Essay Toward the Probable Solutions of this Question: Whence come the Stork and the Turtle, the Crane, and the Swallow, when they Know and Observe the Appointed Time of their Coming." The theory proposed was simple—migrating birds fly directly to the moon and spend the winter there, but "if the Moon will not be allowed, some other place must be found for them."

Until birds acquire space suits, travelers to the moon will not be able to while away their hours in bird watching, for at extreme altitudes where oxygen is reduced birds lose much of their buoyancy and, like men, they have difficulty breathing. In several hundred hours of daylight flying during World War II the ornithologist Eric Simms encountered only a few starlings and lapwings migrating above 2000 feet and he concluded that most migration takes place below 3000 feet. When there are high barriers on their flyways, however, the birds, especially large-winged ones who are least affected by loss of buoyancy in rarefied airs, surmount them. There is one report of a flock of geese whose flight over the Himalayas chanced to be recorded on a photographic plate aimed at an eclipse of the sun. Colonel Meinertzhagen states that the photograph "clearly shows a skein of seventeen geese crossing the face of the sun and flying south. . . . It has been worked out that these geese must have been eleven miles above sea level when the photograph was taken."

Though migration is not toward the moon, as the "Person of Learning and Piety" supposed, and though it takes place at fairly low altitudes where it may be observed, mystery still surrounds many aspects of it. How do birds find their way through the darkness and fog and over countless miles of unmarked flyways? The Baltimore oriole that hangs its nest in some tree on a particular street in a New England town has a winter home in a certain spot far to the south, perhaps in Venezuela. How can it find its way unerringly between these two homes without a map, a compass, and an address book? There is no one, of course, from whom it can ask directions.

The records of banded birds give evidence of unbelievable journeys. Eastern golden plovers breed in the Western Hemisphere north of the Arctic Circle but spend the winter on the pampas of Brazil and Argentina. In the fall after making their way across northeastern Canada most of the adults use an ocean route from Labrador or Nova Scotia to

South America. According to Frederick C. Lincoln, "The golden plover may accomplish the whole 2,400 miles without pause or rest . . . [for] the golden plover in this remarkable journey flies both day and night." What sort of heart and lungs and wing muscles do these eleven-inch birds possess to accomplish such a feat? And what sort of compass is built into their brain to enable them to hold their course through the dark and over the trackless ocean?

The arctic tern is the champion migrant of all. Its extreme summer and winter homes are eleven thousand miles apart and some of these amazing terns may travel as much as twenty-five thousand miles a year on their annual migratory journeys. Who but God could guide these birds and give them the navigating equipment of their tiny brains?

Today there are several theories to account for the astonishing capacity of birds to find their way. Perhaps day migrants get their sense of direction from familiar landmarks, like the course of the Nile. Young birds may learn the route by following their parents. But often birds of the year precede their parents southward and many of them fly during the hours of darkness. Perhaps the earth's magnetic field guides them or certain radio waves keep them on their course. A recent theory proposes that birds may steer their course by the sun or by the stars. These are shifting points, constantly swinging through their orbits. Are the mathematical calculations necessary to navigate by the sun or the stars reduced to instinctive patterns and stored in a bird's brain? Here is one of the great mysteries of living beings. Though one day we will penetrate this mystery, we shall always join with Jeremiah and Job in attributing the seasonal comings and goings of birds along their ancestral migration routes to the wisdom and providence of God.

CHAPTER 17 🖎

The Snare of the Fowler

HUNGER, a constant enemy during forty years in "the great and terrible wilderness," taught the people of Israel that there is more to life than eating and "that man doth not live by bread only." They were grateful for manna and for quails which the Lord caused to fall into their camp. When they arrived at last in the Promised Land it seemed to them, in comparison to the semideserts of their wandering years,

a good land, a land of brooks of water, of fountains and depths that spring out of valleys and hills; a land of wheat and barley and vines and fig trees and pomegranates; a land of olive oil and honey; a land wherein thou shalt eat bread without scarceness.

Deuteronomy 8:7-9

Even in the Promised Land they sometimes experienced famine, for there were long droughts, crops failed, farming methods were often poor, landowners were greedy, and warfare brought frightful devastation to their fields. When they were hungry the people learned that the flesh and eggs of Palestine's abundant birds could make the difference for them between starvation and survival.

Though the Lord forbade them to eat "unclean" birds, He expressly said, "But of all clean fowls ye may eat" (Deuteronomy 14:20), and many Israelites knew the delicious taste of pigeons, the succulent flavor of quails, and, best of all, the delicate flesh of partridges. The Lord had given man dominion over the world: "the beasts of the field, the fowls of the heaven hath he given into thine hand" (Daniel 2:38). While the great birds of prey and all others on the forbidden list dived and glided and circled overhead, safe from the snare of the fowler, the small perching birds and all kinds of "clean" birds fell into traps, were caught in nets or brought down with throw sticks, and men gathered them up by the basketful. Even so, few inroads could have been made on the teeming bird populations of ancient Palestine, for the Lord had put the fear of man "upon every fowl of the air" (Genesis 9:2). Moreover even the most ingenious traps were not very efficient; a law protected parent birds on the nest; and the markets for birds were merely local.

Here and there a bird was captured in a manner such as that described by the prophet Amos. In the rock-strewn pastures near his home at Tekoa he was perhaps guarding sheep one day when he saw a bird on the ground frantically beating its wings in a desperate effort to fly away. Amos perceived that its wings were uninjured and wondered what held it prisoner. Something had robbed the bird of its freedom. Looking more closely Amos found a concealed trap and scattered grains of corn with which it had been baited and he saw that the bird's feet were held fast in a string noose. The poor creature had been

> like a bird fluttering straight into the net—
> never dreaming its life is in danger.
> Proverbs 7:23, Moffatt

The sight of the trapped bird haunted Amos for many lonely days on the hillsides with his sheep. The bird was caught because a snare had been set and baited for it. Almost everyone in those days thought birds could be caught by pronouncing magic words or performing certain rites, but to Amos this was foolishness. Cause and effect marched inexorably together. Amos proclaimed this truth and his words helped to end, for reasonable men, the long reign of superstition and the supremacy of magicians, dreamers, and false priests. Not the least of Amos' contributions to the world was his insistence that in the world God has created there is no capriciousness. On this foundation science is built.

> Does a bird drop into the trap,
>   unless the trap is baited?
> Does the trap spring up,
>   unless there is something to catch?
> Amos 3:5, Moffatt

When his countrymen accused Amos of treason against Israel, he used these words in his own defense. His terrible prophecies were not treason against the nation, he declared, but messages the Lord gave him to deliver. When God speaks, His prophets must prophesy. Cause precedes effect. It is the same with all the evil-doing of Israel. Evil-doing is the cause and it will inevitably reap punishment. Israel was blessed indeed to be a people whom the Lord had chosen for His own, but special privilege entails greater responsibility. It must have occurred to some of those who listened to Amos that Israel was like a bird about to fall into a trap of her own unrighteousness.

While there was still time God had sent His prophet Amos to warn the comfortable, self-satisfied Israelites. In this very fact, had they but considered it deeply enough, they might have perceived the mercy and forgiveness and love of God for His people which Amos' successor, Hosea, was to proclaim. "Whoso is wise and will observe these things, even they shall understand the lovingkindness of the Lord."

When Hosea began to prophesy in Israel, Amos had retired from public life, perhaps to write the book of his prophecies. We have little definite information about Hosea's life, but the kind of man he was emerges from his words. For one thing, he was sensitively aware of the world of nature and a brief catalogue of natural history can be compiled from the few pages of his prophecies. Hosea knew the creatures of the Lord—the beasts of the field, the fowls of the air, creeping things of the ground, and fishes. He mentions mountains and hills, forests and vineyards, furrows in the field and thorn hedges, fallow ground and pastures, and the sand of the sea. Among wild beasts he speaks of the lion, leopard, bear and her whelps, and the wild ass. He names horses, heifers, calves, lambs, flocks and herds. He even mentions so tiny a creature as a moth. If we translate his words correctly, he mentions among the trees that grew in Israel the fig, oak, poplar, elm, hemlock, olive, and fir. He identifies nettles, thorns, thistles, grapes, and the lily. He notes the former and later rains, the morning cloud and early dew, fountains of water, drought, the east wind, and the whirlwind.

Hosea, of course, noticed birds and their ways and mentions them eight times in the brief space of his prophecies. He employs four different words for birds: *oph* (2:18; 4:3; 7:12; 9:11); *tsippor* (11:11); *nesher* (8:1); and *yonah* (7:11; 11:11).

Alive to everything around him, Hosea must have participated deeply in the life of his time. He experienced personal tragedy in his marriage to Gomer and public hostility when he proclaimed the doom that would overtake Israel if the people did not repent. He declared that the Assyrian enemy would "come as an eagle against the house of the Lord, because they have transgressed my covenant and trespassed against my law" (Hosea 8:1). Children were Israel's glory, but these, he said, "shall fly away like a bird" (Hosea 9:11). Hosea saw all nature and even birds suffering under the sins of men and the corruption of Israel.

> Because there is no truth, nor mercy,
>   nor knowledge of God in the land. . . .
> Therefore shall the land mourn,
>   and every one that dwelleth therein shall languish,
> with the beasts of the field,
>   and with the fowls of heaven.
>
> Hosea 4:1, 3

Prophecies such as these were not popular and Hosea's enemies tried to catch him like a bird and silence him. They laid traps for him, but Hosea was God's spokesman sent to warn Israel.

> The prophet is God's watchman,
> placed over Ephraim,
> and yet his paths are snared;
> within the temple of his God
> men are hostile to him!
>
> Hosea 9:8, Moffatt

A single partridge could be taken in a simple snare, but a large net was needed to capture a quantity of birds. When Ezekiel says "my net also will I spread upon him, and he shall be taken in my snare" (Ezekiel 12:13), he is evidently describing such a device. Egyptian wall paintings illustrate the method of suddenly lowering a net over ducks resting on the water. Flocks of quails were often captured in nets thrown over the bushes in which they had taken refuge. When the birds flew up they became entangled in the meshes of the net. Pigeons also were trapped in this way. Jesus mentioned such a net when He spoke of the day of judgment and He said: "as a snare shall it come on all them that dwell on the face of the whole earth" (Luke 21:35). Ecclesiastes notes that "the birds that are caught in the snare" (9:12) are taken suddenly and unawares and "man also knoweth not his time."

Centuries earlier Hosea had prophesied that the day of judgment would overtake Ephraim in this very way. Ephraim behaved like a foolish dove. Because she neither knew nor trusted God, she wavered between Egypt on the one side and Assyria on the other, trusting first one and then the other. In the end her foreign policy would prove disastrous and the Lord would take her as in a net.

> Ephraim is like a dove,
>   silly and without sense,
>   calling to Egypt, going to Assyria.

> As they go, I will spread over them my net;
>   I will bring them down like birds of the air. . . .
> Woe to them, for they have strayed from me!
>   Destruction to them, for they have rebelled against me!
> I would redeem them,
>   but they speak lies against me.
>
> Hosea 7:11-13, RSV

"I would redeem them" expresses the deepest element in Hosea's teaching—the redemptive love of God. Long after Hosea's time, after Israel had suffered the terrible punishment of exile, the postexilic prophets knew that Hosea had been right and that God's love is indeed real. They believed that redemption was at hand and they looked forward to the day when Israel would be faithful to her Lord, and righteousness, love, and mercy prevail. Then men would know the Lord and understand what He is really like, and the mission of Hosea, Amos, and all the prophets would be accomplished.

The birds Hosea imagined flying off to Egypt and Assyria in the eighth century, a postexilic writer saw returning with the exiles in the sixth century or later and he added this postscript to Hosea's book:

> "They shall come eagerly like birds from Egypt,
>   and like doves from the land of Assyria;
>   and I will return them to their homes," says the Lord.
>
> Hosea 11:11, RSV

The birds that once languished because of Israel's sin would soon share with men and other creatures the Lord's covenant of peace.

> And in that day will I make a covenant for them with the beasts of the field and with the fowls of heaven . . . and I will break the bow and the sword and the battle out of the earth, and will make them to lie down safely.
>
> Hosea 2:18

There was no safety in the nests described by the great eight-century prophet Isaiah. He does not mention bird-trapping, as did Amos and Hosea, but he compares the conquests of Sennacherib to robbing a nest of its eggs (Isaiah 10:14) and he describes how parent birds flutter away in alarm from a rifled nest (Isaiah 16:2, Moffatt).

Often enough in the sixth century Jeremiah had seen fowlers at work, perhaps in the fields around Anathoth. They set traps so constructed that when a bird alighted on the perch a stone was displaced and the bird was imprisoned. Sometimes they concealed a noose in a bird run and scattered grain as bait around it. At night they often hung a bag net loosely between two poles set up near roosting places. When the sleeping birds were alarmed by shouts and by lanterns, the hapless creatures fell into the net. Fowlers were skillful, patient men who worked hard for the baskets of birds they collected and sold in ancient market places, but there was something about their trade that offended Jeremiah's sensitive feelings. They reminded him of the evil men of Judah who preyed upon the needy, denying their rights to the fatherless and justice to the poor, and becoming prosperous by fraud and treachery.

> For wicked men are found among my people;
>   they lurk like fowlers lying in wait.
> They set a trap;
>   they catch men.
> Like a basket full of birds,
>   their houses are full of treachery;
> therefore they have become great and rich,
>   they have grown fat and sleek.
>   Jeremiah 5:26-28, RSV

Jeremiah knew that the Lord would punish them for these things and, like all the prophets, he believed that moral blindness would destroy the nation. The Psalmist said of a wicked man: "let his net that he hath hid catch himself" (Psalm 35:8).

There are about a dozen words for "net," "snare," "gin," and "trap" in the Old Testament. No fewer than seven of these are used by the versatile and learned author of Job in 18:18-10; 19:6; and 40:24. In the first of these references he writes the Bible's fullest account of capturing birds and other animals. Moffatt's translation indicates how elaborate and effective snares of all kinds were in Job's time:

> He entangles himself in a net,
>   and sprawls within its meshes,
> his heels are caught in a snare,
>   and the trap closes on him tight,
> a noose lies hid for him upon the ground,
>   a pitfall on his path.
>   Job 18:8-10, Moffatt

The Apocrypha contains three references to capturing birds. Ecclesiasticus, or Sirach, mentions "a decoy partridge in a cage" (11:30, RSV). This was a bird that had been captured, tamed, and placed in a concealed cage from which it uttered its call notes. Lured by the sound, its fellows alighted nearby to investigate and were easily captured when the hunter threw his net over them. Sometimes the decoy bird's eyelids were sewn together and it was tied to a perch from which its piteous cries lured other birds. Larks, linnets, pigeons, quails, and partridges were taken in great numbers in this way, and it may be the method Jeremiah mentioned in 5:26-27.

"One who throws a stone at birds" (Ecclesiasticus 22:20, RSV) usually only scares them away, but a running quail or partridge could be captured by hitting its legs with a stick or stone and thus causing it to fall. This method may be the one David refers to in I Samuel 26:20.

"Those who have sport with the birds of the air" (Baruch 3:17, RSV) may be falconers or hunters with dogs. But the Hebrews did not hunt with falcons, hawks, or dogs, for not only were these creatures considered "unclean" in themselves, but they often tear their prey, making it "unclean."

In addition to the hunting methods mentioned above, bows and arrows were used in Bible times.

> In the Lord put I my trust;
>   how say ye to my soul,
> "Flee as a bird to your mountain?"
>   For, lo, the wicked bend their bow,
>   they make ready their arrow upon the string,
>   that they may privily shoot at the upright in heart.
>   Psalm 11:1-2

This long catalogue of ingenious hunting methods and devices might seem to make it difficult for birds to survive. Birds are, however, protected by very efficient equipment of their own. They scare easily and only on uninhabited islands can birds be found that have never learned to fear man and quickly flee from his presence. The superb eye of a bird is its most important sense organ and its best warning device. Even the despised and lowly English sparrow undoubtedly sees twice as well as a man, while a hawk on a falconer's wrist has been known to cock its eye at a bird so far up in the air as to be out of sight to a man using binoculars.

> Surely in vain the net is spread in the sight of any bird.
>   Proverbs 1:17

When danger threatens, birds simply fly away, leaving earthbound men to gaze after them and sigh:

> Oh that I had wings like a dove!
> For then would I fly away and be at rest.
>   Psalm 55:6

Sometimes a snare was broken by a bird's frantic efforts to escape.

> Our soul is escaped as a bird
>> out of the snare of the fowlers;
> the snare is broken,
>> and we are escaped.
>>>> Psalm 124:7

Sometimes a fowler opened his hand and the bird regained its freedom.

> Deliver thyself . . . as a bird from the hand of the fowler.
>>>> Proverbs 6:5

> And as you allow a bird to escape
> from your hand,
> so you have let your neighbor go,
> and will not catch him again.
>>>> Ecclesiasticus 27:19, RSV

The people of Israel knew that the most effective of all defenses was the Lord's protection, and they prayed: "O deliver not the soul of thy turtledove unto the multitude of the wicked" (Psalm 74:19). Such was their faith that they believed:

> Surely he shall deliver thee from the snare of the fowler . . .
> He shall cover thee with his feathers,
>> and under his wings shalt thou trust.
>>>> Psalm 91:3-4

CHAPTER 18

An Old Testament Naturalist

As THE author of the Book of Job reveals a wider knowledge of natural history than any other Bible person, it is perhaps appropriate to claim for him the title of naturalist. Who this author was we do not know. Did he live during Jeremiah's time or earlier or later? Did he belong to the chosen people of Israel or to another people? Were parts of his book written by other men? Though we cannot give positive answers to these questions, we do know that Job contains the Bible's richest collection of nature lore and that its author made some of the Old Testament's keenest and most penetrating observations about birds.

He knew, as we have already noted, four different ways to capture birds, but he seems less interested in fowling than in bird watching. He may have been like many duck hunters today who evolve into bird watchers and who find greater enjoyment in watching life through binoculars and in photographing it with their cameras than in taking it with guns. Ulysses' wife Penelope expressed the enjoyment of all bird watchers when she said of her flock of twenty geese: "It cheers me to look at them."

Job's qualifications as a naturalist do not end with his birds, for his ostrich monograph is preceded by a fascinating account of wild goats and asses and is followed by a spirited description of a war horse in the midst of battle. This author has as keen an eye and ear for the world in which birds live as for the birds themselves. He listens to "the wild ass bray" and, according to the Moffatt version, "the war-horse . . .

snorting bravely, furiously." He hears "the roaring of the lion" and searches for the dens and lairs of wild beasts. He sees flash floods tear destructively down mountain valleys and with their "torrents wash away the soil of the earth." He identifies papyrus growing in the mire, thistles crowding out wheat and barley, and willows lining the brook. Snow, hail, and rain fall on him and he knows ice, hoarfrost, and dew. He watches the Bear, Orion, the Pleiades, and the constellations of the south moving across the night sky, and he hears again the primal music of creation "when the morning stars sang together and all the sons of God shouted for joy."

The author of Job must have traveled widely, for he describes life in cities, on farms, and in the desert. He knows about sailing, fishing, and mining. He met many kinds of people, but he saw that in the life of almost everyone evil casts its dark shadow upon the splendor and wonder of human existence. It was to the problem of evil that the author of Job devoted his deepest thought and all his superb gift of utterance. If he had been less perplexed by the troubles and suffering of men, he might have written more fully about nature. As it was, he used what he knew about nature's wonders to illuminate his discussions about the meaning of evil. He was intelligent, perceptive, compassionate, and he viewed God's works with humbleness, seeing what is really there and always there. His eyes were focused on reality and though some twenty-five hundred years separated him from us, his book still speaks powerfully to us of unchanging nature and human nature. The Book of Job is the acknowledged literary masterpiece of the Old Testament and belongs among the truly great achievements of man's mind.

The story of Job concerns a good man who suffers terrible calamities. When Job's friends come to "comfort" him, he asks them the agonizing question: If God is just, why does He allow good people to suffer? Parroting the shallow wisdom of their time, Job's friends declare that suffering is sent to punish men for their sins. Sure of the answers they ask Job: "Whoever perished being innocent, or where were the righteous cut off?" They are certain, in their unthinking way, that whoever is innocent and righteous is guaranteed a happy life. But Job knows that this is not true and that innocent and righteous people often suffer grievously. He himself lives an upright life according to a very high moral code. He can be called a righteous man, guilty of no evil, yet his sufferings are almost more than he can bear. Moreover, wicked people everywhere seem to prosper and Job asks: "Wherefore do the wicked live, become old, yea, are mighty in power?" The world seems upside down to Job and the problem of evil insoluble until out of the whirlwind he hears the voice of God. God is not absent as Job feared, for with his own eyes he sees the Lord and his heart finds peace.

In and out of this incomparably brilliant drama fly Job's birds, sometimes adding their note to the evidence, but always bringing life, activity, and an extra dimension to the argument. Job's first birds usually fly away unnoticed, for many versions of the Bible do not perceive any birds in the sentence usually translated:

> Yet man is born to trouble as the sparks fly upward.
>
> Job 5:7

The Hebrew word here rendered "sparks" means literally "sons of flame." This poetic phrase was interpreted by the Septuagint and other ancient versions to mean eagles and vultures, those splendid, swift birds that flash through the sky with meteorlike speed. Some ancient people believed that these birds were filled with sunlight and akin to flame. Others looked into eagles' eyes and saw two bright yellow discs, for the iris of an adult eagle is yellow. These beautiful sunlike orbs seemed to make the eagle a symbol of the sun itself. If eagles were in Job's mind when he wrote this passage about trouble and suffering, his meaning may be, not that trouble is inevitable, "as the sparks fly upward," but that men cause much of the evil in their own lives. Eagles and vultures voluntarily enter the powerful updrafts which bear them aloft. To Dr. Moffatt's translation:

> Suffering? it springs not from the soil,
>   trouble grows not from the ground;
> man brings trouble on himself. . . .
>
> Job 5:6-7

we can perhaps add as a fitting climax the phrase "as eagles soar upward."

Often as Job traveled on foot or on some plodding beast he would have seen eagles and vultures tearing out of the sky at incredible speeds. They were the fastest things he knew. In the ancient world a runner carrying an urgent message or a reed boat lightly skimming over the water were notable for their swiftness, but an eagle was faster. In the modern world, before jet planes and missiles made all previous speed records obsolete, eagles and falcons could hold their own with airplanes. Timed by a stop watch a golden eagle chased by peregrine falcons achieved a speed of 120 miles an hour, while a peregrine falcon diving on prey outflew a plane going 175 miles an hour. These are records achieved by living organisms, not by machines and explosive elements, and they stand unchallenged. It was with speeds such as these that the author of Job climaxed his list:

> My days go quicker than a courier,
>   they fly without one happy ray,
>   they flit as rapidly as skiffs,
>   like eagles swooping on their prey.
>   Job 9:25-26, Moffatt

The man who marveled at the soaring of vultures and the stooping of eagles found the white of an egg tasteless. Surely he had eaten partridge eggs and possibly hen's eggs and the huge three-pound eggs of the ostrich, but with all of these he noticed the difference between the flavorful yolk and the insipid white which needed salt to make it palatable. "Can that which is unsavoury be eaten without salt," he asked, "or is there any taste in the white of an egg" (6:6)? For "the white of an egg" the Revised Standard Version substitutes "the slime of the purslane." Purslane is a gelatinous plant believed to have been eaten only during famines. Either egg white or purslane serve the meaning of this passage equally well: man needs food he relishes rather than loathes, just as Job needed worthwhile life rather than bare existence.

Because birds seemed supernaturally wise to ancient men, the augurs, an early variety of bird watcher, looked for signs of approaching events in the flights of birds. Even today the first robins are regarded as unofficial members of the weather bureau announcing the arrival of spring. We say: "Spring is surely on its way, for the robins know when to come north." Job may refer to the reputed wisdom of birds in an enigmatic verse containing two unknown words, the first of which is sometimes rendered "ibis," while the second is "cock" in the Douay Version. If these renderings are correct, Job's meaning in 38:36 may be:

> Who hath put wisdom in the ibis,
>   or who hath given understanding to the cock?

The cock's sure instinct knows the approach of dawn which he loudly proclaims. The sacred ibis probably arrived in Egypt when the Nile began to flood and departed as its waters subsided. Both birds seemed to ancient men to possess a wisdom only God could have given them.

As birds and other creatures often appear to be wiser than men, Job advises people living in man-made cities and occupied with man-made things to "speak to the earth," or ask the birds Who made them and sustains them. From these creatures men can gain truer understanding of God their Creator.

> But ask now the beasts, and they shall teach thee,
>   and the fowls of the air, and they shall tell thee,
> or speak to the earth, and it shall teach thee,
>   and the fishes of the sea shall declare unto thee.
> Who knoweth not in all these
>   that the hand of the Lord hath wrought this?
> In whose hand is the soul of every living thing
>   and the breath of all mankind.
>
> Job 12:7-10

Besides wisdom, Job knew that birds also possess superb powers of sight. Some, to be sure, might be so unwary and unseeing as to fall into nets and traps (18:8-10), or be captured and caged (41:5). But Job knew that a hawk's vision is outstanding, though he did not understand why. The chief reason a bird's eye excells that of any other vertebrate including man, is that the image-forming tissue lining the eye's interior is richer in visual cells than the eye of other creatures. The number of visual cells determines the ability of the eye to see small objects at a distance. While the retina of a man's eye contains some 200,000 visual cells per square millimeter, most birds have three times that number, and hawks, vultures, and eagles have a million or more per square millimeter. Job could not have chosen better birds than vultures and hawks to make his point. What these birds cannot see is hidden indeed.

In addition to its greater density of visual cells, a bird's eye is more sensitive than ours to red light rays. These rays give sharp focus to far-off objects. From a distance at which no man can distinguish anything so small, a hawk sees a mouse and watches it scamper away. An eagle once spotted a dead fish floating in a lake three miles away and made a diagonal dive to the exact place. Not only was the eagle able to see a small object at a far greater distance than a man could, but the bird kept the fish in constant focus through its three-mile dive.

But with all their astonishing perfection the eyes of birds cannot see beneath the ground to hidden veins of sapphire and gold, nor find the path to the secret abode of wisdom.

> No vulture knows the path to it,
> no hawk's eye ever spies it.
>
> Job 28:7, Moffatt

At this point Job asks:

> "Where is wisdom to be found?
> And knowledge, where does it abound?

For she is hid from every living creature,
even from the eyes of a wild bird."
Job 28:20-21, Moffatt

Wise as birds were commonly supposed to be, the author of Job knew that God gives more wisdom to men than to birds. In a passage of rare insight he described how men cry to God for help, but their cry is empty and their petitions remain unanswered, for men want only God's help, not God Himself. True faith sees God as our Creator, One who endows us with wisdom and turns our midnight sorrow into rejoicing.

They cry out by reason of the arm of the mighty.
But none saith, "Where is God my maker,
who giveth songs in the night,
who teacheth us more than the beasts of the earth,
and maketh us wiser than the fowls of heaven?"
There they cry, but none giveth answer,
because of the pride of evil men.
Job 35:9-12

Job's disease denied him the pleasant company of friends and he had not yet experienced the joy that comes when God "giveth songs in the night." He felt himself to be "a brother to dragons and a companion to owls" (30:29). These were possibly jackals and ostriches, whose howling Micah and Isaiah associated with desolation. As the voice of the cock ostrich is a loud, sepulchral cry sounding like the "neighing of a horse, the bellow of a bull, and a shriek of savage laughter," it is no wonder that these creatures suggested grief and woe.

Some Jewish rabbis found a fantastic bird in Job 29:18, for the word translated "sand" in the authorized Version they understood to be the phoenix. This fabulous creature was supposed to live five hundred or a thousand years through an entire cycle of history and then set its nest on fire, making a funeral pyre on which it burned itself alive. From its own ashes it rose with restored youth to begin a new cycle. Tacitus and Pliny, though they made no claim of having seen the phoenix themselves, said that the bird had been seen. St. Clement narrates the phoenix legend in an early Christian document and this mythological bird became a Christian symbol of the resurrection. Most Bible translators, however, do not include the phoenix among Job's birds, real or mythological.

The peacock, though a real enough bird, should also be dropped from Job, for the Hebrew *renanim* of 39:13 is now usually rendered ostrich.

From the whirlwind the Lord mentioned four birds: the raven, hawk, eagle, and ostrich. They and other aspects of nature taught Job the immense difference between God's measureless wisdom and power and his own. Only when he acknowledged his limited wisdom and feeble power did he gain true understanding of God. "Can you do what God does?" Job was asked. "How foolish!" Job surely exclaimed. "Of course I cannot!" But the questions continued inexorably. "Are you the one who feeds the young ravens? Does the hawk migrate southward with your guidance? Does the eagle soar at your command? Are you responsible for the behavior of ostriches?"

As might be expected, Job's monograph on the ostrich contains penetrating observations; indeed, two modern ornithologists, Dr. Robert Cushman Murphy and Dr. Dean Amadon, state: "Few readers of the Bible realize how exact is this passage."

> The ostrich flaps her wings in pride;
> but is the feathered creature kind?
> She leaves her eggs upon the earth
> to warm and hatch out in the dust,
> forgetting that a foot may crush them,
> or a wild beast tread on them—
> harsh to her young, as if they were not hers,
> unheeding though her labour is in vain;
> for God makes her devoid of sense,
> he denies her intelligence.
> Let hunters come, and she will scour the plain,
> scorning the horse and its rider.
>
> Job 39:13-18, Moffatt

Despite his exact observations Job, as we shall discover, is not fair to ostrich parents when he judges their behavior by human standards and accuses them of dealing cruelly with their young. He also thought God had deprived this bird of wisdom—a well-taken point, for ostriches are among the most primitive of living birds, blindly relying on their instincts to a greater degree than do the more highly organized birds. It is well known that ostriches swallow hard objects like nails and stones, a habit mentioned in Shakespeare's line: "I'll make thee eat iron like an ostrich." To Tristram's dismay an ostrich ate his pocket-knife and buckle. But there is "wisdom" even in this apparently sense-less act, for hard, indigestible substances help to grind up food in a bird's gizzard. For all their stupidity, creatures belonging to an order of birds that has managed to survive the catastrophic changes of the past twelve million years or so must be endowed with some kind of "wisdom."

The smallest bird in the world is the bee hummingbird of Cuba which, as its name indicates, is not much larger than a bumblebee. It lays two pea-sized eggs in a nest only slightly bigger than a thimble. The largest of living birds is the ostrich, the males being about eight feet tall from head to toe and weighing up to three hundred pounds. As far as we know only the roc, sometimes called the elephant bird, was larger. This creature was said to have carried off elephants in its talons —a flight of the imagination indeed, for the bones of the roc found on the island of Madagascar indicate that it was a flightless, ostrichlike creature, standing twelve feet tall and having gigantic bones and a two-gallon egg. The roc is a veritable dinosaur among birds and like the dinosaurs it perished before history began. The ostrich succeeded to the roc's title as largest bird and survives today in zoos and on ostrich farms where it is bred for its plumes. Six forms of the ostrich are known in Africa and Arabia, the Syrian ostrich, *Struthio camelus syriacus,* undoubtedly being the one Job described. This bird was abundant in the Arabian and Syrian deserts in Job's time and until 1914 was often encountered by caravans traveling in these regions. Today, however, this subspecies is believed to be extinct.

Body feathers of male ostriches are black, but their beautiful soft wing and tail plumes are pure white. Their heads and necks, being practically featherless, appear pink or sometimes red, which is the color of the skin. The female is nearly as large as the male, but her plumage is entirely grayish brown, a protective device, as it is she who generally broods the eggs during the day. Ostrich chicks also are protectively colored, having mottled dark brown and buffy white feathers. Ostriches have small, flattened heads no larger than an orange and their brains are said to be the size of a walnut. With their muscular legs and thighs, massive bodies, long flexible necks and huge eyes, two inches in diameter and possibly the largest among land vertebrates, ostriches have a curiously prehistoric appearance. They have been called "living fossils."

Ostrich feathers are depicted on Egyptian monuments as proud emblems of high rank, but they are more decorative than useful. Even before the time of the pharaohs, men prized these soft, airy plumes as ornaments, but ostriches cannot fly with them, though they do increase the bird's running speed. It has been suggested that ostriches, and also penguins, may be descended from flightless ancestors, entirely distinct from those of flying birds. If so, ostrich wings may not be degenerate but actually better developed today than ever before. According to another theory, however, ancestral ostriches were flying creatures whose wings lost the power of flight and so caused their descendants to become earth-bound. Ostrich plumes lack the tiny hooks which lock together all parts of a feather, making it a somewhat rigid structure, impervious to air and water and capable of sustaining flight. Even if ostrich feathers were equipped with these all-important tiny hooks, ostriches still could not fly, for their breastbones are flat and lack the characteristic keel to which the flight muscles of other birds are attached. They walk with a swaying, mincing gait, their bodies too heavy, their necks too long, and their legs too massive to be graceful.

Though a failure as a flier and awkward as a walker, the ostrich is a superb runner. With its wings spread out to give lift to its heavy body, with its feet adapted to running, the larger of its two toes being provided with a soft, fleshy pad, and with long legs that give the bird a bounding stride of fifteen feet or more, ostriches can indeed "scour the plain," running forty miles an hour and easily outdistancing the fastest horse. In his *Anabasis* Xenophon mentions "many ostriches" the ten thousand Greeks encountered in 401 B.C. as they marched southward along the Euphrates through level country abounding in wild asses, bustards, and gazelles. It was the remarkable running speed of the ostriches that amazed the Greek cavalry, as well it might, for it is faster than the speed of a horse or an antelope. Even today an ostrich hunter riding in a jeep may have to chase the bird for an hour or more at high speed before overtaking it. Xenophon's amazement at the performance of these birds is preserved in this comment:

No one succeeded in catching any of the ostriches. The horsemen who hunted these birds soon left off pursuing them, for running ostriches use their wings like sails and can far outstrip horses.

Hunters using crafty stratagems were more successful than the Greek horsemen, and captured many ostriches. There is a record of eight pair harnessed and marching in a day-long procession of animals through the city of Alexandria in the reign of Ptolemy II. The parade was a fabulous one including 96 elephants, 120 goats, 24 antelopes and hartebeests, wild asses, camels, sheep, oxen, bears, leopards, one giraffe, 24 lions, a rhinoceros, thousands of dogs, and cages of such birds as parrots, peacocks, guinea-fowls, pheasants, and "Ethiopian birds" which may have been ibises or egrets.

Ostriches, though large, conspicuous birds, are well-adapted to their home in sandy plains and open, desert country, for with their huge eyes set on necks that act like periscopes they can see distant objects in a wide field of vision. When they spot danger they can outrun all their natural enemies. Their keen sense of smell alerts them to danger approaching from the windward. Grass, leaves, fruit, snakes, insects, and small desert mammals are their food and if necessary they can survive for many days without water. They are a veritable camel among birds as their scientific name *Struthio camelus* suggests.

As parents they are outstanding. "Cruel, like the ostriches in the wilderness" (Lamentations 4:3) is as mistaken a statement of their parental behavior as is the statement that they hide their heads in sand to avoid danger. The cock ostrich scoops a shallow depression in the ground where the hen lays her clutch of twelve to twenty eggs. Often two hens use the same nest, for these birds are polygamous. The cock is the chief guardian of the family nest, watching over it and incubating the eggs for a month and a half. In the wild, the hen usually takes over the incubating from eight in the morning until four in the afternoon. The eggs are large and have strong, thick shells. Their breaking strength has been measured at 55 kilograms while that of a hen's egg is only 5.1 kilograms. The glazed shell, six times thicker than that of a hen's egg, protects the embryo within from desert heat and an ostrich can safely leave her eggs exposed during the noonday. When parent birds sense danger they run from the nest, apparently careless of the safety of eggs or young. As the desert affords no good hiding places, however, the best safety for ostrich young lies in the protective coloration of eggs and chicks and the diversionary tactics of their parents. As soon as the chicks break through their shells the cock assumes all their care while the hens generally go off together. Job observed this behavior very accurately, but he interpreted and judged it by human rather than avian standards.

Not long ago Carl R. Raswan crossed the Nefud and wrote of his adventures in *Black Tents of Arabia*. As he and his party crossed the red sand dunes of this desert where gazelles, antelopes, ibex, eagles, and panthers live, they came upon an ostrich family. Though the men approached cautiously, the birds became alarmed and frantically flapped their wings. At first the seven bristly chicks ran hither and thither, scurrying after their mother, while the cock remained in the rear covering their retreat. He looked back frequently as he ran and when he saw the horsemen gaining on him he dashed straight ahead, then zigzagged abruptly. As it was impossible to overtake him on horseback, he was chased in the direction of an ambush where a man with a gun waited and soon shot him. The hen, meanwhile, ran in a wide curve back to her nest and called to her scattered chicks. When they unfroze and came out of hiding, she herded them away. Had Job seen this sight, he would hardly have written "harsh to her young, as if they were not hers."

Ostriches have been hunted for millenniums and their plumes have always been greatly prized. King Tut-ankh-amen's ostrich feather fan can still be admired in Cairo. During the Victorian era every fashionable lady adorned herself with these plumes. Charles M. Doughty in *Travels in Arabia Deserta* tells of meeting on the pilgrim road to Mecca an Arab ostrich hunter so poor that he often went without food, but he was mounted on a good riding camel and his hunter's tools were of the best. When he found ostrich tracks he dismounted and waited patiently, his gun ready, for the bird to return. Usually he caught two birds a year and sold them to a certain Damascus feather merchant who gave him the price of a good camel for each skin, for the plumes were in great demand in Paris, London, and New York. Some Arab hunters used to disguise themselves in gazelle skins and stalk ostriches on all fours; other hunters rode specially trained horses and, carrying their own supply of water, chased the birds for several days. When the ostriches became exhausted they could be captured.

Today among primitive African tribes ostrich eggs are sometimes used as water bottles. With their glazed outer surface and their thick, strong shell they are durable enough to be decorated as ornaments for churches and mosques. During the Renaissance they were sometimes mounted in silver and used as drinking cups. Ostrich eggs hang above the lamps in the Church of the Holy Sepulchre in Jerusalem, suggesting that Christ's care of His Church is like that of an ostrich for its eggs.

It is said that ostrich eggs are delicious and a one-egg ostrich omelette will feed as many people as an omelette made with two dozen hen's eggs. An egg can be cooked by setting it on end in a fire while its contents are stirred through a hole pierced in the upper end. In *Seven Pillars of Wisdom* T. E. Lawrence describes how, in the Arabian Desert during the Arab revolt of 1917-1918, he cooked an ostrich egg over a fire made of shredded blasting gelatine. He found the egg "tough and strong, but good." Before Lawrence discovered the egg he had seen "little puffs of dust" that "scurried into the eye of the wind." These his Arab companions identified as dust stirred up by running ostriches, but, like the famous English traveler Gertrude Bell who had been in this region a few years earlier and had seen tracks and eaten ostrich eggs, Lawrence did not see the birds themselves.

More than thirty years earlier Lady Anne Blunt and her husband on their pilgrimage to the Nejd were presented with a fresh egg, but, though they kept a sharp lookout for ostriches, they saw none of these creatures. In 1914 Captain Shakespear, while encamped with his British soldiers at Nefud, was presented with an ostrich chick. A live ostrich, said to have been caught south of Beersheba, was exhibited by Bedouins

Doves Were Familiar to Jesus from His Childhood

Sitting upon His mother's lap, the Child Jesus turns from the symbolic pomegranate seeds toward little St. John the Baptist. Mary has been pensively reading her Magnificat. Behind her stretches an ideal landscape. A lifelike dove in the foreground bears symbolic meaning. Raffaellino del Garbo (1466-1524) painted this lovely scene now in the National Museum, Naples. [Page 235]

"The Spirit of God Descending Like a Dove"

Jesus hears the words of His Father, "Thou art my beloved Son," as He comes out of the Jordan. John the Baptist begins to understand what is taking place and his eyes express wonder and awe as he kneels. One of the angels on the opposite bank sees the heavenly dove which is invisible to mortal eyes. Soft clouds of a summer sky and a quiet landscape invest the scene with beauty. This "Baptism" in the Pinacoteca, Dresden, was painted by Francesco Francia of Bologna (1450-1517). A goldsmith before he became a painter, he is known for the meticulous finish of his appealingly simple pictures and for his beautifully painted birds. [Page 237]

The Symbol of God's Holy Spirit

A dove brought Noah the message of peace. Jesus told His disciples that at His
baptism the Spirit of God descended from heaven like a dove and alighted upon
Him. In this exquisite illumination from a book of prayers the artist has represented that which no man can see—the Holy Spirit of God. Angels sing praises to
the radiant symbol and saints adore Him. The sixteenth-century vellum manuscript
was written and illuminated at Tours, probably for Pierre de Rohan of France.
[Page 238]

"He Was There in the Wilderness . . . with the Wild Beasts"

After His temptation, Jesus tranquilly rests amid desert rocks. He accepts the friendship and homage of wild creatures. A lion sleeps beside Him, a snake slithers harmlessly at His feet, a fox and a bear lie down before Him, while the deer is unmistakably kneeling. The birds approach Him fearlessly and seem to be curious about Him. Painted by Moretto da Brescia, a contemporary of Giorgione and Titian, the picture embodies Moretto's simplicity and tenderness, and his sense of what is spiritually significant. [Page 242]

Birds Look on As the Disciples Make Their Huge Catch

Raphael designed this Vatican tapestry portraying Luke's story of the miraculous draught of fishes. Two of the three cranes in the foreground are trumpeting their resonant call. Birds flying above and white birds floating on the lake give a sense of space to the beautiful composition. On the far shore crowds have assembled to see Jesus. He sits serenely in the stern of one of the laden fishing boats. While others strain to haul in the heavy catch, Peter and Andrew adore their Lord. [Page 242]

"Behold the Birds of the Air"

Surrounded by His disciples Jesus sits on a rock beneath a tree to teach the people. At His feet some of the "lilies of the field" are blossoming. In the distance is a little town sheltered among the hills of Galilee. "Behold the birds of the air," says Jesus, making a motion toward the flock flying above. The engraving is from an old German Bible, the *Biblia Strasburger* of 1630, which contains Martin Luther's translation. [Page 243]

St. Francis Preaching to the Birds

Against a background of burnished gold, the beloved St. Francis preaches to his "little brothers and sisters." His message startles the fierce owl, but the spoonbill and cranes seem to be inspired by it. The Brother in the foreground may be merely waiting, but it is possible to see in him one who is bored with birds. This page from a thirteenth-century Flemish Psalter was painted earlier than Giotto's familiar fresco at Assisi. Both pictures celebrate the new spirit of the twelfth and thirteenth centuries when men recognized God's goodness manifest in the beauties of His creation. The story of St. Francis and the birds typified men's joy in the creatures of God. [Page 246]

"Behold a Sower Went Forth to Sow"

A farmer broadcasts his seed over good ground, stony ground, a trampled wayside, and ground choked with thorns. Birds fill the air and settle in hungry flocks on the exposed seed upon the wayside. Men are shown plowing and harrowing in this engraving from the *Biblia Strasburger* of 1630. The devil shouts temptations to laborers asleep under the trees. A quiet river winds past little medieval towns. [Page 249]

"As a Hen Gathereth Her Chickens under Her Wings"

Christ's lament over Jerusalem evidently suggested this appealing decoration in the Vatican in Rome. The barnyard scene was painted by Mantovani on one of the candelabra in the Loggie famous for its series of Raphael's Bible scenes. Here a grapevine curves through the background and adds its symbolism of the Church to the tender symbolism of the hen and chickens. [Page 253]

"Take These Things Hence!"

His basket of pigeons balanced on his head, the birdseller rushes past the overturned money table toward the Temple gate. Jesus wields His whip with indignation and majestic power. Cupidity darkens the face of the money-changer. While a stampeding animal drags its owner, an escaping bird is pinned to the ground. The barking dog reflects all the noise and violence around him. Though the high priest appears secure in his exalted position, one of his attendants turns toward the unruly scene with a hint of anxiety. Rembrandt's powerfully-conceived **etching** is dramatic and full of life and shows his reverence and deep feeling. [Page 255]

"While He Was Still Speaking the Cock Crowed"

A bright fire burns in the courtyard of the high priest's palace while Jesus is on trial within. Among those warming themselves at the fire is the serving maid on the left who points accusingly at Peter. His face shows he is deeply troubled. To the malicious people crowding around he gestures with his right hand: "No! I do not know him!" At that moment the cock crows from his perch. Far to the right Peter departs, wringing his hands in remorse and sorrow. The expressive drawing is from the *Holkham Bible Picture Book,* which has been called "one of the most lively graphic products of the Middle Ages." [Page 259]

"Their Eyes Were Opened and They Recognized Him"

One of Palestine's swallows is silhouetted against the fading light. It is the evening of the day His disciples found the tomb empty. The perching bird brings to the scene a note of reality and a hint of spring. In a house at Emmaus the risen Christ breaks bread with Cleopas and his companion. Carefully-painted details of everyday life surround the figures, while outside is an Italian landscape in twilight. Jacopo Bassano (1510-1592) painted this picture now in the Duomo, Cittadella, Italy. [Page 260]

"In It Were All Kinds of Animals . . . and Birds of the Air"

Peter recoils in horror from the suggestion that he eat ritually "unclean" meat. While praying on Simon's housetop at Joppa he sees a vision and hears the Voice. Meanwhile in the street below three men approach Simon's house with an invitation from a Roman centurion for Peter. The engraving is from *Historien des Ouden en Nieuwen Testaments,* published in Amsterdam in 1700. [Page 261]

The Chalice of Antioch

A symbolic eagle with outspread wings perches upon a basket of Eucharistic bread. Christ's throne is above the bird, as though supported by its wings. While He stretches out His arm in blessing, a dove flies above. The grapevine encircling the chalice represents the Church. Besides the eagle and dove eight other birds are depicted, together with the apostles and small decorative creatures. This fourth- or fifth-century silver vessel, used in the sacrament of the Lord's Supper, was discovered near Antioch by Arabs digging a well. [Page 264]

St. John and His Eagle

The upward gaze of the eagle, itself a superb creature, enhances the serene majesty of this saint whose visions are recorded in the Book of Revelation. He stands in deep thought, his finely-modeled head turned toward the volume on his left arm. The gesture of his right hand indicates the act of writing. This eleven-inch bronze statue is one of the four evangelists designed by Giovanni Bologna in the sixteenth century for the high altar of the Carthusian monastery near Florence. [Page 265]

Four Winged Beings Surround Christ in Glory

With their courage, strength, wisdom, and speed these heavenly creatures surround Christ in the Last Judgment and illustrate the paeon of praise in Revelation. The wonderful figure above the central portal of the west front of Chartres Cathedral is one of the most powerful representations of Christ in medieval art. With His attendant figures He has looked down in sublime majesty upon Christian worshipers for seven and a half centuries. [Page 265] at the Levant Fair in 1929. These reports are the last records of the Syrian ostrich, the subspecies so plentiful in Job's time and in the days of the Greeks. Its immense sharp eyes, its keen smell, and its running speed that "scorneth the horse and its rider" enabled this huge, ungainly bird to survive in the deserts since the Pliocene period. Already becoming rare, it was doomed by the automobile and the efficient firearms which flooded Arabia after World War I. In *Birds of Arabia,* Colonel Richard Meinertzhagen says that the ostrich has been extinct in the Syrian and Arabian Deserts since 1941. Thus this fascinating bird joins the hippopotamus, crocodile, reindeer, lion, leopard, Syrian bear, and all the other animals which have become extinct in this region.

The ostrich is possibly mentioned more frequently in the Old Testament than the Authorized Version indicates. Both the *renanim* of Job and the *yeenim* of Lamentations are translated "ostrich," but other translations, including the Revised Standard Version and Moffatt's, render the Hebrew *bath yaanah,* literally "daughter of howling" or "of the wilderness," as "ostrich" rather than "owl" in the following passages: Leviticus 11:16; Deuteronomy 14:15; Job 30:29; Isaiah 13:21; 34:13; 43:20; Jeremiah 50:39; Micah 1:8. On the other hand, Dr. Driver observes that as the ostrich needs some water, does not haunt ruined cities, and booms but does not wail, it cannot be the bird mentioned in all of the verses cited above.

Job's poor opinion of birds as parents is further seen when he accuses the raven of abandoning its young.

> Who provides for the raven its prey,
>   when its young ones cry to God,
>   and wander about for lack of food?
> Job 38:41, RSV

According to the folklore of Job's time ravens desert their nestlings and it is God, the Psalmist declares, who feeds "the young ravens which cry" (Psalms 147:9). Job's spiritual insight here was truer than his natural history. His mistaken notion, however, persisted for hundreds of years and as late as the seventeenth century Izaac Walton wrote: "When the raven hath hatched her eggs she takes no further care, but leaves her young ones to the care of the God of nature. . . ."

Actually ravens, like ostriches, are devoted parents. The male and female pair for life and generally return to the same nest in some tall tree or high cliff where they share the task of incubating their five or six eggs. They feed, guard, and care for their nestlings during many weeks, even after the young birds have left the nest. They continue to stay with their young ones throughout the summer, teaching them the ways of ravens. Though raven nestlings cry for food, it is their parents, as God has ordained, who hear their cry and feed their own young. Ravens are bold and fearless in defending their young, and Gilbert White reports that "a pair of ravens nesting in the rock of Gibraltar would suffer no vulture or eagle to rest near their station [nest], but would drive them from the hill with an amazing fury."

Among the most devoted parents of the avian world are eagles and vultures. The eggs of some of these large birds take one or two months to hatch and the nestlings must be fed and guarded for two or three months more. From their eyries built on inaccessible crags the parent birds "mount up" to heights from which they can scan an immense area for food for their young.

Tristram reported in *The Survey of Western Palestine* that griffon vultures were "the most striking ornithological feature of Palestine. It is impossible in any part of the country to look up without seeing some of them majestically soaring at an immense height, and their eyries abound in great colonies in all the ravines of the country." There "toward evening every jagged rock in the cliffs is the perch of one or more of these noble birds." These griffon vultures may be the "eagles" of Job's passage below, for they always nest on cliffs, whereas eagles sometimes nest in treetops.

> Doth the eagle mount up at thy command,
>   and make her nest on high?
> She dwelleth and abideth on the rock,
>   upon the crag of the rock, and the strong place.
> From thence she seeketh the prey,
>   and her eyes behold afar off.
> Her young ones also suck up blood,
>   and where the slain are, there is she.
>
> Job 39:27-30

Men match their human strength against mountains and reach the highest summits on earth; they match their knowledge against nature's secrets and discover the forces within the atoms and the galaxies; they invent machines to take them through the air like birds or beneath the seas like fishes. But all this has not changed the basic situation of men since the days when Job surveyed the manifold wonders of God's creation and acknowledged that all his human strength and ability were no match for the power and wisdom of God. Job had neither the wisdom to feed young ravens, nor the authority to command eagles, nor the skill to direct hawks on their southward migration. From some vantage point on an autumn day, perhaps on the Sinai Peninsula or near the shores of the Red Sea where tens of thousands of migrating accipiters have been observed, Job may have watched armies of hawks pass majestically by, riding the thermals and setting a course toward the southern goal of their migration.

> Doth the hawk fly by thy wisdom
> and stretch her wings toward the south?
>
> Job 39:26

Only dimly comprehending what he saw, Job watched in fascination and wonder as the wild, free creatures flew on, symbols of the ineffable wisdom of God by whom all things were made. In moments of beauty like these God writes a message across the sky for men to read. Here God spells out the marvels of His workmanship of the world, His loving care of all His creatures, and all His might, majesty, dominion, and power. In the fullness of time God was to speak more clearly to men through His Son, and as one said who witnessed those days:

> In many and various ways God spoke of old to our fathers by the prophets; but in these last days he has spoken to us by a Son, whom he appointed the heir of all things, through whom also he created the world. He reflects the glory of God and bears the very stamp of his nature, upholding the universe by his word of power.
>
> Hebrews 1:1-3, RSV

PART V

Birds in the New Testament

CHAPTER 19 ✐

She Could Not Afford a Lamb

THIS story opens as a new era of history begins. The Old Testament world of the patriarchs, of the splendid but sometimes wicked kings, and of the inspired prophets already belongs to history and all its birds are dust. For a half century and more, Rome has dominated Palestine. Men still tell their children the old hero stories, teach them the royal names, and hear them recite the words of the prophets, for Israel is proud of her history as God's people of the Covenant, chosen to uphold His Holy Law. One by one the old empires have come and gone—Egypt, Assyria, Babylonia, Persia, and the Hellenistic rulers. Now from his marble palace in Rome Caesar Augustus rules an empire extending from Britain to Arabia and from the Rhine and Danube to the Sahara. Cyrenius, the governor of Syria, sends the tax revenues from his province to Rome; under Roman authority Herod the Great, and later his son Archelaus, rules Judea; and in Jerusalem one of the Sadducees is high priest. Power is in the hands of Rome, but God's ancient Law still binds the sons and daughters of Israel as they hope and pray for the coming of the Messiah. Even now a young woman with a strange hope in her heart is on her way up to Jerusalem to fulfill all that the Law requires.

Lulled by the gentle motion of the donkey on which they ride Mary's Son sleeps in her arms. Early that morning when they left the stable in Bethlehem Mary wrapped herself in a warm cloak to protect her Baby from the chill air. The Holy City is only five miles away, but the donkey will not be hurried. Joseph walks at the beast's head, leading it lest it stumble over stones in the rough path. In his other hand Joseph carries a wicker cage from which come the squeaking and peeping of two young pigeons. These birds are for the ancient sacrifice of purification which the Law of Moses requires and which Joseph and Mary, loyal members of the holy people of Israel, are glad to offer. "Think not that I am come to destroy the law or the prophets," Mary's Son will say in later years. "I am not come to destroy, but to fulfill." The Law that was given to Israel in the Wilderness was not to be abolished but brought to completion by this wondrous Child.

The donkey jogs along, the pigeons squeak in their cage, Joseph hums to himself, but Mary is silent, listening to the incredible music of angelic hosts singing in her heart: "Glory to God in the highest and on earth peace, good will toward men." In Jerusalem she will present her first-born Son to God and offer the ancient sacrifice.

In Bethlehem their new-found friends advised against the journey. "The child is so young and the way long and rugged. Our priest here in Bethlehem will perform for you all the necessary rites." But Mary and Joseph love the House of the Lord and want to visit it on this great occasion in their lives.

Soon the walls of Jerusalem come into view and Mary and Joseph begin the traditional song often sung by pilgrims on their way to the Holy City:

> I was glad when they said unto me,
> "Let us go into the house of the Lord!"
> Our feet shall stand within thy gates,
> O Jerusalem!
>
> Psalm 122:1-2

As Mary sings the old words she still hears in her heart the new strains of "Glory to God in the highest" soaring like a descant above the ancient melody. In her the Old Israel and the New meet. It is recorded:

> And when the time came for their purification according to the law of Moses, they brought him up to Jerusalem to present him to the Lord . . . and to offer a sacrifice according to what is said in the law of the Lord, "a pair of turtledoves, or two young pigeons."
>
> Luke 2:22, 24, RSV

Mary and Joseph are too poor to offer the lamb which the Law in Leviticus usually requires, and so they avail themselves of the kindly provision which permits those who cannot afford a costly sacrifice to offer two birds instead. It was not difficult for Joseph to find a pigeon's nest and take from it two young birds. These are with the infant Jesus on His first entry into Jerusalem.

From His birth He had been surrounded by the humble creatures of God, for was He not born in a stable? Outside in the courtyard the cock crowed each morning and doves fluttered in their cotes. Horses and camels, so often depicted in paintings of the three Wise Men, were well-known creatures in Palestine at this time.

Some of those who in later years meditated on the birth of Christ wove legends about the birds and other animals that were among the first to greet the Lord. Not a few of these unscriptural, fanciful tales enshrine a nugget of truth. One of these stories is about a small olive-gray bird asleep on the branch of a tree near Bethlehem. Suddenly he was awakened by the sound of angel choirs, but nearby, beside their dying fire, the shepherds still remained asleep. The bird felt that these heavenly splendors belonged to some extraordinary event and he began to warble the angels' song and to fan the embers of the fire with his wings in order to awaken the shepherds. The flames turned his breast a rich orange and from that day all his family of Old World robins have worn the brightly-colored feathers with which they were invested, so it is said, the night when Christ was born.

According to another tale, a little brown bird, plain, shy, and song-less, slept that night near the stable. The shining light and the singing angels awakened him and, though he had never sung before, when he tried to join the heavenly chorus he discovered his own glorious voice. On and on this nightingale sang with his new-found voice, so rich and musical, and from that day nightingales have continued to sing out of the darkness the marvelously brilliant crescendo of their "Glory to God in the highest."

In the stable itself, according to one legend, all the animals gathered around to adore the Lord and ever since, when midnight strikes on Christmas Eve, they are said to kneel while all the birds sing praises.

When Christmas Day dawns the cock awakes and some hear him call out: "He is born!" Out of the dusk the little owl asks: "When?" "This night, this very night," warbles the robin. "Where, where, where is He?" twitter the swallows. Softly the doves coo their answer: "In Bethlehem, in Bethlehem." The great owl hoots deep in the woods: "Who is He? Who is He?" High in the sky on quivering wings the lark pours forth his song which like heavenly sunshine fills the world: "He is the Christ, our Lord and King!"

Forty days after the legendary birds and beasts recognized their Lord, Joseph carried a cage in which actual pigeons fluttered. These Mary offered in the Temple for her purification after the danger and mystery

234   All the Birds of the Bible

of childbirth. While the rite was so ancient that its meaning was all but forgotten, it afforded Mary an occasion to thank God for His wonderful gift to her of this new Life. The two pigeons Mary sacrificed were to be among the last of the many victims offered upon the altars of Israel since the days of Abraham, Isaac, and Jacob. He whose mother offered the birds was Himself to be the true and perfect sacrifice. Before His century closed, the Temple was burned, its old altar destroyed, and all the sacrifices ended. By Christ's own sacrifice men entered into a deeper relation with God and the New Covenant was established between God and His people.

Under the New Covenant of Christ the old sacrifices were sometimes remembered and symbolically re-enacted. When a new saint is canonized in St. Peter's in Rome, the offering of bread and wine is carried in solemn procession down the long aisle to the pope seated upon his throne. H. V. Morton in *Through Lands of the Bible* says that bread and wine are not the only offerings, for in the procession are many black-clad figures holding silvered cages in which doves and songbirds coo and chirp. In the hush of this ancient ceremony the pope extends his hand to bless each offering. The birds, unaware of the presence of the pope and dazzled by the brilliance of lights surrounding him, gaze about them uttering cries and calls, their lively chittering and chattering mounting into the silent vaults of the great church. Long ago when St. Francis was made a saint, birds were doubtless presented in symbolical sacrifice before St. Peter's throne. Surely on that occasion they sang their happiest songs in honor of the saint who called them his "little brothers and sisters."

But all this remained far in the future the day Mary offered the pigeons. In the second rite she and Joseph presented their first-born Son to God to whom all Israel and especially all first-born sons belonged. It was customary to redeem the eldest son with five silver shekels paid into the Temple treasury. Though Luke's Gospel does not specifically mention this payment, merely stating that Joseph and Mary "brought in the child Jesus, to do for him after the custom of the law," undoubtedly His parents paid His redemption fee as dutifully as He Himself in later years paid His annual half-shekel Temple tax.

Unnoticed among the Temple crowds, Joseph and Mary prepared to return to Bethlehem. Would no one in the sacred place recognize the holy Child? There had been angels and shepherds, the Wise Men, the birds and beasts, and of course His mother. When the aged prophet Simeon met Joseph and Mary and the Child, he took the Infant in his arms, exclaiming in wonderment and thanksgiving to God: "Mine eyes have seen thy salvation!" Joyfully the old man knew he had been granted his heart's desire, for this Child in his arms would accomplish God's salvation for all peoples. As Simeon ended his blessing, the prophetess Anna entered the Temple. For all her eighty-four years, most of which were spent in the service of God, her eyes were as keen as Simeon's to perceive the things of the Lord. As soon as she saw Mary's Child she recognized Him and spread the news of the Messiah's coming among the devout people of Jerusalem.

From the moments of glory in Bethlehem and of prophetic exaltation in the Temple, Joseph and Mary returned with their young Son to the everyday life of their home in Nazareth. Theirs was the common world of all men in which rest follows toil, hunger is satisfied by bread, and thirst is quenched by water drawn from the well. They did not live among the splendors with which the artists of later centuries endowed them, but the goldfinches and doves which often appear in paintings of Mary and her Child were birds they surely knew. Theirs was a world of bird song and the marvel of bird flight. It was the world in which children grow up to be men.

And the child grew and waxed strong in spirit, filled with wisdom. And the grace of God was upon him.

Luke 2:40

CHAPTER 20 ❧
Like a Dove Descending

A CROWD is gathered at one of the fords of the Jordan where John is baptizing. He is the son of Zacharias and Elisabeth, both of well-known priestly families, but John has lately come from the wilderness where, so it is reported, he lived on locusts and wild honey. He wears a mantle woven of camel's hair and belted with a leather girdle. The preaching of this strange man has already kindled a fire among the people of "Jerusalem and all Judea and all the region round about Jordan," and they assemble in multitudes on the bank of the Jordan to hear his message and to be baptized by him.

"Who are you?" the religious authorities of Jerusalem ask John in considerable alarm.

"I am the voice of one crying in the wilderness, 'Make straight the way of the Lord!' " John replies. Then he tells them of the coming of One mightier than himself.

The multitudes at the Jordan press closely around this uncouth prophet as he exhorts them: "Repent ye!" And their hearts are lifted up on a mighty wave of hope as John proclaims: "The kingdom of heaven is at hand!" It is a day of fervor and tense expectancy as people repent and confess their sins and come down to the water's edge, waiting to be baptized.

Quietly making His way through the crowd comes Jesus to be baptized by John. His thirty years of silence are ended. Behind Him now lie the unrecorded years of His boyhood and young manhood in the carpenter's shop in Nazareth. He has "increased in wisdom and stature, and in favour with God and man." The one saying preserved from His childhood, "I must be about my Father's business," now seems to guide Him as He becomes maturely conscious of His mission. The glory of which the angels sang on the night of His birth in Bethlehem is about to become manifest.

The crowd makes way for Jesus, such is the quality of His person, but His identity remains hidden from the multitude. Quietly He enters the Jordan for the simple rite of baptism. When He steps out of the water and is praying, something unusual happens: the heavens open and the Spirit of God descends "like a dove" and alights upon Jesus. Then from heaven comes a Voice, saying: "Thou art my beloved Son, in whom I am well pleased."

All four Gospels mention the dove: Matthew 3:16; Mark 1:10; Luke 3:22; John 1:32. None states, however, that an actual bird was present, though Luke contains the phrase, "in a bodily shape like a dove."

Here, then, was no marvel, no amazing spectacle to astonish the multitude at the Jordan. No bird rushed down from the sky for all to see and no thunderous voice spoke out. Only Jesus and John saw and understood the meaning of the event. Afterwards John remembered that he had not even recognized Jesus when He first came forward. John's exclamation, "And I knew him not!" underlines the simplicity of the first public appearance of Jesus. John testified later that he saw "the Spirit descending from heaven like a dove, and it abode upon him" (John 1:32), but he left no record of hearing the Voice. The event was a spiritual one, fully experienced by Jesus alone, but transmuted by His consummate artistry into a story of inexhaustible meaning. He told it to His disciples who told it to others, until it was finally enshrined in the Gospel record. It must be to Jesus Himself that we owe this story and our sight of the heavenly dove of His baptism.

Doves living in the dovecotes around Nazareth enlivened His days with their gentle cooing. He admired the purity of their feathers and the swiftness and arrowlike directness with which they flew to their goal. Quickly observant, He noticed that, unlike eagles and vultures, they ate seeds, grain, dates, and figs rather than flesh. In the village school at Nazareth Jesus learned the Scriptures beginning with the story of creation and with the other boys He recited the majestic words: "The Spirit of God moved upon the face of the waters." Here the high-pitched, childish voices would pause while their teacher, the rabbi, added the customary explanation, "like a dove." The rabbi also used to tell the children that the "still, small voice" of God was soft and low like the cooing of a dove. Every boy knew that Noah's dove returning to the Ark with an olive twig in its beak was God's messenger of forgiveness and love and peace. When Jesus visited Jerusalem as a boy of twelve, He saw the costly sacrifices offered in the Temple by the rich and powerful, and the lowly doves which were the sacrifices of the poor. His own mother had sacrificed two of these gentle birds and it was said that doves were the only victims that offered themselves willingly to the priest's knife.

Doves and men have had a long association. Since the dawn of history doves have flourished in the neighborhood of man, being perhaps the first winged creatures that learned to live near human beings. They are depicted in Egyptian bas-reliefs, in Babylonian terra-cotta models, and they adorn many monuments found throughout the ancient Middle East. These birds, earlier perhaps than any other living creature, won the attention, the delight, and even, sometimes, the worship of men.

When the disciples gathered around Jesus to hear from Him the meaning of His ineffable experience of baptism at the Jordan, He told them about a dove. This familiar bird with all its rich associations was the one He chose to symbolize God's Holy Spirit and to convey the meaning of His consecration.

It was, he said, as a dove that God's Holy Spirit descended and rested upon Him and endowed Him with the spirit of wisdom and under-standing, the spirit of counsel and strength, the spirit that knows and reverences God. In this manner Christ was ordained to His ministry as the Son of God.

After His baptism, when Jesus stepped from the waters of the Jordan, the Voice He heard naming Him the beloved Son was like the voice of a dove. He was God's new Creation and over Him the Spirit of God hovered like a dove. This dove prefigures qualities of Christ's own life: gentleness, love, purity, lowliness, swift action toward His goal, and willing sacrifice. This baptismal dove is the first of many birds to carry a message of Jesus.

Later it became a symbol of the Christian Church, for the dove's feet are red as were the feet of the early Christians who followed their Master to martyrdom. During the Middle Ages the vessel in which the Eucharistic wafers were reserved was sometimes made in the form of a dove, and artists portrayed this bird when they were asked to represent that which no man can see—the Holy Spirit of God. The dove and the eagle are the birds most often represented in Christian art and they are the two most frequently mentioned in the Bible. The eagle symbolizes God's care of His people, and the dove, His Holy Spirit active in the world—two aspects of the basic message of the Bible.

CHAPTER 21 🙢

His Eye Is on the Sparrow

To Jesus it was all God's world. From His home on one of the narrow streets of Nazareth He could climb "unto the brow of the hill whereon their city was built" and look out upon one of the most extensive prospects in Palestine. From this sixteen-hundred-foot elevation all the grandeur and soul-lifting wonder of a vast panorama came into view and He could see how marvelously God had wrought the world. Directly below, sheltered in the cup of its green hills, Nazareth's white houses seemed "like a handful of pearls in a goblet of emerald."

To the south the vast fertile Plain of Esdraelon shimmered in the sun's heat. On the highways which crossed the Plain caravans bound for Egypt encountered those going to the coast or to Damascus. The Roman road from Syria passed through Nazareth and crossed the Plain on its way to Jerusalem. The Plain was a highway for armies as well as for commerce and here, long ago, Sisera had been defeated. Nearby on Mount Gilboa, Saul and Jonathan were slain. To the west the long wooded ridge of Elijah's Mount Carmel pointed to the Mediterranean, glimpses of whose blue waters, specked with sails and stretching far away to the distant horizon, must have stirred the imagination of a boy living in an inland hill town. On the far seashore He could see clusters of white houses marking the towns on the bay now called Acre.

Leaving the coast and looking northward He saw in the pure air of this region the highlands of Galilee, a veritable sea of hills, and beyond them, the mountains of the Lebanon ranges culminating in the snow-capped summit of Mount Hermon on the northern border. Looking eastward toward the deep gorge of the Jordan, Jesus could plainly see beyond its rim the mountains of the long Gilead range framing the horizon. The words of the old psalm were appropriate here.

> The earth is the Lord's and the fulness thereof,
> the world and they that dwell therein.
>
> Psalm 24:1

And the angel chorus Isaiah heard long ago must have echoed in Jesus' heart: "Holy, holy, holy, is the Lord of Hosts. The whole earth is full of his glory!"

All creatures that live beneath this vast expanse of sky belong to God,

> For every beast of the forest is mine,
> and the cattle upon a thousand hills.
> I know all the fowls of the mountains,
> and the wild beasts of the field are mine.
>
> Psalm 50:10-11

Standing on the hill above Nazareth, Jesus may have found Israel's great chorus of praise appropriate to this high point. He was nurtured in the glories of the psalms and their phrases often clothed His thoughts. Here while His eyes swept over the extensive panorama He could, as it were, hear triumphant praise issuing from all things and all creatures God has made.

> Praise ye the Lord!
> Praise ye the Lord from the heavens,
>   praise him in the heights! . . .
> Praise the Lord from the earth . . .
> Mountains and all hills,
>   fruitful trees and all cedars,
> beasts and all cattle,
>   creeping things and flying fowl.
> Kings of the earth and all people,
>   princes and all judges of the earth . . .
> let them praise the name of the Lord,
>   for his name alone is excellent.
> His glory is above the earth and heaven . . .
>   Praise ye the Lord!
>
> Psalm 148:1-14

Jesus was a true Son of Israel, for to Him the heavens declared the glory of God and the firmament proclaimed God's handiwork. Nature speaks a different language to those who do not know God, for to these it cannot reveal its ultimate secret. Some understand nature's meaning to be indifference or blind chance or brutality—a "nature red in tooth and claw." Others see in it the proof of some brilliant theory or mathematical equation. Jesus perceived the reality beneath these superficial masquerades of nature and gave His followers the clue to its meaning. Because God made them, Jesus saw the lilies of the field and even its lowly grasses arrayed in a glory not even Solomon could outshine. "He has made everything beautiful in its time; also he has put eternity into man's mind" (Ecclesiastes 3:11, RSV). Birds belonged to God and this made Jesus cherish them. The Bible is rich in its appreciation of nature, but it contains nothing to equal Jesus' awareness of the wonder and beauty and meaning of creation. All nature was to Him a finger pointing to God.

Birds were especially significant to Jesus. Their freedom from worry and their trust in God gave Him deeper insight into His Father's love. He saw hope and courage incarnated in them. In their obedience to the Father's will they became patterns for men to follow. God loved these frail, vital creatures and Jesus loved them too.

Since early childhood Jesus had doubtless delighted in birds, nests, eggs, and young. Perhaps He threw crumbs to the half-domesticated doves and saw them flutter down to consume His bounty. He may have recognized the different melodies of songbirds and learned to distinguish one bird from another by its plumage. Surely He loved the humble sparrows and robins and the chaffinches with their rollicking song. He would have seen the same species of birds that Cunningham Geikie described a century ago around Nazareth in *The Life and Words of Christ*.

The bright colours of the roller, the hoopoe, the sunbird, or the bulbul, catch the eye as one or other darts swiftly past. . . . The song of the lark floods a thousand acres of sky with melody; the restless titmouse, the willow-wren, the blackcap, the hedge-sparrow, the whitethroat, or the nightingale, flit or warble on the hillside, or in the cactus hedges, while the rich notes of the song-thrush or blackbird rise from the green clumps in the valley beneath. The wagtail runs over the pebbles of the brook . . . the common sparrow haunts the streets and house-tops; swallows and swifts skim the hillsides and the grassy meadows; and, in winter, the robin redbreast abounds.

When Jesus went down to the Jordan to be baptized by John some of the brightly-colored birds slipping through the lush foliage of that semitropical region were new to Him, for some of the species there are found nowhere else. Peculiar to the Jordan Valley, we are told, are twenty-three species among which are two owls, a dove, a starling, a thrush, two larks, a martin, a bunting, and six warblers.

After His baptism Jesus went into the wilderness and lived amid its sparse vegetation and barren rocks during the forty days of His temptation. Even here He found teeming life and innumerable birds that God has taught to live in dry, inhospitable places. Desert birds are grayer and more somber than those of favorable climates, but they have adapted themselves to arid regions and are lively, cheerful, and full of song. It is said that desert birds successfully raise their young in completely dry areas by flying themselves to the nearest oasis to drink. Some return with water stored in their crops for their nestlings. Others may come with wet breast feathers from which their young suck moisture. Such were the birds Jesus watched during His lonely days in the wilderness. From there He "returned in the power of the Spirit into Galilee and there went out a fame of him through all the region round about."

In the beginning of His ministry He went into the synagogues and taught. He entered people's homes and healed the sick. Wherever He went crowds followed, for they saw that He was "full of grace and truth." His deeds were performed with power, and His words brought men face to face with reality. News that He was within a house spread like wildfire and there would be sounds of hurrying feet, "and straightway many were gathered together, insomuch that there was no room to receive them, no, not so much as about the door. And he preached the word to them." He chose twelve stalwart disciples, hard-working, dependable men, for the most part, men of courage, quick to catch His meaning, and filled with immense desire for a better world. With these men He fought the fear, sorrow, sickness, selfishness, and insanity of the world. The record of one crowded sabbath day in Capernaum (Mark 1:21-37) shows the pressure of human need upon His boundless sympathy.

All that He wrought could not be hidden. At first "all the city was gathered together at the door." Then as the good news about Him spread far and wide "a great multitude from Galilee . . . and from Judea and from Jerusalem, and from Idumea and from beyond Jordan, and they about Tyre and Sidon . . . when they had heard what great things he did, came unto him." Always lurking in the crowds were unfriendly faces, scribes and Pharisees hoping to trap Him in an incautious statement or waiting to catch Him breaking the Law.

With His disciples Jesus withdrew from the cities of Galilee to gain uninterrupted time in which to teach His twelve chosen followers. They climbed a mountain; they put out from the shores of the Sea of Galilee in a boat, encountering perhaps some of the flocks of pelicans, flamingos, Indian darters, and giant herons which are found only in this one place in Palestine. The birds would have taken wing at the approach of His boat, but crowds of people followed Him, eager for the touch of His healing hand and for the sound of His amazing words. "People pressed upon him to hear the word of God" and they were astonished at His teachings, for "he taught them as one having authority." He taught His disciples to pray. It is the humble, He told them, the kindhearted, the pure in heart, and those who desire goodness whom God blesses. To convey one of His deepest messages He told them a story, so casually, so simply, that its weighty meaning floated as lightly as thistledown.

They are in the open air. His disciples press close around Him and beyond them mills the crowd. Unspoken in each heart lies the troubling questions: Does God really care? Does He care about me? Does He care if my children are hungry? Even the disciples sometimes worry about how things are going at home while they are absent. Is the fishing prospering and do the children have enough to eat? Were we foolish to leave our work and come with Jesus? What shall we eat and drink and wear tomorrow? Jesus Himself had known these worries in His home in Nazareth among His brothers and sisters and later during His lonely days of temptation in the wilderness.

Pointing upward to a flock of birds cleaving the air on buoyant wings, Jesus says: "Behold the birds of the air!" (Matthew 6:26).

Every eye gazes into the clear blue to whatever nameless creatures are at that moment flying or soaring or fluttering above the multitude.

"They sow not, neither do they reap nor gather into barns," remarks Jesus, giving the well-known fact a humorous twist. The crowd is delighted with this flight of fancy. Bird-farmers and bird-barns indeed! Ridiculous! The children laugh gleefully.

"Yet," continues Jesus, deeply serious after His humorous sally, "yet your heavenly Father feedeth them."

The truth, illuminated with such liveliness, lies for them at the heart of life. God cares for every one of His creatures, even the insignificant sparrow and the despised raven (Luke 12:24). In the abundant granaries of God each bird that searches diligently finds its special food. As the proverb says: "God gives to every bird its proper food, but they must all fly for it."

The disciples understand the point Jesus is making even before He asks them the question: "Are ye not much better than they?" (Matthew 6:26). They know that if God cares for ravens and sparrows, He certainly cares for men.

Patiently explaining His point from other angles Jesus continues to

speak, but the birds of His story have already flown away. Few who
hear Him this sunny day in Galilee will ever see birds again without
thinking: "My heavenly Father provides for them, and He provides
for me. Underneath are His everlasting arms."

In another lesson Jesus teaches His disciples that God is like a father
and will never trick or deceive His children, for He loves them and they
can rely on Him. Many of the disciples are fathers themselves and
know how willingly they give food and whatever is needed to their own
children. Jesus is sure of their answer to His question:

> "What father among you, if asked by his son for a
> loaf, will hand him a stone? . . .
> or, if asked for an egg, will he hand him a scorpion?"
> Luke 11:11-12, Moffatt

A scorpion at rest rolls itself into an egglike shape, but it is a small,
poisonous animal which no father would feed to his hungry child.

On another occasion it was of the death of sparrows that Jesus spoke.
Jesus and the disciples had often seen them in the market place—small
dead birds laid out on trays awaiting a purchaser. Among the measures
of wheat, the jars of oil or wine, and the mounds of brightly-colored
fruits and vegetables the birds looked pathetic indeed. Some of them
were stripped of feathers and threaded on long strings or trussed with
wooden skewers. They were a cheap food for those who could afford
nothing better. With their eyes glazed and their songs stilled, the different species could hardly be distinguished one from another, and
even those still in their plumage appeared dingy, the colors of their
feathers dulled by death. Usually there were many kinds of birds for
sale, their species varying according to the seasons of the great migrations through Palestine. There were always common house sparrows,
wheatears, goldfinches, and crested larks. Sometimes a person could buy
a golden oriole, a European greenfinch, a chaffinch, a skylark, or any
one of dozens of other songbirds caught in clever traps and snares. But
who would bother to name these creatures? Names are found and
learned for the birds and trees and flowers people love, but in the
market places of Galilee "sparrow" was good enough for the innumerable species of little dead birds offered for sale. In Jesus' day their
regular price was two for a penny, but sometimes a bargain was offered
of five birds for two pennies, though the fifth bird was likely to be small
and thin and unsalable at the usual rate.

To One who delighted in birds and shared His Father's love for all
living creatures, the dead birds of the market place must have been a
painful sight. Even more so was the cruel game in which boys tied a

string to a bird's leg and let it fly up a little way before jerking the string to make the creature fall. Perhaps these distressing sights were vivid in Jesus' mind one day as He and the disciples returned from the market of some Galilean town after buying their provisions. The sparrows Jesus saw were to achieve immortality and their frail bodies become the text of one of His best-remembered sermons.

As the twelve men gather around Him, Jesus engages their attention with a question: "Are not two sparrows sold for a penny?" (Matthew 10:29, RSV).

How, the disciples wonder, can the penny price of sparrows affect them! But they have learned to listen with all their minds and hearts, always expecting Him to surprise them with a fresh revelation of truth. Afterwards one of them was to remember the opening question in a slightly different form: "Are not five sparrows sold for two pennies?" (Luke 12:6, RSV). The fifth sparrow, thrown in because it was of no value to the merchant, underlines the cheapness of the birds.

Jesus continues and His voice has authority when He says: "Not one of them is forgotten before God." The truth He sees beyond the pathetic little bodies is that not even the least of His creatures lies outside God's care. He feeds them and is with them to the end, knowing even the hour of their death. "Fear not therefore, ye are of more value than many sparrows" (Luke 12:7; cf. Matthew 10:31).

Later one of the disciples, remembering perhaps the cruel sport of boys or the nets stretched between trees, reported a different version of Jesus' words: "And not one of them will fall to the ground without your Father's will" (Matthew 10:29, RSV). The underlying meaning of both sayings is the same: God's love is at the heart of things and it embraces even the death of a sparrow. Cicero had no such faith when he declared, in an all but forgotten sentence: "The gods care for the great, but they neglect the lowly."

Christ's words about sparrows were almost a commonplace fifteen hundred years later when theater audiences in Elizabethan England heard Hamlet declare: "There's a special providence in the fall of a sparrow." Martin Luther, on seeing a bird perching on a branch and closing its eyes for the night, said: "It abides under the shadow of the Almighty. It sits on its tiny twig content, and lets God take care."

The Christian faith that God loves and watches over all His creatures and knows even when a sparrow dies has practical consequences. If God loves His creatures, should not we love them too? One of the signs that a man is a Christian may be his response to the other creatures of God. One remembers St. Francis of Assisi of whom St. Bonaventura wrote:

As St. Francis went forth to preach he found a great multitude of birds gathered together, and when he saw them he ran to them and saluted them and with great joy he beheld them. And it was great marvel, for there was not one of them that removed from their place, but all stood in peace and bowed their heads and stretched their necks, and attentively beheld him. When the holy man saw this he reasoned with them and urged them to hear the word of God. Then he said to them in this wise, "Fair brother and sister birds, you ought greatly to praise God who is your maker, who has clothed you from the rain with feathers, who has given you wings to fly with, and has granted you your living in the purity of the air without labor, who sustaineth and feedeth and governeth you." When he had said many words to them the birds put out their necks and stretched their wings and opened their bills and beheld the man of God attentively, and with all their bodies made great joy after their fashion. And the holy man passed among them with great joy of spirit, and his coat touched them, and yet none of them removed from their place nor stirred their wings until he had given them his blessing and leave to depart from him. And when they had his blessing they all flew away. And his fellow that accompanied him beheld all this and marvelled much, as well he might. And when the holy man came to his fellow he blamed himself greatly for his negligence, that he had not preached to the birds before that time.

In the fifteenth century when pilgrimages to Jerusalem were fashionable among Christian folk, a certain Bishop of Saintes made the journey. Part of his journal is quoted in H. F. M. Prescott's *Friar Felix at Large*. The Bishop was evidently an observant man with kindly sympathy for humble creatures, for he noted the plight of the sparrows in Jerusalem during the dry season. At this time men and animals used water stored in deep cisterns, but small birds found it difficult to drink from these. The sparrows of Jerusalem, however, had a friend in a certain Stephen Talivelli whose heart was filled with the teachings of Christ. The Bishop of Saintes noted with approval that Stephen put shallow pans of water on his window ledge and there nearly all the little birds of the city gathered to drink.

In Africa a white owl sat under Albert Schweitzer's piazza roof, a pelican above his door, and a stork on the ridgepole—all friends of the great doctor whose phrase, "reverence for life," includes in a boundless ethics all that lives. Albert Schweitzer, writing of his own childhood, said:

It was wholly unreasonable to me—this was even before I had gone to school—that in my evening devotions I should pray only for men. So when my mother had prayed with me and kissed me goodnight, I used secretly to add another prayer which I had myself composed for all living creatures.

It ran like this: "Dear God, guard and bless everything that breathes; keep it from all evil and give it quiet sleep."

From the bird stories Jesus told them and from His other teachings, His disciples gained confidence in God's love. Eleven of them soon faced the storms of a hostile world, but they had been given an anchor in the love of God. They were ordained to preach the good news of the Kingdom and as apostles they were especially valuable in God's sight. But evil was to befall them and each took up a cross to follow Christ. The picture of their future that Jesus sketched would have been as dismal as the sight of dead birds were it not set against the radiance of God's loving care. Christ promised that in losing their lives for His sake they would find life and He unfolded to them the glorious prospect of being acknowledged by Him before the throne of God. The meaning of suffering and death He did not disclose, but His assurance that God knows and cares, even when a sparrow falls, is proof enough that these dark events have a meaning.

In His own darkest moments on the cross, Jesus cried out at the ninth hour the words of the 22nd Psalm: "My God, my God, why hast thou forsaken me?" But God, who watches over the death of a sparrow, was at Golgotha. When those looking on heard Jesus say at the end, as the dark cloud rolled away, "Father, into thy hands I commend my spirit," they saw that He died in triumph.

CHAPTER 22

In Him Was Life

LITTLE feathered embodiments of highly-charged energy; great buoyant, graceful bodies joyfully soaring in the free space of sky—these were the creatures Jesus knew and loved. In the thirty silent years before He began to preach in Galilee Jesus must have stored up a fund of accurate bird observations which later became useful to Him in His preaching. Birds are God's jeweled handiwork, masterpieces of form, color, motion, and sound, fashioned out of earthly stuff according to inconceivably intricate patterns. So astonishing is the perfection of birds and so vivid and intense are their lives that they seem, at times, to transcend the earthly limits of other creatures.

Measured, weighed, and tested in every possible way with modern scientific equipment, birds are found to be champions of living. Their bodies, which are so marvelously designed for activity, can produce energy very rapidly. Normally a man's heart beats 70 times a minute, but a bird's heart has a much higher rate, a pigeon's being 192 per minute, a sleeping black-capped chickadee's 400 to 600, a house sparrow's 800, and an excited canary's 1000 or more. The bodies of birds are designed to maintain high temperatures, so high in fact that in man they would constitute fatal fevers. The song sparrow's regular temperature is 109.1 degrees Fahrenheit; the American robin's 109.8 degrees. Even in the extreme cold of an Antarctic winter when thermometers register 40 to 70 degrees below zero Fahrenheit, emperor penguins maintain a body heat of 102.1 degrees, warm enough to hatch their one egg.

To produce all this amazing vitality birds not only need quantities of high-energy food, but they must have a great deal of oxygen; consequently they breathe very fast. At rest a man usually breathes about 18 times a minute, but a sparrow's rate is about 90 and a hummingbird's 250. When active a bird increases its breathing rate and a flying pigeon is said to breathe 450 times a minute. In addition to their extraordinary hearts and lungs, most bird have comparatively large brains which are well-developed in the areas controlling sight, hearing, and the intricately co-ordinated motions of flight.

The vitality and beauty and vividness of birds must have delighted Jesus for He Himself possessed these qualities supremely. "In him was life," declared the apostles, remembering His amazing words and acts during the years they accompanied Him in Galilee and Judea and still experiencing within themselves that upwelling of vital energy with which He had endowed them. They had known Him well. He "dwelt among us and we beheld his glory," they testified. Their ears had heard, their eyes seen, and their hands had touched Him. They had talked with Him and eaten with Him, and one of them had seen Him die. Yet these were the men who, out of their own experience, proclaimed that "in him was life and the life was the light of men." They had come to Jesus and from His life and teachings they had received for themselves and for others real life, vivid, joyful, and abundant, both in time and in eternity. He gave what He Himself possessed: Life and Light. It was true as He had said: "The words that I speak unto you . . . are life."

Among His words are a few swift allusions to the ways of birds which give point to His teachings. His birds are entirely unspectacular; they are the common feathered creatures everyone knows: sparrows, pigeons, eagles, seed-eaters of many species, and the familiar barnyard fowls. His birds do not talk as do those in fables, nor do they perform prodigious feats, and not one behaves like a feathered caricature of a man. They are just birds, lowly and unassuming, each living in its own proper sphere. They chirp and fly about, build nests, lay eggs, and protect their young from danger. In their unceasing search for food they peck at grain, alight on seed-bearing bushes, or gather in multitudes around their prey. Some coo gently, others crow vociferously. Though they are neither preachers nor theologians, they speak to us through the alchemy of Jesus' words and tell us of God and His love for us, of His Kingdom and our discipleship. Fantastic creatures confuse us with their imaginary qualities; only real birds can convey to us the great realities.

In the parable of the sower Jesus mentioned seed-eating birds such as sparrows, finches, and crows. These voracious eaters can be a problem when a farmer sows his fields in spring. But the sower in Jesus' story must have expected to lose some seed to the birds, for he scattered it broadcast and

> as he sowed, some [seed] fell by the way side,
> and the fowls of the air came and devoured it up.
> Mark 4:4; cf. Matthew 13:4; Luke 8:5

A well-trodden path is inhospitable to seeds and few will germinate there; most will lie inert upon the hard soil and be plainly visible to hungry birds. The only crop these seeds yielded was perhaps a wing-beat or a moment of song. Despite the seed devoured by the birds and the seed lost in thin soil or among thorns and briars, the farmer of the parable reaped an abundant harvest from his good ground, thirty, sixty, and sometimes as much as a hundred times what he had sown. This is the way the Kingdom of God grows.

God's Kingdom, Jesus said, is also like a mustard seed which is the smallest of all the seeds commonly planted in the fields and gardens of Palestine. Though the seed of the cypress tree is actually smaller, the mustard seed was better known and had become proverbial for. anything tiny and insignificant. But is the Kingdom of God either small or of no significance? This is what Jesus said:

> "The kingdom of heaven is like a grain of mustard seed which a man took and sowed in his field; it is the smallest of all seeds, but when it has grown it is the greatest of shrubs and becomes a tree, so that. . . ."
> Matthew 13:31-32, RSV; cf. Mark 4:32; Luke 13:19

The facts are impressive, but Jesus was too consummate an artist and teacher to end here. He proved to His listeners that mustard actually grows into a veritable tree and at the same time He painted for them a delightfully unforgettable picture in His concluding words: ". . . so that the birds of the air come and make nests in its branches."

Birds are attracted to mustard for its minute black seeds which they pick out of the pods. People also enjoy the sharp, pungent flavor of mustard seed oil and flour, and in the East the plant is widely culti-vated for this purpose as well as for fodder. Mustard is a wild flower that long ago spread from its original home in western Asia to the grain-fields of the East. In Palestine's climate it grows luxuriantly, often attaining a height of ten to fifteen feet. Some mustard thickets grow so rank and tall that a man on horseback cannot see over the plants. In the fall the stems and branches become hard and rigid like wood so that great numbers of sparrows, finches, and linnets can perch on them and find shelter from the rain or shade from the sun. The original Greek word translated "make nests" in this passage means "to rest as in a tent" and has been variously translated "lodge," "settle," "perch," "roost," as well as "nest."

At this point in His story the kindled imaginations of Jesus' hearers leaped from the treelike mustard to the great trees of Scripture. Ezekiel's gigantic cedar, they knew, represented mighty Assyria and "all the fowls of heaven made their nests in his boughs . . . and under his shadow dwelt all great nations" (Ezekiel 31:6). Daniel described Nebuchadnezzar's dream of a tree that "grew and was strong and the height thereof reached unto heaven . . . and the fowls of the heaven dwelt in the boughs thereof" (Daniel 4:11-12). These "trees" were kingdoms and empires and the birds nesting in their branches symbolize the subject peoples brought under their control. History records that the world powers of antiquity were hewn down like trees and destroyed. There was another cedar, however, which Ezekiel said the Lord planted on Israel's lofty mountain. This cedar grew from a tender shoot into a noble tree and "under it shall dwell all fowl of every wing; in the shadow of the branches thereof shall they dwell" (Ezekiel 17:23). It remained for Jesus to transform this Old Testament vision of a mighty kingdom into the all-embracing Kingdom of God which Jesus now proclaimed to be at hand. Growing from a tiny beginning, as small and inconspicuous as a mustard seed, the Kingdom will become a huge plant extending "unto the uttermost part of the earth."

With such stories Jesus taught the multitudes, and especially His disciples, the realities concerning the Kingdom of God. There is an interesting use of birds in this connection in the Gospel of Thomas, one of the ancient Coptic gnostic papyri found by Egyptian peasants in 1946, and published by Pahor Labib in a collection of photographs. The Gospel of Thomas was long ago placed in a jar which was put in a tomb cut in the limestone cliffs of Upper Egypt. This apocryphal gospel, in addition to many sayings of Jesus identical to those in the canonical Gospels, also contains hitherto unknown sayings ascribed to Him. One of these mentions birds:

Jesus said: "If those who lead you say to you: Behold, the kingdom is in heaven, then the birds of heaven will precede you; if they say to you that it is in the sea, then the fish will precede you. But the kingdom is within you and it is outside of you."

Jesus also taught His disciples their own part in the Kingdom and three times He used the ways of birds to make His meaning clear. The cost of discipleship is high, He told an enthusiastic would-be follower who is identified only as a "certain scribe." He was probably a young man, fired with zeal for God's Kingdom, for he came to Jesus to offer his services. We can still hear the almost breathless eagerness with which he promised: "Teacher, I will follow you wherever you go!"

But Jesus perceived that the scribe's enthusiasm was as shallow as thin soil in stony places. Did this young man imagine that he would share with Jesus a triumphant progress through Galilee and Judea? Did he expect the adultation of crowds and hospitality in the largest house of every town they visited? Did he foresee that he would experience loneliness when he cast loose from his small scribal world with its well-known rules and customs and its comfortable security? Following Jesus meant launching out into the unknown. Jesus challenged the young scribe, saying:

"Foxes have holes, and birds of the air have nests; but the Son of man has nowhere to lay his head."

Matthew 8:20, rsv; cf. Luke 9:58

When He spoke these words Jesus probably stood outside Capernaum near the fertile Plain of Gennesaret at the northwestern end of the Sea of Galilee. Colonies of thousands of field sparrows breed in the low pine trees growing there and, according to William M. Thomson in *The Land and the Book,* the bushes "are stuffed full of bird's nests." The excited chirruping of countless nesting sparrows may have risen in a lively counterpoint above Jesus' voice. Even birds with their frail nests and uncertain resting places are better off than Jesus and His disciples whose homelessness was that of the pioneers of faith. The young scribe knew the stories of Abraham and Moses, but he also remembered the cautious proverb about the "bird that wandereth from her nest" (Proverbs 27:8) and the sad plight of Moab, "a wandering bird cast out of the nest" (Isaiah 16:2). With the cost of discipleship made vividly clear to him, did the "certain scribe" leave his home and the safe shelter of his ancient scribal traditions for the perils and uncertainties of following the Master? The Gospels do not say.

To those who did follow Him Jesus gave practical advice. "Behold," He said, "I send you forth as sheep in the midst of wolves; be ye therefore wise as serpents and harmless as doves" (Matthew 10:16). They were to need all the wisdom proverbially attributed to serpents, but not their deceitful cunning. Treachery and guile were to have no place among their weapons in combating the evil in the world for their defense would be wisdom and the gentle innocence of doves.

There was warning, too, in the grim picture of birds of prey darkening the sky as they swoop down to pick the bones of a carcass, "for wheresoever the carcass is, there will the eagles be gathered together"

(Matthew 24:28; cf. Luke 17:37). This behavior of eagles and vultures had been observed since the days of Abraham and had become proverbial, as in Job 39:30. Vultures are usually gregarious, but some of the eagles of Palestine have similar habits. In the word "eagles" Jesus may suggest the silver eagles surmounting the standards of the Roman legions. In their talons these eagles grasped the thunderbolts which legend said they brought to Jupiter for his battle against the Titans. Was the Jewish nation a corpse to be picked by the Roman "eagles"?

But Christ brings life, not death, and eagles symbolizing speed, ferocity, and power are not His birds though they may at times bear His warnings. He might have rejoiced in the eagle as a symbol of freedom, but the bird to which Jesus finally compared Himself, in one of the tenderest passages of Scripture, is the familiar hen of the poultry yard. Jesus was not interested in the hair-splitting arguments of the rabbis concerning this bird. In their fantastic zeal to observe the Sabbath they decided it was not proper to eat an egg laid by a hen on the Sabbath, that is if the hen was one kept to lay eggs, for her egg would represent work done on the Sabbath. But one of the liberal rabbis decided that it was lawful to eat the Sabbath egg of a hen kept, not for laying, but for eating.

The scene Jesus paints of this bird is unforgettable. It may have been an event He witnessed in some Nazareth farmyard. A brood of just-hatched, fluffy, yellow chickens scamper across an open space, peeping shrilly, while the troubled hen clucks nervously at them. Swiftly out of the sky a hawk plummets, its wings folded, its keen eyes gleaming, its talons ready to seize a hapless chick and bear it away. But the hen's eye is keen also and swiftly she collects her chickens and hides them beneath her wings. This farmyard drama came vividly to Jesus' mind as He stood on a hill commanding a view of the sacred city and uttered His lament:

O Jerusalem, Jerusalem, thou that killest the prophets and stonest them which are sent unto thee! How often would I have gathered thy children together, even as a hen gathereth her chickens under her wings—and ye would not!

Matthew 23:37; cf. Luke 13:34

Under the wings of God Israel long ago escaped from bondage and entered the Promised Land. "I gathered you as a hen gathers her brood under her wings" (II Esdras 1:30, RSV), says the Lord in a later Christian writing which here echoes Jesus' words. But when Christ offered His tender protection, His care and His love, Israel rejected Him. His final days with their drama and all their deep significance are at hand.

CHAPTER 23 ❦

Bird Cages in the Temple

As Jesus enters the Temple in Jerusalem on Monday morning, He hears a roar of confused sound swelling within the great colonnaded Court of the Gentiles. Lost in the tumult is the low, throaty, repeated cooing of pigeons and doves. If anyone is praying here, he is surely not disturbed by the gentle sound issuing from cages where doves and pigeons utter their pitiful, muffled plaints.

It is the Passover and Jerusalem is thronged with devout Jews from Babylonia, Egypt, Rome, and many other places far and near, come to make their sacrifices in the Temple. All Jewish men will pay their annual half-shekel Temple tax. Among the crowds of Jews are many Gentiles who are attracted by the holiness, purity, and righteousness of the Lord God of Israel and who prefer to worship Him instead of their old pagan gods. Gentiles are allowed to enter the sacred precincts of the Temple and in its outer Court people of all faiths may pray. Signs are posted, however, warning Gentiles not to penetrate beyond this large area, for the Court of the Women, the Court of the Israelites, and the Temple building itself are for Jews only.

With Jesus and His disciples are many enthusiastic hangers-on who have recently sung hosannas to Him. As they pass through the Temple gates, Jesus strides ahead of the crowd into the Court of the Gentiles. There the din, turmoil, and stench are overpowering. How could a man pray here? The place is really not a temple at all, but a bustling market place or a great yearly fair at which thousands of animals are sold for the sacrifices. There is indignation in Jesus' eyes as He looks around.

From the reeking stalls and pens filled with lambs, goats, and oxen come mingled animal cries. Tied in baskets or imprisoned in cages stacked one above the other, pigeons and doves to be sold for the rites of purification flutter helplessly and moan. Nearby stand tables piled with silver coins, the ancient Hebrew half-shekels in which the Temple tax must be paid. The half-shekels make a sharp, metallic clink as they are counted out for Roman and other foreign coins, and there are often outraged cries as clients protest the exorbitant rate of exchange the money-changers demand. Cattle traders shout the merits of their beasts and pigeon dealers cry: "Come buy!" Business is flourishing and profits are piling up.

People carrying heavy bundles use the Court of the Gentiles as a short cut and this adds to the general confusion. Members of the Sadducean hierarchy walk up and down observing everything with watchful eyes. By virtue of the fact that they control Temple revenues, the Sadducees issue licenses to traders and money-changers and inspect the sacrificial animals offered for sale before pronouncing them unblemished and ritually clean. Some say there are very sharp practices in connection with money-changing, the five per cent charge for exchange usually being increased by tricks and dishonesty. It is believed that the Sadducees are enriching themselves by graft, that the sale of pigeons and doves is secretly in the hands of the priests, and that the high priest himself derives huge profits from his dovecotes on Mount Olivet.

All this Jesus sees and knows as He stands in the Court of the Gentiles. The crowd waits for Him to speak His gracious and wonderful words, but when they see indignation blazing in His eyes they step back a little. There will be no sermon for them today. This desecration of God's house of prayer demands vigorous, forthright action.

On the pavement at His feet lies a length of rope used, perhaps, to drag some protesting animal into the Temple. Jesus bends over and picks up the rope, quickly twisting it into a rough whip. Then He begins to drive out those who are buying or selling, and He overturns "the tables of the money-changers and the seats of those who sold pigeons" (Mark 11:15, RSV; also Matthew 21:12; John 2:14-16; Luke 19:45-46).

For a few minutes there is pandemonium—cries, shouts, the crash of coins on stone pavement, a stampede of animals, the crack of the whip in Jesus' hand. Then there is silence and His voice can be heard in the farthest corners of the colonnade: "Take these things hence!" He shouts, pointing to the bird cages and baskets. "Make not my Father's house an house of merchandise" (John 2:16).

The birdsellers, seizing the cages and baskets in which their pigeons and doves still moan, hurriedly make their way amid overturned benches and tables, stepping carefully over the mounds of silver coins. As there is no chance to make a sale today, they hasten to take their birds back to the safety of the dovecotes. By tomorrow order will surely be restored and they and the cattle traders and money-changers will again be in their accustomed places. The priests and Sadducees will see to that. Is it not in their interest to do so?

When the people recover from their stunned surprise they eagerly await the climax of the drama. It is time now, they know, for the chief priests and scribes to assert their authority and power by taking action. What will the action be? But these religious leaders, incensed though they are by the unexpected attack against their prerogatives, are afraid of Jesus' popularity with the people and do nothing at all—for the moment. They stand silently looking on while Jesus explains to the crowd the reason for His action. The explanation is in the form of a question:

> "Is it not written, 'My house shall be called a house of prayer for all the nations'?"
>
> Mark 11:17, RSV

How can a Gentile worship in this place? The scribes know the quotation well, for it is from the prophecies of Isaiah, and they dare not argue against the Scriptures. While they hesitate and look about at their splendid marble and gold Temple and wonder what reply to make, Jesus challenges them in words that come like a thunderclap:

> "But you have made it a den of robbers!"
>
> Mark 11:17, RSV

Now their rage boils over. This teacher from Nazareth has caused them trouble enough already, but His invasion of the Temple and His overt attack against long-established customs, which yield them comfortable revenues, cannot be endured. One by one the priests and scribes make their way out of the Court of the Gentiles, following closely the retreating birdsellers. Meeting in their own quarters in the Temple the chief priests and scribes seek "a way to destroy him."

CHAPTER 24 ～

Peter and the Cock

THE crowing of the cock on the morning of the crucifixion is the best-known bird sound in history. In Jerusalem today, on the supposed site of the ancient high priest's palace, there stands, amid the shrubs and pines of Mount Sion, a church named Gallicante for the cock Peter heard there that fateful Friday morning. During the three days since the birdsellers fled from the Temple with their cages, secret meetings had been held between the chief priests, the Sadducees, and the Pharisees. Usually split into rival factions, the religious leaders of Jerusalem were now united on one plan: Jesus must die. He, meanwhile, continued to teach and preach openly in the city and to prepare His disciples for the coming ordeal. By Thursday evening when Jesus and the Twelve ate their last supper together, the conspiracy against Him was complete and the authorities had arranged, because of His great popularity with the people, to arrest Him stealthily.

After supper, according to John's Gospel, Judas rose from the table and went out into the night, but the eleven disciples and their Master remained in the upper room to sing a hymn before going into the moonlit city streets. It was now several hours before midnight and while the paschal moon rose higher into the sky Jerusalem slept in a quiet broken only by footfalls and muffled voices. The hearts of the disciples were so full of love for their Master that the way seemed neither dark nor deserted to them.

At midnight from city courtyards and neighboring farms would come the first crowing of cocks which was a signal to the Roman garrison that the midnight watch had ended and the third night watch had begun. "Cockcrowing" lasted until three in the morning when the cocks usually crowed a second time and awakened the fourth or dawn watch. Jesus had mentioned the four Roman night watches in His parable of the household: "Watch ye therefore, for ye know not when the master of the house cometh, at even, or at midnight, or at the cockcrowing, or in the morning" (Mark 13:35).

As they made their way through silent streets to the Garden of Gethsemane outside Jerusalem's walls, Jesus told the disciples what was to happen and He warned them that it would shake their very faith. The old prophecy of Zechariah would come to pass: "Smite the shepherd and the sheep shall be scattered."

Brave, impetuous, vehement Peter brushed the warning aside. Other men might scatter at the first hint of danger and desert their Master, but not he.

"Even though they all lose their faith in You, Master, I will not!" he exclaimed, his earnest, excited voice ringing out in the darkness.

How like Peter it was—enthusiastic, impulsive! Jesus turned and looked at him in the darkness and knew that in Peter's rocklike character there was a hidden vein of instability. Peter needed to be warned lest he fail when his test came.

Jesus said to him: "Truly, I say to you, this very night, before the cock crows twice, you will deny me three times" (Mark 14:30, RSV; cf. Matthew 26:34; Luke 22:34; John 13:38).

Events moved inexorably forward. Under the olive trees of Gethsemane Jesus prayed to His Father while the disciples slept. Suddenly in the distance appeared the light of lanterns and torches, coming from the city and approaching nearer and nearer to the Garden. It was a crowd of Temple guards armed with swords and clubs and accompanied, perhaps, by Roman soldiers. Judas led them. There was his kiss of betrayal, a brief scuffle between disciples and guards, and the arrest. As they led Jesus away His disciples deserted Him and fled, escaping into the dark shadows of the olive trees in the Garden.

Peter, however, followed his Master at a safe distance and when Jesus was taken into the high priest's palace, Peter waited outside in the courtyard. The night air was cold and when Peter approached the fire where the servants and guards warmed themselves, the flames lit up his face and a sharp-eyed serving maid spotted him.

"You were with Jesus of Nazareth!" she accused Peter, pointing her finger at him.

Quick as a flash Peter defended himself. "I do not know Him!" he declared, moving out of the firelight toward the gateway. Mark reported that at that moment "the cock crew" (Mark 14:68). If so, the time would have been near midnight.

The hours dragged by while inside the high priest's palace the religious authorities of Jerusalem examined their Prisoner and listened to false witnesses against Him. Out in the courtyard Peter still waited. The maid whose suspicions had been aroused could not let the matter rest. "He *is* one of them!" she insisted to the guards around the fire.

A second time Peter denied her charge.

But Peter spoke with a distinctive Galilean accent and this was all the guards needed to believe the maid's suspicion, for it was well-known that Jesus and many of His followers came from the northern province of Galilee. The bystanders, bored with their long wait and ready for any small diversion, began to harass Peter. "You are surely one of the band," they declared, "for you are obviously a Galilean."

"I swear I do not know this man of whom you speak!" Peter declared vehemently.

And immediately the cock crowed a second time. And Peter remembered how Jesus had said to him, "Before the cock crows twice, you will deny me three times." And he broke down and wept.

Mark 14:72, RSV; cf. Matthew 26:74-75; Luke 22:60-61; John 18:27

As Friday dawned over Jerusalem, other birds besides cocks began to stir and sing, for it was spring, the season of nest-building and of the great migrations through Palestine. The aerial flyway above the Holy City was alive with feathered creatures, unaware of what we believe to be the central event of human history taking place below them at Gethsemane, in the palace of Caiaphas, before Pilate's judgment seat, on the rocky mound called Golgotha, and in the new stone tomb. In every tree and field and rocky valley near the city were innumerable birds, singing, searching for food, or engaged in their customary springtime activities. But of all of this there is no hint in the stark Gospel records of Christ's passion. There is only a suggestion, in the account of the darkness that covered the earth during His final three hours on the cross, that nature paused in silent homage as Jesus laid down His life for men. When He died, we are told, nature spoke in the voice of an earthquake and the rending of rocks.

Though the only authentic bird in the narrative of the passion is the cock, devout people have embroidered the factual Bible record with the bright colors of the goldfinch, the robin, and the crossbill. According to the legends, these birds witnessed the Lord's sufferings on the cross and in their attempt to help Him they themselves suffered. The crossbill struggled desperately to wrench the nails from His hands and feet only to twist its beak so that its mandibles became crossed in the way they appear today. The robin's breast, they say, was wounded and stained red when it tried to pull the thorns from His crown. And the red face of the European goldfinch and its habit of eating among thorns and thistles betoken the aid it, too, gave the Savior as He hung on the cross.

These fanciful bird legends belong to the realm of pious imagination, not to that of the canonical Gospels which report events in a world of reality where real tears of remorse are shed in a palace courtyard, a man dies on an actual cross, and a rock tomb is found to be indeed empty. The Gospels give testimony concerning the resurrection of Christ from many different sources: from Mary Magdalene and the women, Peter and the nameless disciple, the guards at the tomb, Thomas and the other disciples, Cleopas and his companion, and a crowd of five hundred brethren. To the followers of Christ His death and resurrection were not idle, imaginary tales, but events whose meaning and reality they hammered out on the anvil of sorrow, despair, persecution, and their own boundless joy. The difference between Peter on the morning of the memorable cockcrow and Peter forty days later at Pentecost attests the reality of the events on which Christianity stands. Jesus had died on a cross, but the apostles knew Him risen and glorified and they experienced His living presence still with them. The resurrection was the decisive event which changed Peter. As the cock crowed he had protested: "I do not know the man." A few weeks later he proclaimed to a vast crowd in Jerusalem:

"This Jesus God raised up, and of that we all are witnesses. . . . Let all the house of Israel therefore know assuredly that God has made him both Lord and Christ, this Jesus whom you crucified!"

Acts 2:32, 36, RSV

It was the new Peter of Pentecost, chief of the apostles, who stood one day at Joppa looking out to sea. Several years had passed since the wind of the Holy Spirit, blowing in a mighty gale through the early Church, had swept Peter and his fellow Christians from their old, safe moorings. They had become new men and women, able to do and willing to suffer what was formerly impossible for them. After the stoning of Stephen, Christ's followers in Jerusalem suffered persecution and many fled to Judea, Samaria, and safe places in Syria. Peter now traveled up and down the land, visiting his scattered brothers in Christ, feeding his Master's sheep. At Joppa he remained for many days with Simon the tanner whose house was near the harbor.

To a fisherman like Peter, accustomed to the inland Sea of Galilee, everything at Joppa was new and exciting—the salt waves approaching the sandy beach, the pounding breakers, the smell of sea breezes blowing in from the Mediterranean. He listened to the Joppa boatmen singing as they brought their rafts and barges through heavy surf safely to shore. The fish caught here were different, he saw, from those he netted in Galilee. He recognized few of the birds patrolling the skies or skimming along the shore just out of reach of the foaming waves. He watched gulls wheel and flap and soar and float down to a graceful landing. He heard the terns scream as they hovered and plunged for fish. Here were shore-loving plovers, and sandpipers attentively examining the beach. Peter saw that the sparkling waters of the Mediterranean were not contained within a bowl of mountains like those encircling the Sea of Galilee. These salt waters beating upon the Joppa shore stretched to the very limits of the world and carried on their tossing surface the ships of many peoples. From Simon's housetop Peter could see ships from distant ports riding at anchor. Here were drying sails that had been made in Tarsus, home of that new and somewhat disturbing convert Paul. There were Greek ships from Miletus and Corinth and heavy galleys from Alexandria bound for Puteoli and Ostia with grain to feed the swarming populace of Rome. At Joppa Peter looked out to sea and his imagination moved toward "the uttermost part of the earth."

It was noon and Peter was hungry when he climbed to Simon's housetop to pray. His labors among his fellow countrymen, the chosen people of Israel, in Jerusalem, Judea, and Samaria had been fruitful, but had not the Lord commanded him to carry the Gospel to all those who lived beyond the Mediterranean in the farthest parts of the earth? Peter, for all his impetuous daring, still preferred safe inland waters and clung to the Law and the enclosed world of Judaism. Musing on these things Peter fell into a trance in which he saw a vision of heaven opened and a great sail-like sheet let down by its four corners. In the sheet he saw "all kinds of animals and reptiles and birds of the air" (Acts 10:12, RSV; also 11:6). A voice commanded him to eat these creatures, but all Peter's Hebrew training made him recoil from eating ritually "unclean" meat. The long list of "unclean" birds in Leviticus and Deuteronomy he knew well: such creatures as vultures, eagles, kites, kestrels, ravens, owls, herons, cormorants, and hoopoes. Peter had never eaten their flesh and in his trance he refused to eat anything "common" or "unclean." But the voice came a second time, still commanding him to eat, and saying: "What God has cleansed, you must not call common."

Was this Christ's new teaching? Peter remembered that Jesus had said: "Not what goes into the mouth defiles a man, but what comes out of the mouth, this defiles a man." And he knew Christ's words that "nothing is unclean in itself"—a saying which Paul preserved in his Epistle to the Romans. The old Hebrew ritual laws were abolished for the followers of Christ.

As the vision faded, Peter heard three men outside the gate calling and asking if Peter were within. They were messengers from Caesarea sent to invite Peter to preach the Gospel of Christ to their master Cornelius. Cornelius was a Gentile, a Roman centurion, who desired to hear the message from Peter himself. Was it to prepare Peter for this opportunity that the vision had been sent to him? It had taught him that he no longer needed to have scruples about entering a Gentile home. He was free to eat with Gentiles. Christ had repealed the prohibition against "unclean" foods.

Cornelius' relatives and friends crowded into his house at Caesarea to hear the message of the chief apostle of the new faith. As he preached to them Peter was astonished when he saw the Holy Spirit fall on these Gentiles and he baptized them, glorifying God who had "also to the Gentiles granted repentance unto life."

Peter carried a burden of remorse for his three denials, and the cock-crow of the Friday morning in Jerusalem haunted him to the end, but he conquered his instability and became the "rock" of Christ. At a climax of his apostleship, in the home of the Roman centurion at Caesarea, Peter stood at the growing edge of Christianity where barriers to the expanding life of the Church were overthrown. Peter at Caesarea faced the whole Gentile world and was like the gilded cock on an old church weathervane catching the first light of dawn and crying out: "Rise up, ye that sleep, for Christ is giving His light unto the whole world!"

CHAPTER 25 ~~~
Flying Eagles of Revelation

THE burning sun smote John with terrible fury as he labored with his fellow prisoners in the stone quarry on Patmos. This penal island was surrounded by the Aegean Sea whose beautiful blue waters appeared as "a sea of glass like unto crystal." But the sea and the sun were not playthings to John nor was the lovely island of Patmos a holiday place, for here he was always hungry and thirsty. The sea was like prison bars separating him from the mainland and from those he loved, and preventing his escape from the intolerable dust, noise, and danger of the quarry. The Romans had condemned him to hard labor on Patmos because he remained loyal to Christ and refused to worship the emperor. Yet beyond the great tribulations of the present time John saw future blessedness for those who love Christ. In the midst of his own trials he dared compose a hymn of sublime faith for his fellow Christians:

> They shall hunger no more, neither thirst any more;
>   neither shall the sun light on them nor any heat.
> For the Lamb which is in the midst of the throne shall feed them,
>   and shall lead them unto living fountains of waters;
> and God shall wipe away all tears from their eyes.
>   Revelation 7:16-17

John saw the new heaven and the new earth brought into being at the end of time, when all suffering has passed away. In his vision Patmos was no longer a prison for "there was no more sea."

On Patmos John continued to hammer rock in the quarry whose mid-day heat was like that of a furnace, but his mind soared on wings of the spirit into the limitless, cool spaces of sky. Though his body remained in Roman custody, his mind was free, for it belonged to Christ. In freedom his imagination conceived the wonderful things now collected in the Book of Revelation which helped to sustain the faith and courage of a persecuted Church. Remembering the days of old, John saw the great symbolic eagles flying again, moving through the heavens in graceful flight, free, fearless, and superb—creatures ordained to carry out God's will and worthy to guard His throne.

Egypt had once oppressed the people of God, then Babylon had defeated them, and later the Seleucid kings, but these three earthly powers had vanished and now imperial Rome assumed the oppressor's role. The young Christian Church, heir to the Israel of Moses and the prophets, now stood pitted against the Rome of Caesar Augustus, Nero, and Domitian. Armed only with her faith, hope, and courage the new Israel of God appeared doomed by the terrible might of Rome. To John it was clear that the struggle was not between invincible Roman legions and unarmed men and women, but between the powers of evil and all the power of God. John knew that the issue of the coming battle was never in doubt, for Christ had already won the victory.

Long ago at Sinai the people of God were confident that the Lord bore them, as it were, on eagles' wings out of Egyptian bondage. He brought them through all Wilderness perils and made of them a holy nation, a kingdom of priests. With wonder and a sense of elation they watched the grandeur and grace of the eagles and vultures of Palestine and they dreamed of symbolic eagles moving in heavenly realms. Later, during Israel's captivity in Babylon the prophet Ezekiel saw a vision of the Lord's throne guarded by creatures with the faces and wings of eagles (Ezekiel 1:5-11; 10:14). When Antiochus Epiphanes persecuted Israel, Daniel saw a strange, eaglelike being (Daniel 7:4, 6). Still later many a synagogue was decorated with the figure of an eagle carved on the lintel over a doorway or pictured in mosaics on a floor. These magnificent birds reminded the worshipers that God had helped them through past ages and promised them spiritual deliverance in the coming Messianic age. Eagles bore this meaning for Christians also. The unknown silversmith of the fourth or fifth century A.D. who made the famous Chalice of Antioch depicted Christ as the Good Shepherd with His sheep while below Him, as if to uphold Him with its outspread wings, flies the eagle of God's protection.

When John pondered the events of history he saw visions of strange, wonderful, and sometimes terrible things: horsemen, trumpets, angels, the dragon, and a jeweled city. Rome, which he called "Babylon the great," was to him "a cage of every unclean and hateful bird" (Revelation 18:2). Somewhere he had seen vultures tearing at carrion for he painted a gruesome picture in which all the evil forces of the kings of the earth and their armies are finally overcome. After they are slain "all the fowls are filled with their flesh" (Revelation 19:21). But John's chief birds are neither vultures of retribution, nor ravens of disaster, but the keen-eyed, swift, strong eagles of God. These birds became John's emblem. Christians of a later period heard the Scriptures read from lecterns ornamented with eagles carved with outspread wings to remind them of John's flying eagles and of the outreach of the Gospel to the ends of the earth.

John saw an eagle messenger suddenly appear in the sky and he heard it warn men that judgment was about to come upon the pagan world:

Then I looked, and I heard an eagle crying with a loud voice, as it flew in midheaven, "Woe, woe, woe to those who dwell on the earth . . . !"

Revelation 8:13, RSV

It would be, as on eagles' wings, that the people of God would again be borne above all perils and brought to a safe place. John saw the ancient drama re-enacted in his vision of the woman, the dragon, and the eagles' wings. The dragon is Rome; the woman is the Church of Christ; and the wings of eagles are, as in the time of Moses, the sustaining, protecting power of God.

And when the dragon saw that he had been thrown down to the earth, he pursued the woman. . . . But the woman was given the two wings of the great eagle that she might fly from the serpent into the wilderness, to the place where she is to be nourished for a time. . . .

Revelation 12:13-14, RSV

One day, while a wretched prisoner on Patmos, John saw the very door of heaven open and God's shining throne surrounded by the rainbow "like unto an emerald." Guarding the heavenly throne were the four beings who served God with their courage, strength, wisdom, and speed. The first was like a lion, the second was like an ox, the third had a face like a man, and the fourth "was like a flying eagle" (Revelation 4:7). Day and night they chanted the song heard long ago by Isaiah: "Holy, holy, holy, Lord God Almighty, which was, and is, and is to come!" Heaven resounded with the song the four angelic beings and the twenty-four elders sang to God upon His throne:

"Worthy art thou, our Lord and God,
to receive glory and honor and power,
for thou didst create all things,
and by thy will they existed and were created."
                          Revelation 4:11, RSV

In the end, as at the beginning, God reigns. The long Bible story
reached its glorious climax as a song was sung to Christ, the Lamb of
God, who redeemed men "from every tribe and tongue and people and
nation." They praised Him, for He had

". . . made them a kingdom and priests to our God,
and they shall reign on earth."
                          Revelation 5:9-10, RSV

"Ten thousand times ten thousand" angelic voices joined the chorus
of the elders and the four winged beings, and still the music swelled
as "when the morning stars sang together, and all the sons of God
shouted for joy." Finally John heard the voices of "every creature
which is in heaven and on the earth and under the earth and such as are
in the sea." All joined the full chorus of creation and sang praises to
God and to Christ in a vast, resounding cosmic symphony:

Blessing and honour and glory and power
Be unto him that sitteth upon the throne,
And unto the Lamb for ever and ever!
                          Revelation 5:13

Then the heavenly winged lion and the ox and the man and the
flying eagle cried: "Amen."

INDEX OF BIBLE
BIRD REFERENCES

OLD TESTAMENT

NEW TESTAMENT

APOCRYPHA

APOCRYPHAL GOSPEL OF THOMAS

INDEX OF
NAMES AND SUBJECTS

Hebrew bird names are printed in italics. Page numbers in boldface type refer to identifiable birds appearing in the illustrations.